NEWS WRITING IN A MULTIMEDIA WORLD

Tom Clanin, Andi Stein and Anthony Fellow
California State University, Fullerton

KENDALL/HUNT PUBLISHING COMPANY
4050 Westmark Drive   Dubuque, Iowa 52002

We dedicate this book to journalists around the world who put their lives at risk each day to provide their readers, viewers and listeners with information that is vital to an informed and educated people.

Contents

This textbook addresses the new reality of today's journalists: Reporters who excel in their profession can no longer consider themselves simply print reporters, broadcasters or Internet-content providers. They have to be multimedia journalists.

Journalists today work in all media. Print reporters do stand ups for broadcast news; broadcast reporters write stories for their station's or network's Web sites; and Web reporters use their cell phones not only to call in breaking news but also to shoot and transmit photos for their Web sites.

The Internet is the catalyst for this media convergence. The World Wide Web has allowed traditional print and broadcast news media to easily move into other areas and give audiences expanded perspectives of what's happening locally and around the world.

Consider the front page of The New York Times on April 1, 2004, the day after four civilian security personnel were murdered in Fallujah, Iraq. The lead story was staff writer Jeffrey Gettleman's account of the killings and how a mob mutilated and displayed the bodies. Also on Page One was a news analysis by Baghdad bureau chief John Burns headlined, "U.S. Optimism is Tested " and one photo from Fallujah.

Web users expect up-to-the-minute news, and the Times had posted an account of the killings the same day they occurred. By the next morning, April 1, the fact that the killings occurred was old news on the Web, so the top story on the Times' Web site was the reaction to the previous day's events: Burns' analysis on how the killings would affect U.S. policy. Gettleman's story was also on the Times' home Web page, as was a third story titled "Shock Waves: Americans Are Jolted by Gruesome Reminders of the Day in Mogadishu," about Americans' reactions to the killings and gruesome images of mutilated bodies, and comparing coverage to news media's reports of the deaths of Marines in Somalia in 1993.

The Times does not use its Web site simply as a new way of distributing the newspaper. The site offers much more than what the Times could offer its newspaper readers. At about the same time that Times' subscribers were opening their newspapers, the Web site featured TV news footage of the mob attacking and mutilating the charred bodies, a TV report by Burns that had aired the night before on PBS's "News Hour with Jim Lehrer," and an audio report by Gettleman describing what he had seen. Nine photos of the bodies and cheering crowd flashed on the screen during his narration. Some of the photos were not included in the Times' print edition.

Two news stories were on the Web site by early that afternoon. One was about the Marines defending their decision to stay out of Fallujah after the killing, and the other was about how the Iraqi news media reported the killing.

This constant updating of Web sites is why the Internet transcends time and space. People looking for a specific news item — a sports score or election results, for example — don't have to wait for the newspaper to be delivered or for the item to be mentioned in a TV or radio 30-minute news cycle. They go to the Internet for instant news. Someone living in Fairbanks, Alaska, has the same easy access to the Guardian or The Washington Post as do people living in London or Washington, D.C. Geography has no relevance to people who use the Internet as their source of news.

The Internet can do much more than supply up-to-the-minute information anywhere in the world. It can also involve people in their communities.

After Minnesota Gov. Tim Pawlenty proposed a two-year, balanced budget in 2003 that reduced spending by $4.2 billion, Minnesota Public Radio introduced its "Budget Balancer" Web site that allowed the public to decide how to balance the budget. The 19-page Web game asked visitors which programs — including education, health and human services, criminal justice, transportation, state government, local aid, and the environment — they would reduce funding for and how much the funding should be reduced. Participants also were asked which, if any, taxes and fees should be increased and by how much, and if slot machines should be allowed at race tracks.

The Democrat and Chronicle newspaper in Rochester, N.Y., launched a program in 2003 called "Fighting For Rochester's Future" that allowed residents to help make decisions regarding the city's public safety, health care, economy, taxation and education. In response to complaints that taxes were too high, the Web site offered a taxation calculator that allowed people to compare their taxes with people in other cities. Visitors to the Web site also were invited to give recommendations on how to rebuild the deteriorating downtown area.

These two projects are only a sample of how the news media are using the Internet to connect with their audiences. As more people connect to the Internet and high-speed access becomes the norm, the news media will find other ways to involve readers and listeners and to form partnerships with their audiences to shape public policy.

ACKNOWLEDGMENTS

The authors wish to thank Professor Beth Evans at California State University, Fullerton, for her invaluable help in writing this book. We also thank Professor Gail Love at California State University, Fullerton, for contributing Chapter 16, Writing for Advertising.

Chapter 1

NEWS IN A MULTIMEDIA WORLD

This chapter:

☑ Explains the differences between information from the mass media and other forms of communication

☑ Discusses the characteristics of news

☑ Explains why some news stories reported by the media have instantaneous and dramatic impact while others have little or no impact

☑ Explains the external pressures that shape news

☑ Addresses some of the criticisms of the news media

Singer Janet Jackson's stunt during the 2004 Super Bowl half time show in which she, with the help of fellow celebrity Justin Timberlake, revealed her right breast on national television was news — or so many members of the press thought. Some television anchors considered it such a big story — or a way to boost ratings — that it was played ad nauseum two weeks after the unveiling.

It caused a stir with the Federal Communications Commission, which readied an investigation into the incident and promised fines. Congress also wanted answers. CBS executives were called to Washington, D.C., to explain why they polluted the airwaves. Meanwhile, the Grammy Awards disinvited Jackson and allowed Timberlake to make a guest appearance only after he apologized profusely. The stunt generated calls by politicians and the public to clean up television programming.

CBS's "60 Minutes," America's popular source of information, produced a similar national stir years ago when it reported that middle-aged American men were three times more likely to die of heart attacks than Frenchmen of the same age.

How could it be? The average Frenchman eats 30 percent more fat, smokes more and exercises less. The secret, according to "60 Minutes" correspondent Morley Safer, is in the wine. The average Frenchman drinks 10 times more wine — mostly red wine — than does the average American. "For years ... doctors in many countries [have believed] that alcohol — in particular, red wine — reduces the risk of heart disease," Safer reported.

The media in this cholesterol-clogged nation bannered the story the next day, and wine sales across the United States increased some 46 percent over the same period the previous year. When "60 Minutes" rebroadcast the story nine months later, wine sales jumped even higher — some 49 percent over the same period the year before.

A health story in 2003 had a similar impact. Media coverage of the popular high-protein, low-carbohydrate Atkins diet caused a national fad, attracting some 32 million "health-conscious" Americans. Seeing a 40 percent drop in bread consumption from the previous year, the bread industry called a crisis "bread summit." The story also shook the restaurant and fast-food industries, prompting urgent meetings concerning the future of diners' palates. Again, the French chuckled. The average American eats 54 pounds of bread a year, barely a third of the quantity consumed by the French and Italians.

And who can forget Oprah Winfrey's April 1996 broadcast that sent beef prices into free-fall for nearly a year? Former cattle rancher Howard Lyman, touting the benefits of vegetarianism, told Winfrey and her national audience that practices by the beef industry could lead to an outbreak of mad cow disease. Winfrey told her audience "The presentation stopped me cold from eating another hamburger!"

The National Cattlemen's Beef Association felt so threatened that it initiated a $2-million lawsuit against Lyman and the talk show host. The beef industry sued under Texas' little-used "veggie libel" law that forbids false and disparaging remarks about agricultural products, claiming the nationally televised comments caused beef prices to tumble and cost ranchers millions of dollars.

MEDIA, NEWS AND THE PUBLIC

Information via America's media — newspapers, magazines, radio, television and the Internet — has had a profound impact on American culture, society, politics and, in recent years, eating and drinking behaviors. And the patterns of consumption of this information are constantly changing.

According to a 2004 survey of 1,506 American adults by the Washington-based Pew Research Center for the People & the Press, about 42 percent got their information about the 2004 presidential election from local television. That is down 6 percent from 2000.

Network news viewing fell by 10 percent and newspapers readership dipped 9 percent from 2000 to 2004 as more Americans turned to the Internet. About 13 percent of Americans — a percentage twice that from 2000 — said they regularly visited the Internet to find out about the candidates and issues. Thus, the Internet now boasts as many visitors to political and news Web sites as people who watch public television, Sunday morning news programs and weekly news magazines.

Surprisingly, 30 percent of adults said they get their news from late-night comedy shows, such as NBC's "Saturday Night Live" and Comedy Central's "The Daily Show." About 23 percent said they get their news about political races from the nightly news, down significantly from the 39 percent in 2000. However, 38 percent said they get their news from cable news networks such as CNN and Fox News.

The public turned to cable news when the nation was hit with back-to-back historic events — the disputed presidential race of 2000 between George W. Bush and Al Gore, and the Sept. 11, 2001, terrorist attacks. They wanted more and immediate news and better journalism because their own interests were at risk. According to Leonard Downie Jr. and Robert G. Kaiser in "The News About the News," pandering to the popular appetite for scandal and celebrity had been commercially rewarding for some, but the terrorists reminded us all of the difference between pap and serious journalism.

The events also showed that news organizations knew how to respond to what was happening even if it hurt their pocketbooks. Television news organizations, for example, suspended commercials, and newspaper chains spent heavily on extra editions and expanded news coverage to get out information they thought was important.

Those two events defined the characteristics of mass communications and the product — information — they disseminate.

CHARACTERISTICS OF MASS COMMUNICATIONS

Perhaps the greatest difference between information from the mass media and other forms of communication is that most mass media are commercial. Most of the more than $123 billion a year American mass communication industries generate comes directly from advertisers. In their book "Interplay of Influence," Kathleen Hall Jamieson and Karlyn Kohrs Campbell note that other distinct differences between information from the mass media and other forms of communications are due to the media's audience, messages and sources.

The Audience

The audience for mass media information is large, anonymous and heterogeneous. Some 98 percent of American households have television sets; 99 percent own radios; 62 percent of all adults read a daily newspaper; 86 percent of all adults read a newspaper at least once a week; adults read an average of 10 magazines a month; half of all Americans buy at least one book a year; and the average library user borrows 15 items a year.

This mass audience is anonymous in that producers of mass media information don't know exactly who is watching, listening or reading. In turn, if writers or producers know their audiences at all, it is generally in terms of their aggregate market characteristics: age, sex, occupation, political orientation or brand preferences.

The mass audience is also heterogeneous. People of different ages and educational and socio-economic levels watch, listen or read mass media information.

The Message

These mass audiences receive information that is simple in form and content, transient, transmitted rapidly, and limited to time and space. Disseminators of information are conscious of what Wilbur Schramm, the founding father of communications research, called the fraction of selection. That model dictates that producers of information should make the consumption of information by audiences as effortless as possible. To do that, messages must be written simply, concisely and precisely. According to Schramm, simple messages will bring about the greatest reward — large readership for the mass media and a greater understanding of the information by the consumer.

Mass media information is transient. It is composed of short-lived messages that are meant to be consumed immediately because they are usually useful only for the moment. We treasure a Matisse or Renoir, carefully store a recording of Beethoven and Mozart, spend a lifetime collecting the works of D.H. Lawrence or Ernest Hemingway, but put our newspaper in the recycling bin after one day.

Mass media information is transmitted rapidly, and most consumers receive it at the same time. Together Americans watched live television coverage of the rover Spirit criss-crossing planet Mars in 2004; the Sept. 11, 2001, terrorist attacks on the World Trade Center; and U.S. bombing raids in Afghanistan and Iraq. Mass media information is limited to time and space. With the exception of the Internet, mass media usually have a finite number of pages or minutes in which to convey their information. That time or space is dependent on the amount of advertising. The timing of the information and amount of important information also determine whether it will be available to the consumer. What else is happening on a particular day, when tied to the time and space limitations, becomes relevant when media decide which information to disseminate to consumers.

The Source

Finally, according to Jamieson and Campbell, sources of mass media messages must be organizational or institutional — radio and television networks, newspaper chains, publishing firms, Internet service providers and conglomerates owning different media or a variety of industries — because sending messages is costly and complex.

What messages, then, do these impersonal organizations disseminate to their audience?

NEWS AS INFORMATION

Messages called *news* are at the core of mass communication's information function. However, it is unlikely that any two journalists would come up with the same definition of the term. An often-used definition is that news is a report of what is happening now, a report of anything of interest to a large number of people.

For most of the 20th century, journalism schools taught that news also should be "objective" — free of political bias from the publisher and free of personal bias from the reporter and editor. However, in their role as *gatekeepers* — people who control the flow of information to others, selecting what is important and what shall be discarded — reporters and editors make personal judgments whether to share the information with consumers.

This gatekeeping process colors all news. Gatekeepers embellish, delete and improve messages. For example, reporters decide which events to cover and which sources to use. Sources decide what information to tell reporters. Reporters decide what information to report. Editors decide what information should be included, combined or deleted from the final product. Except for live reporting, news seldom reaches its audience in its purest form.

CHARACTERISTICS OF NEWS

In their role as gatekeepers, reporters and editors are trained to recognize and value issues that are "newsworthy" by virtue of how much the issue reflects, or can be made to reflect, newsworthiness criteria. News judgment is the understanding of what is newsworthy. It is the process of selecting and evaluating news and visuals to determine if they should be used, if they should be used in part or full, and where they should be used.

No two Web sites, publications or broadcast news programs look the same every day because no two people exercise their judgment in exactly the same way. However, criteria do exist to help editors and producers evaluate the news. A medium's audience is the most important criterion. No two newspaper audiences may be exactly alike. News and visual selections of a newspaper whose circulation area is comprised largely of senior citizens may be different from those of a newspaper that caters to a younger readership. With the help of readership studies and focus groups, editors have a feel for the tastes and interests of their audience. Still other important newsworthy criteria are impact, conflict, proximity, unusualness, timeliness and prominence.

Impact

The magnitude of the event, action or crime and its impact on individuals may determine the news value of facts or images. How many are dead? What is the extent of the property damage? How many people will be affected? The 6.7-magnitude quake that struck the ancient Iranian city of Bam in 2003 found its way onto the world's front pages and prime-time broadcasts only after reports filtered out that some 20,000 people may have been killed or injured and that 70 percent of the houses were flattened.

Impact also deals with information and images that are personalized and individualized so that audiences can identify with them. It is one thing to write about or show photographs of the crippled landscape of Bam. It is another to show or report about a 17-year-old girl who lost her parents, grandmother and two sisters under the rubble.

Conflict

Much of the news we see and hear involves conflict. Stories about terrorism, wars and crimes all involve conflicts. The Iranian earthquake story could be described as a conflict between man and nature or between rescuers searching for survivors and the clock. Describing news events in terms of conflicts makes the narrative more dramatic and compelling, and these stories attract a greater number of viewers and readers. Even political stories are often framed in terms of conflicts, with reporters focusing more on how the campaign is fought rather than where candidates stand on the issues.

Proximity

Stories in our own backyard have more news value than those thousands of miles away. Finding the local angle of a national or international story will heighten reader interest. The newsroom word for this is *localizing*, which can be done with breaking stories as well as features. How will new state tax laws affect readers in my community? How did local schools rate on state or national tests? How did your city or state rate in the annual list of best places to live?

Unusualness

Novel, deviant or odd information is newsworthy. The news value is heightened by the more novel, deviant or odd the information is. In his book "On Press," Tom Wicker writes, "The dull, the routine, the unexciting, is seldom seen as news, although ... the dull, routine, unexciting management of rates and routes for the railroads, truckers, and airlines may affect far more Americans in their daily lives than some relatively more glamorous presidential directive or congressional action." Most newscasts end today with some unusual or odd piece of information.

Issues not only receive mass media coverage because of these newsworthy qualities and others — such as progress, science and sex — but the information also must be timely, which is perhaps the most important criterion for newsworthiness.

Timeliness

News is important when it happens. Nothing is more stale or of less value than yesterday's news. The "breaking" quality of news is its most important characteristic. That's why media provide updates to old stories. Updates are attempts to make old stories timely by presenting new perspectives or information. The mass media's constant need for new information partially explains why it is so unusual for a public issue to stay on the evening news and on the front page for very long. Once an issue receives media coverage, it usually remains on the news agenda for a fairly short time.

Prominence

Prominent individuals are newsworthy. Information from or about the famous and infamous influences news selection. And the more famous or infamous the individual, the more likely the mass media will use the information. For example, thousands of Americans get married and divorced each year, but only high-profile figures such as Julia Roberts, Jennifer Lopez and Liza Minnelli make the news each time they walk down the aisle.

Prominent individuals help us humanize and individualize information, making the information more credible and understandable. For example, the abstract ideas of President Ronald Reagan's economic theory were personalized as "Reaganomics."

In addition, prominent individuals lure audiences to mass media information. Interviews with "stars" in government, science, medicine, education and economics allow reporters to call upon experts who help draw attention to information.

Elements of impact, proximity, unusualness, timeliness and prominence determine the newsworthiness of information for the mass media. However, external forces can influence this information as well.

EXTERNAL PRESSURES ON THE NEWS MEDIA

The mass media's information function is influenced by numerous pressures: consumer pressures, political pressures and commercial pressures.

Individuals, groups and organizations attempt to influence information by manipulating deadlines and access and by packaging events. Presidents manipulate information through photogenic pseudo-events, news conferences, exclusive interviews and news leaks. Federal agencies manipulate information in the name of national security, while state and local governments manipulate information by threatening the financial base of the media organizations.

Besides consumer and political pressures, news can be influenced by commercial pressures such as loss of advertising or the threat of lawsuits. Advertising revenues partly finance newspapers and magazines and completely finance most radio and television stations. More than one advertiser has threatened to pull its advertisements or sponsorship as a means of manipulating the media. Besides pulling advertisements, companies have threatened media organizations with libel suits. The threat has made many news organizations think twice about pursuing investigative reports on controversial issues.

The characteristics of newsworthiness and external pressures on the news media enable journalists to sort information into categories such as hard news, straight news, and soft news or feature stories.

CATEGORIES OF INFORMATION

Hard news is the factual account of a timely event — one that occurred in the previous 24 hours or one that treats an issue of ongoing concern. Traditionally, hard news stories were written in the inverted pyramid style of writing. That is, the most important news elements — the *who, what, when, where* and sometimes, the *why* and *how* included in an opening sentence, the lead of the story.

Various types of hard news stories exist: *spot, enterprise* and *investigative*. Spot or breaking news is up-to-the-minute coverage of events as they happen. The most dramatic in recent years occurred following the terrorist attacks on the World Trade Center and the U.S. invasion of Iraq. Enterprise stories occur when editors and reporters think up story ideas on their own and ask questions others may not have asked in an effort to present the public with new information it may never have imagined. Investigative news reporting involves efforts by reporters to expose wrongdoing, crime or disturbing trends in society.

Straight news is synonymous with this hard-news type of reporting. However, it is considered a factual style of writing more than a type of news. That is in contrast to a feature treatment, in which the writer relies heavily on quotations and descriptions.

Soft news or feature stories are less timely, often of less consequence and not always based on current news. Take the Orange County (Calif.) Register's story of a woman who shed some 621 pounds, her house and her husband. Readers could live without the information, but it made for a good feature — which provided much fare for the tabloids and television talk shows. She became a regular guest with some "gurus of gab" such as Maury Povich.

Her debut on the TV talk show is just one example of the blurring of lines between information and entertainment.

THE RISE OF "INFOTAINMENT"

This convergence of information and entertainment has appropriately been labeled "infotainment." The blur between "substance and fluff," between "journalism and hype," between "news and entertainment," according to Los Angeles Times media critic David Shaw, has been caused by the proliferation of "fact-based docudramas, tabloid TV shows such as 'Access Hollywood,' 'Hard Copy' and 'Inside Edition' and local TV news shows that emphasize murder and mayhem — flash, crash and trash."

At one time news constituted only a small part of the television networks' empires. Today, it has become an extension of their entertainment businesses and a way to promote them. The networks and local television devote portions of their news programs promoting features about their parent networks' entertainment shows. Furthermore, Downie Jr. and Kaiser in "The News About the News" wrote that the network-owned television newsmagazines feature crime and celebrity stories to compete for prime-time ratings with dramas and situation comedies. They reveal that "NBC decided that such 'infotainment' was a better prime-time product than old-fashioned entertainment — much cheaper to produce, easy for an network to control and attractive to advertisers." For example, ABC's prime-time broadcast of an interview with former White House intern Monica Lewinsky drew an audience of 49 million people, bigger than any previous audience for a network news program.

CHANNELS OF INFORMATION

The rise of infotainment may have to do more with the network where the information is carried than with the nature of the information. At first, it may appear that Marshall McLuhan was correct: "The medium is the message." But McLuhan's logic is too simplified.

Different kinds of news stories can be told about identical events, depending upon which medium does the telling. In their book "Nightly Horrors: Crisis Coverage in Television Network News," Dan Nimbi and James E. Combs write that it may not be that "the medium is the message" as McLuhan said, but, rather [that the medium is] the stylizer of the message."

Certainly information broadcast on television — a medium for creating image — is more dramatic than the same information published in newspapers — a medium for presenting ideas. Reporters who create reality by telling stories that are dramatic, colorful, novel and sensational capture the largest audience. Does this explain then why some stories reported by the media have instantaneous and dramatic impact while other stories have little or no impact at all? And why some stories disseminated by one medium have more impact than others?

CHARACTERISTICS OF HIGH IMPACT NEWS STORIES

As we have seen, the characteristics of information, specifically the news value of facts, determine why some information presented by the mass media is more important than other information. The question is: Why do certain stories disseminated by the mass media have more impact than others? First, how does one measure the impact of mass media's information function?

High-impact stories, according to Shaw, generally are dependent on three sets of reactions:

☑ Do other major media pick up the story and extend both its reach and its life?

☑ Do social and political institutions respond, with an investigation if the initial story alleges wrongdoing?

☑ Does the public at large become caught up in the story?

High-impact stories also possess these attributes: issue gratification, issue credibility and issue familiarity.

Issue Gratification

Schramm distinguished between two types of information presented by the news media: immediate- and delayed-reward stories. Immediate-reward stories provide instant gratification for readers, listeners and viewers. Audiences obtain immediate rewards from information that can be used at once. The heart-wine connection story by "60 Minutes" was an immediate-reward story. It produced an array of immediate rewards for listeners. Delayed-reward stories provide information that consumers will file away and use at some other time. For example, information on the dangers of measles for pregnant women may be useful to couples and recalled at a later date when they are planning a family.

Issue Credibility

Besides providing immediate gratification, high-impact stories must be credible. According to sociologist Herbert Gans, author of "Deciding What's News," "news that is not believable is short-lived."

For example, it took a long time for Watergate to have any impact. The public could not believe that White House officials could have orchestrated the burglary of the Democratic Party headquarters. Even more incredible were stories that the president of the United States was involved in a massive cover-up of covert action.

Issue Familiarity

In addition to providing immediate gratification and being credible, high-impact stories must deal with facts with which the public has some familiarity. Studies have shown that media's influence is "contingent on the audience's pre-existing issue sensitivity." Simply, a story will have more impact the more the listener or reader knows about the issue.

Issue gratification, issue credibility and issue familiarity, then, help determine which news stories will likely be high-impact stories. But do media play a role in what impact a story will have?

MEDIA'S INFLUENTIAL ROLE

In a 2003 poll by the Pew Research Center for the People & the Press, 55 percent of Americans interviewed said the media's influence is growing, not decreasing. This is a view that has been consistent since the mid-1980s. However, those under the age of 30 are most likely to see media influence as increasing.

A story's impact may depend on the medium. Let's revisit the "60 Minutes" story on the wine-healthy heart connection. Some 18 months before "60 Minutes" aired the program about the longevity of Frenchmen compared to American men, the same information appeared in the magazine In Health. The San Francisco Chronicle and the Los Angeles Times then published it. None of the stories generated much public interest. The interest generated by the "60 Minutes" story underscored the power of television.

Not only do more Americans get their news from television, but results of a recent poll show that television has replaced newspapers as the most trusted medium in the minds of most Americans. That doesn't mean, however, the public is without criticism of their main providers of information.

CRITICISMS OF THE NEWS MEDIA

Everyone has an opinion about mass media's performance as a provider of information. The most heard criticisms are these: the news media are biased; the news media rely on sensationalism to attract an audience; and the news media invade the privacy of individuals.

Journalistic Bias

The 2004 Pew Research Center for the People & the Press survey revealed that 61 percent of Americans believe the news media were biased in coverage of the 2000 presidential election. Nearly 33 percent of Democrats believed the television coverage of the election is biased toward the Republicans while more than 40 percent of Republicans said the election news is skewed toward the Democrats. What is astonishing is that 16 years ago — before Rush Limbaugh, the Internet and Fox News — some 62 percent believed the news was unbiased and objective.

Conservatives, such as Limbaugh, have been the most vocal in charging that the media are biased, favoring Democrats over Republicans and liberals over conservatives. It used to be that most journalists were liberals while management was conservative. In their study, "The American Journalist: A Portrait of U.S. News People and Their Work," researchers David Weaver and Cleveland Wilhoit found that most journalists identified themselves as independents, more so than the number of people in the general population who see themselves as independents, although a large percentage of reporters voted for Democrats.

But the charge of journalistic bias is likely to stick. Why? First, news is concerned with change because that is more interesting than the status quo. Because conservatives favor the status quo, they are more likely to find news coverage on change or proposals for change more threatening and uncomfortable. Second, implicit in the First Amendment is the belief that the news media should serve as watchdog. Journalists consider themselves members of what is referred to as "the Fourth Estate," as if they are a branch of government. This makes it their duty to serve as a check on the other branches of government by keeping government honest and responsive to the people. The problem is that watchdogs are sometimes critical and antagonistic, a style foreign to the more conservative elements of society.

Reliance on the Sensational

The news media are criticized for using sensationalism to attract audiences. However, some media owners are quick to point out "that is what sells newspapers." It certainly is what's selling the growing number of TV infotainment programs: "Hard Copy," "Access Hollywood," "Inside Edition," "Entertainment Tonight" and "Extra." And don't forget "Oprah Winfrey" and the sleazier talk shows of "Jerry Springer" and "Jenny Jones." The problem is that about a fourth of the general public lumps this "new media" in with "the news media."

Do the mainstream media deserve this rap? Probably. Conscious of ratings, television news programs are not averse to leading with the most sensational, sexy, attention-getting story available. Take Janet Jackson's 2004 Super Bowl stunt that bared her right breast on national television, or Madonna and Britney Spears' television kiss. Both were replayed until the public took them as legitimate news.

In addition, the successful national newspaper USA Today, the print version of television, has had a profound impact on newspapers. Newspapers across the nation now emulate its superficial approach to news — short and snappy stories that are accompanied by colorful and glitzy graphics.

Invasion of Privacy

Finally, the news media have been criticized for invading the privacy of individuals. Many people blamed the news media for Princess Diana's death in a car accident. Others are horrified that the media photograph people's grief at murder scenes, funerals and disasters. However, many members of the news media believe the image of a murder's impact on one family may rush society into fighting crime and violence.

Consumers appear to be attracted to news media for their storytelling function – media that fashion information in a dramatic and colorful way. But they consider journalists biased and the news media sensational, and it bothers them that the news media are not respectful of people's privacy.

New Communication Technologies and the Commercialization of Information

The reliance on television has had an influence on news consumption, but converging technologies are also changing communication. The telephone is a key component of the technological revolution. For example, semiconductors are allowing more voices to be carried simultaneously on a single cable, while optical fiber cable is allowing greater capacity to carry messages with better quality at less cost. The result is digital computerized mass communication — tagged as the "new medium." Digitization allows a message — whether sound, words or pictures — to be reduced to millions and millions of signals.

What does this mean for society? The good news is that more information will be available, whether by computer or television. The bad news, according to many media observers, is that the new medium will bring about a widening polarization along social class lines of those who have the technology available to them and those who do not.

High Speed on the Information Superhighway

Ideally, the new medium will allow more information to be provided to more people at greater speeds. In his book "Creating Tomorrow's Mass Media," Harry Marsh predicts that the new medium may contribute to "a new environment of intellectual activity, an open environment that will diminish the constraints of time and space." Marsh notes that "providers of information will have the maximum opportunity for complete exposure through multimedia." In addition, for information of specialized interest, "providers can strive for the maximum in detail but also the perspective and background that gives the information meaning."

More importantly, Marsh predicts that the new medium will allow society to acquire, organize and contribute information freely. The end result, according to long-time media observer Leo Bogart, will be "a free-flowing, freely accessible electronic information stream."

The Haves and the Have Nots

"The danger lies in the possible creation of information haves and have-nots," according to John Maxwell Hamilton, commentator for Minnesota Public Radio's "MarketPlace." In his article "Areopagitica Redux: In Defense of Electronic Liberties," Hamilton writes that this concern is often framed in terms of money. "Can people afford computers and modems?"

However, the real determinant is likely to be more difficult to overcome, according to Hamilton, who supports the notion that anyone who can buy a Nintendo can buy into the Information Age thanks to decreasing costs. He also notes that education and interest are going to be the filters.

Hamilton also predicts the new medium will likely bring about "the relentless commercialization of information." Information is big business, and with it comes the promise of big profits. Conglomerates like Time Warner, Disney, News Corp. and Westinghouse are making mega bucks on information. And the intense competition that is likely to arise among these conglomerates, however, may not be all bad. According to Hamilton, intense competition in the news and information business could encourage serious, in-depth, engaging coverage of public policy issues. However, he sees danger on the horizon if competition and fixation on the bottom line drive everyone to design news products that achieve a high level of marketability and discourage them from enticing people to take information they may not particularly want but need in order to be good citizen-voters.

For instance, Bogart says the growing preference today for entertainment over knowledge may produce a polarization along social class lines of entertainment consumers and knowledge consumers. He writes, "An information highway that's jammed with the likes of the Jackson family, Madonna, and Ice-T can easily be a road to nowhere."

THE INFORMATION FUNCTION OF MASS COMMUNICATION

Mass media's most important function is providing information. Messages called news are at the core of mass communication's information function. News is determined by gatekeepers who determine what information to pass along to their audiences. Gatekeepers are trained to recognize elements — conflict, impact, proximity, unusualness, timeliness and prominence — that make information newsworthy. What is deemed newsworthy also is influenced by external pressures: consumer pressures, political pressures and commercial pressures. Impact of media information also depends on how much gratification the information produces and the believability of and audience's familiarity with issues being reported. But members of the public also are critical of the media. They consider them biased, sensational and disrespectful of people's privacy. Finally, and most importantly, the news media are agents of change that have had the most profound impact on the nation's social, cultural and political institutions — as well as its eating and drinking behaviors.

Exercise 1: Media Use

Keep a daily journal of your news reading, viewing and listening habits for a week. Track the program and the time you spent with the program. Then arrive at a percentage of time you spent with each medium.

Name:	Date:

Exercise 2: News Media Criticism

Write a brief essay in which you discuss your greatest criticism of today's news media.

Exercise 3: Characteristics of News

Clip from a newspaper examples of the various characteristics of news — conflict, impact, proximity, unusualness, timeliness and prominence, among others. Label each story and explain why it fits that category.

Exercise 4: Feature Stories

Clip a feature story and a news story from a newspaper. Explain the differences in the structure and writing style of each.

Chapter 2

WRITING ACROSS THE MEDIA

This chapter:

☑ Explains the strengths and weaknesses of different news media

☑ Discusses how different media gratify audience needs

☑ Shows how news stories in each medium are presented

☑ Explains some of the terms used in the news industry

No matter which medium — newspapers and magazines, radio, television or Internet — reporters are writing for, they are telling stories to a mass audience. These nonfiction stories contain the characteristics of news that we explained in Chapter 1. They are timely stories about newsworthy people and events. They relate information about someone or something (the *who* in stories), tell us *what* occurred, *when* it happened, *where* it happened, *why* it happened and *how* it happened.

All news stories contain the *who, what, where* and *when*; and complete news stories also explain *why* and *how*.

Newsmakers can be our neighbors, celebrities or the movers and shakers of world events. Stories about events might include an elementary school program, a sports contest or the Academy Awards, natural disasters or a war somewhere in the world. Many newsworthy events are not reported in the news; the media don't have enough space or time to share every story. *Gatekeepers* evaluate stories' newsworthiness and then decide which news stories will be reported, how much broadcast time or newspaper space will be given to the stories and where in the broadcast or newspaper they will appear.

While each medium requires specific skills, reporters have many skills and characteristics in common. They are inquisitive; they possess excellent critical-thinking skills and know how to ask probing questions; they have empathy for many of the people they interview and report about; and they possess the writing skills needed to create clear, accurate and precise news articles.

Reporters are not stenographers for governments or powerful special interests. They are disinterested and unbiased chroniclers of events, and they talk to numerous sources on both sides of an issue before they begin to write their stories.

Reporters put stories in a context that their audiences can relate to. They make the stories relevant. For example, a story about labor unrest and threats of a military takeover in Venezuela would mean little to an American audience; it is in a distant country, and events there seem to have no impact on our lives. The impact would be greater if the story explained that Venezuela is a major supplier of oil to the United States and the conflict could result in higher fuel prices.

July 2, 2003

New Newsday Editor to Focus on Convergence

By Joe Strupp

NEW YORK — Incoming Newsday Editor Howard Schneider plans to increase convergence between the newspaper and its Web site, radio, and television links when he replaces retiring Editor Anthony Marro, who announced his resignation Wednesday.

Schneider, 57, who has been at the paper since 1969 and is responsible for the Web-related coverage, said more staffers will be trained to work in multiple mediums, while new hires will be looked at with more of an emphasis on convergence training.

"We will find people in the newsroom who have an appetite for this and begin to cross-train them," said Schneider, who currently serves as managing editor and vice president/content. "Some people will have to come into the newsroom with multiple skills as well."

Newsday, owned by Chicago's Tribune Co., currently does some cross-promotion with Tribune-owned WPIX TV in New York, including story teasers on the station's morning and evening news casts. In addition, a Newsday staffer conducts a twice-daily newscast from the paper's newsroom for WALK Radio of Long Island, while a nightly business report for News 12 Long Island originates from Newsday as well.

Schneider said those relationships will be expanded. "I see more collaboration [with WPIX] and more content sharing," he said. "Some special reports and more with the morning show."

Reporters also understand that people select the source of news that best gratifies their needs at a specific time. Newspapers and the Internet offer in-depth coverage of the day's events, but they also demand more of the readers' time and attention than television and radio. People must concentrate on what they're reading in order to comprehend the story. The Internet is more demanding than newspapers because readers can choose how much of the story and in what order they want to read it. They also have the opportunity to use Internet *links*, shortcuts to other Web sites, to read related stories and background information or to view a broadcast version of the story. Internet users also have the option of reading different versions of the same story on various Web sites.

Most network and 11 p.m. TV news reports are 30 minutes long, and news radio recycles stories about every 30 minutes. Early evening local TV news reports are often 60 minutes. Radio and TV audiences know they need only make a 30- to 60-minute commitment to learn about the day's events. Newspaper subscribers and Internet surfers can spend several hours a day poring over the news. Newspapers also offer a larger number of stories with more details and explanations than broadcast's "headline news."

Getting news from radio and television is a passive activity; these media don't demand as much of the audience's attention. People can make or eat dinner while watching the news, for example, or listen to the news while driving. Someone reading a newspaper while driving, however, might find himself in the news.

Broadcast news presentation is linear. We watch or listen to news in a prearranged order. We cannot fast forward through news stories we're not interested in or immediately go to the sports news. We also are forced to sit through the commercials, which support almost all mass media in this country. We can skim a newspaper's headlines and pause to read only the stories we care about. We also can go immediately to the section of the paper we're most interested in, and we can ignore the advertisements.

Newspapers and magazines also have the greatest mobility. We can read in any room in the house or office, take a newspaper to breakfast or lunch, or read it on a plane while flying across the country. Radio, and to a lesser degree television, have some mobility, but they are limited by the station's broadcast range — unless the viewer also has a portable satellite dish. The day may be fast approaching when wireless Internet access is so cheap and convenient that we can remain online all day anywhere in the world.

Broadcast news, on the other hand, is the most timely. A radio reporter with a cell phone can be on the air within seconds of arriving at a news event. A TV crew with a satellite truck can be on the air within minutes. Newspapers only publish once a day, and stories in papers' morning editions, which are written the day before, are more than 12 hours old by the time readers open their papers. Stories can be uploaded onto the Internet as soon as they are written, so the news is more timely than what's in a newspaper, but it takes time to write and edit stories and format them for the Internet. Television and radio always will be first with breaking news stories.

In summary, broadcast news doesn't demand 100 percent of our attention and allows us to perform other tasks while offering brief summaries of the day's events, while printed publications and the Internet demand more of our attention and time while providing in-depth accounts that better explain the stories. Newspapers also offer greater mobility. One gratifies our need to obtain information easily and quickly; the other gratifies our need for in-depth information. Print and the Internet also give us the option of skipping news stories we're not interested in and moving on to the next story once we feel we have enough information.

Savvy news consumers rely on both broadcast and print/Internet. They watch news summaries in the morning or listen to them during their commute to and from work or school and later read the rest of the story on the Internet or in their newspapers. People cannot expect to be fully informed if they rely solely on television or radio as their source of information. All the words in a 30-minutes news broadcast would not fill the first page of a newspaper. Venerated former CBS News anchor Walter Cronkite, in his memoir "A Reporter's Life," wrote, "The nation whose population depends on the explosively compressed headline service of television news can expect to be exploited by the demagogues and dictators who prey upon the semi-informed."

Each of these media tell their stories differently using different writing styles. Here's an overview of the characteristics of print, radio, television and Internet reporting:

PRINT

Many stories are written by the newspaper's staff, and others are provided by wire services such as The Associated Press and Reuters. A paper's reporters and their editors usually agree before the story is written how long it will be based on the story's importance and complexity.

The average newspaper story is about 500 to 700 words long, or about 14 to 20 *column inches*. A column inch is type set for a newspaper column that is one inch deep. Most newspaper pages contain six columns about 21 inches long, or about 126 column inches per page. Feature stories, analyses and important stories can be much longer than 14 column inches, sometimes more than 100 column inches. Newspapers also run briefs, which are four- or five-sentence stories about less important events, such as a transit strike in another state.

Newspapers usually are organized into topics, which are traditionally main news (the front section, which often contains the most important local news plus regional, national and international news), local news, business, sports, entertainment, features, and classified advertising and other advertising sections. Features will include stories on fashion, home decorating or profiles as well as advice columns and comics. Larger newspapers put each topic in separate pull-out sections. Smaller papers might combine local and non-local news, business and sports, and entertainment and features.

Stories can be written in many styles, which we'll explain later. The traditional style, called the *inverted pyramid*, starts with a first sentence, called the *lead*, that gives a summary of the latest and most important information in the story. The rest of the story explains what happened in order of importance. This style is

---

Newspaper Terms

Attribution — The source of information

Byline — The name of the story's author at the top of the story

Breaking news story — A news event that's happening right now

Column inch — Type set for a newspaper column that is one inch deep, about 30 to 35 words

Copy — A news story

Deadline — When a completed story is due to the editor

Editor — A reporter's supervisor, or someone who handles copy after it has been written

Headline — The text above the story explaining what the story is about

Inverted pyramid — A style of writing where the most important information is at the top of the story

Lead — The first sentence of a story

Package — A story with photos, graphics, sidebars etc. displayed together

Sidebar — A story related to and often packaged with the main story

Summary lead — The story's first sentence that summarizes what the story is about

much like how someone would describe an incident he or she witnessed. It's what would come after the question, "Guess what I saw today?"

Reporters can't rely on photographers to show readers what has happened. The writers have to paint pictures with words to show what has occurred. They accomplish this by using strong verbs and adjectives.

Let's examine how a newspaper would report Shakespeare's tragic story of "Romeo and Juliet," the doomed star-crossed lovers. Every story answers the questions *who, what, when* and *where*, and a complete story also answers *why* and *how*. In this story:

Who: Romeo and Juliet

What: committed suicide

When: Thursday

Where: the Capulet crypt in Verona

Why: each thought the other was dead and didn't want to go on living

How: Romeo took poison; Juliet used a knife

Here's a morning newspaper's version. The story is about 680 words, or about 19 column inches. The average sentence length is 19 words.

VERONA — The bodies of three teenagers from the city's prominent families were found in a family crypt Thursday in what authorities say was a slaying and double suicide.

Guards discovered the bodies of County Paris, a kinsman of Verona's Prince Escalus; Juliet Capulet; and Romeo Montague in the Capulet family crypt and alerted Escalus and the Montague and Capulet families. Romeo and Juliet were lying side by side in a pool of blood in the musty, dark chamber. Paris' bloodied body was found near the entrance of the crypt.

Juliet had been interred Wednesday after she apparently died Tuesday night, but authorities now say she committed suicide Thursday.

Romeo also apparently committed suicide, and Paris is believed to have been killed in a sword fight with Romeo and then dragged into the tomb. Juliet, 13, was to have married Paris on Wednesday morning.

Friar Lawrence, who was apprehended near the tomb along with Romeo's servant Balthasar, said he had given Juliet a sleeping potion that simulated death so that she could avoid marrying Paris. She had secretly married Romeo on Monday, with Lawrence performing the ceremony.

"Romeo, there dead, was husband to that Juliet; and she, there dead, that Romeo's faithful wife," a visibly shaken Lawrence said.

Lawrence said he sent a messenger to Mantua to tell Romeo what had occurred and to order him to return to Verona so he could open Juliet's casket so she would not suffocate when she awoke.

Romeo fled to Mantua after Escalus exiled him for killing Juliet's cousin, Tybalt, in a street fight Monday. The fight was one of many between the feuding Montague and Capulet families. Tybalt had killed Romeo's cousin, Benvolio, moments earlier in a fight. Escalus broke up a larger fight Monday after Lord Capulet, Lord Montague and their kinsmen confronted each other with drawn swords. The prince threatened to execute anyone involved in another fight.

Escalus blamed the two families for their children's deaths.

"See what a scourge is laid upon your hate, that heaven finds means to kill your joys with love."

Lawrence, who married the couple in his chamber, said he had hoped the marriage would end the feud, which has taken many lives. Romeo met Juliet for the first time Sunday night when he crashed a party hosted by the Capulets to look for another teenager, Rosaline, who had broken up with him. Romeo and Juliet met secretly later that night and agreed to marry. Romeo made the wedding arrangements Monday and relayed them to Juliet through her nurse.

Romeo, who killed Tybalt later that afternoon after the wedding, spent Monday night in Juliet's bedchamber and fled to Mantua early Tuesday at Lawrence's urging. The friar hoped to negotiate for Romeo's return and the families' acceptance of the marriage.

Lawrence gave Juliet the potion to feign death after her parents told her that she was to marry Paris on Wednesday.

The friar said he learned Thursday that his messenger never reached Mantua, and, fearing that Juliet would awaken sealed in her casket, he rushed to the tomb to free her and to hide her in his room until he devised a new plan. He said Romeo and Paris were already dead when he arrived, adding Romeo apparently had taken poison. Romeo had returned to Verona to see Juliet's tomb after Balthasar told him that Juliet had died, Balthasar told authorities.

Lawrence said Juliet became hysterical when she saw Romeo's body. The friar said he was afraid the guards would find them, and he urged Juliet to come with him.

"And she, too desperate, would not go with me," he said.

Lawrence said she apparently killed herself with Romeo's dagger after he fled from the chamber.

He added that if he's responsible for the deaths, "Let my old life be sacrificed, some hour before his time, unto the rigors of the severest law."

Romeo's death was a second blow to Montague family in as many days; Lady Montague also died this week.

"Grief of my son's exile hath stopped her breath," Lord Montague said.

Montague and the Capulets have agreed to end their fighting and to build gold statues to their children.

RADIO

Fewer radio stations offer news today than in the past because the Federal Communications Commission no longer requires them to broadcast news. Most radio stations rely on news services for what little news they offer, and, for the most part, the only stations that do much original reporting today are all-news channels and National Public Radio.

Most news stories for broadcast are short, less than two minutes, and good broadcast reporters know how to relate a great deal of information in a few words; they don't waste words. A typical 90-second broadcast-news item is about 225 words long.

News stories on the radio are written for the ear. Reporters are concerned about how the story sounds, and they often edit their copy by reading it out loud. Reporters on the radio also need to be able create pictures for listeners by using ambient sound and by giving vivid descriptions. This requires a keen eye for detail and strong writing skills to share those details in tightly written copy.

Because of their brevity, broadcast stories usually focus on providing information rather than explanation. They give us the *who, what, when* and *where* of the story but very little of the *why* and *how*. Newspapers, magazines and the Internet often do a better job of explaining an event's *why* and *how* because they have more space to devote to the story. Research shows that many people who listen to or watch news on radio and television also read newspapers to better understand the significance of the story.

Broadcast news stresses immediacy, something that is occurring right now, and reporters use the present tense

---

Broadcast Terms

Anchor lead-in — The anchor's introduction to a reporter's story

B-roll — Video images shown while reporters are talking that illustrates what they are talking about

ENG — Electronic news gathering; the process of gathering news for broadcast

Live shot — A reporter's package live from the scene of breaking news

Lockout — The last sentence in a package that gives the reporter's name and location

Package — A completed news story that is edited and ready to go on the air

Phoner — A telephone interview or live report

Producer — The person in charge of the newscast

SOT — Sound on tape; a subject on tape with an interview or sound bite

Sound bite — A taped quote used by radio and television

Standup — reporter speaking to the camera at the scene of a news event, usually a head and shoulders shot

VO — Voice over; video of a news scene with the reporter's narration added later

as much as possible. "Says" is often preferred to "said," the most common word for attribution in print journalism. Showing irony or humor is easier with broadcast than print because reporters can use their voices to signal the tone of the story. Reporters also must be careful that their body language does not show bias.

Both radio and television news are presented in a more conversational style than printed stories. Broadcast reporters write the way they talk, and the conversational style is simple and informal. Contractions such as "aren't" and "he's" are common. Sentences are short and direct. Appositives, phrases and clauses like this one set off by commas, are avoided because if a listener is distracted, he or she will not understand such a long sentence. The previous sentence would be broken into smaller sentences for broadcast news:

Appositives are phrases and clauses set off by commas. Listeners have trouble comprehending long sentences with appositives. Good broadcast reporters don't use them.

We often speak in sentence fragments and start sentences with "and" and "but," and these grammatical faux pas are allowed in broadcast-news copy. However, this conversational style does not mean you make other grammatical errors, such as with subject-verb agreement or noun-pronoun agreement, or that you can use slang or off-color expressions. Reporters do not want to offend their viewers and listeners.

This radio report on the deaths of Romeo and Juliet would take a little more than one minute to present. Anchors or news readers in a broadcast newsroom serve the same purpose as a newspaper headline: They tell us a little about the story's content. In broadcast news, however, these introductions also attract the audience's attention. The average sentence length is 12 words.

ANCHOR:
Tragedy struck three of Verona's prominent families today. Here's reporter Bill Shakespeare with the details.

SHAKESPEARE:
I'm here at the Capulet family crypt in Verona, where the bodies of three teens were discovered today inside this dark, damp chamber. The Capulets' daughter, Juliet, and Romeo Montague both committed suicide. The body of County Paris was found nearby. Romeo apparently killed Paris, who is related to Prince Escalus.

Juliet was brought here Wednesday after her family thought she was dead. But family friend Friar Lawrence says he gave her a potion to fake her death. Guards apprehended Lawrence near the tomb. He says Juliet took the potion to avoid marrying Paris. Lawrence says he secretly married Romeo and Juliet on Monday.

Romeo was supposed to be at Juliet's side when she awoke in the tomb. But Romeo didn't know the death was faked and took poison when he reached her crypt. Juliet killed herself when she found his body.

Lawrence said he hoped the marriage would end the years of deadly fighting between the Montague and Capulet families.

These deaths may accomplish what the marriage couldn't. The families have agreed to end their longtime feud.

As you can see, many of the details had to be omitted, but the main points, the *who, what, when* and *where* of the story, remain. We know a little about the *why* surrounding the deaths but know exactly *how* the deaths occurred. The last paragraph of the story probably would not be appropriate for a newspaper story because it's the reporter's opinion. Because broadcast stories are in a casual style, it is appropriate here.

TELEVISION

TV news often has two characteristics that are not essential for stories in newspapers: simplicity and imagery. Like radio, TV reporters must condense stories to their simplest elements in order to tell the story in a short amount of time. Television news reports run 30 seconds to two minutes, or about 90 to 300 words. At the same time, reporters must avoid oversimplifying stories to the point of making them meaningless; consequently, news producers and reporters tend to choose easily explainable stories such as a police chase, new chimpanzee quarters at the zoo, police crackdown on drunken drivers and other non-complex stories. Even the TV news-magazine programs such as "60 Minutes" or "Dateline NBC," which air multifaceted stories eight to 10 minutes long, condense and simplify stories.

Compelling images are also a factor in TV news selection. Television uses visuals to tell the story, and the story's text is written to complement the images, but reporters do not repeat what is seen in the pictures. A house fire is more likely to get prominent play on TV than in a newspaper or on the radio because of the dramatic video images. Conversely, an ongoing story about a political standoff over the state budget and how it could affect schools and government services might be the lead story in a newspaper because it has impact on the readers. However, it most likely would not be the lead story on television, if reported at all, because it is difficult to explain in 60 seconds and lacks compelling visuals.

Television's images also can affect its audience differently than how words on paper or a computer screen do. We absorb printed information cognitively; we apply reasoning to what we read. Images affect us emotionally; we feel empathy, horror, rage etc. at what we see. During the U.S. invasion of Iraq in 2003, newspaper stories about U.S. casualties did not spark public outcry. Many people, however, were angry and upset to see the dead American soldiers on television.

Television news often stresses immediacy by having journalists report live from the scene of a news event that occurred earlier in the day. For example, a reporter will begin a news segment with a standup at the intersection where a truck jackknifed earlier in the day, spilling toxic chemicals on the road. The reporter will describe what happened while viewers see B-roll, footage of the accident shot earlier in the day. The live standup at the beginning of the segment gives the news immediacy.

Both radio and television sometimes emphasize the "what's next" aspect of the story to reinforce the sense of immediacy. The reporters focus on the next phase of what's happening rather than on what has occurred. Here is how a TV reporter's story on Romeo and Juliet might appear. Shakespeare's play is nearly three hours long. This TV news report would run a little more than 90 seconds. We won't worry about how TV news copy is formatted. The average sentence length is just under 13 words.

ANCHOR:
Two tragic suicides may have brought an end to the long, deadly feud between the Montagues and Capulets. Here's reporter Bill Shakespeare with the story.
SHAKESPEARE [STANDING IN FRONT OF THE ENTRANCE TO THE CRYPT]:
I'm at the Capulet family crypt, where the grieving Capulets and Lord Montague have finally put aside their differences.
[B-ROLL OF BODIES ON GURNIES BEING PUT IN A CORONER'S VAN]
The bodies of Juliet Capulet and Romeo Montague were discovered today inside this chamber. The body of County Paris was found just inside this entrance. Romeo apparently killed Paris, who is related to Prince Escalus. We can still see the blood on the ground here by the entrance.
Juliet was brought here Wednesday after her family thought she was dead. But family friend Friar Lawrence now says he gave her a potion to fake her death. He says Juliet took the potion to avoid marrying Paris. Romeo and Juliet were secretly married Monday by Lawrence.
[SHOT (SOUND ON TAPE) OF LAWRENCE]:
Romeo, there dead, was husband to that Juliet; and she, there dead, that Romeo's faithful wife.
[SHAKESPEARE STANDUP]:
Lawrence says Romeo was supposed to be at Juliet's side when she awoke. But Romeo didn't know the death was faked and took poison when he got here. Juliet killed herself when she found his body.
Lawrence says he hoped the marriage would end fighting between the Montagues and Capulets.
These deaths have accomplished what the marriage couldn't. The families have agreed to end the bloodshed and will build gold statues of their children.
Reporting live from Verona, this is Bill Shakespeare.

The last sentence, the *lockout*, signals to the audience that the story is completed.

INTERNET

The Internet is the first new mass medium in more than 50 years. Although the Internet is not much more than 10 years old, a study by the Pew Internet and American Life Project in the spring of 2003 found that about 72 million American adults go online each day and that 32 percent — more than 23 million people — use the Internet to get news.

The most popular Web sites for news are those maintained by traditional news media such as The New York Times, CNN and other mainstream news outlets. Internet users are more likely to read newspapers than the public in general, though recent studies indicate this trend may be ebbing. Many of the prestige newspapers — including the Los Angeles Times, The New York Times and The Washington Post — require visitors to register in order to download stories. This is to help the companies that advertise on the Web sites better understand the newspapers' audiences. Knowing the age, education, income, occupation and location of Web users helps companies determine if their ads are effective.

Many newspapers fill their Web sites with their print-edition stories along with news updates from The Associated Press. Critics deride this as "shovelware" and say it does not fully gratify the needs of people who go to the Web for news. Reading a story on a computer screen causes more eye strain than reading a newspaper, and Web users are more likely to scan stories than read every word. Stories for the Web are written more in the style of broadcast journalism than newspapers. The sentences are short for faster comprehension, and the stories are short so the reader doesn't have to scroll through several screens. Studies show that readers often click away from a site rather than scroll through a long story.

Internet news outlets have no deadlines. Stories can be *uploaded*, or posted, as they develop. Some newspapers now require their reporters to write a short story for their papers' Web site before they write a longer version for the next day's edition. This immediate publication means that, as with on-the-spot broadcast reports, stories are more prone to errors than articles in newspapers, where editors have more time to vet the stories. Initial statements from officials and eyewitnesses at breaking news events are often incomplete, inaccurate and contradictory. Reporters must make sure they don't sacrifice accuracy and credibility in order to be the first with a story.

Internet users also scan stories because they are in a hurry and don't always want in-depth accounts. They want a summary of what occurred and the ability to read the parts of the story they are interested in. News stories on the Web don't waste words; they are fact filled and concise. Many Web sites offer a headline and one- to three-sentence summary, similar to a newspaper's headline and summary deck head or TV's headline news. A link will take interested readers to the rest of the story. This was all the Los Angeles Times reported about an economic report on its home page:

> ### Factory Orders, Stocks up
> Demand for furniture and nondurable goods produces more new orders than expected.

Readers will have to click on the underlined headline to read the *why* and *how* of the story.

Reporters working on longer, multifaceted stories write several short articles about different elements of the story that are then linked to the short summary on the home page; readers decide which parts to read and in what order.

When the United States offered a $25 million reward for Saddam Hussein, CNN's home page featured an Old West wanted poster with Saddam's photo on it. This text was under the photo:

$25 million for Saddam

U.S. officials today offered a $25-million reward for information that leads to the capture of Saddam Hussein or proof that he is dead and $15 million for his sons Uday and Qusay. A group of senators back from Iraq stressed the importance of finding Saddam: "When we do, then the people of Iraq will no longer live in fear of his return," said Sen. Pat Roberts, R-Kansas.

FULL STORY
Gallery: The faces of Saddam Hussein
TIME.com: The war that never ends
Video: Bush talks tough on Iraq
Bush 'bring 'em on' comment under fire

Let's see how VeronaTimes.com would report on Romeo and Juliet.

Suicides, homicide in family crypt

The bodies of three teenagers from Verona's prominent families were discovered in a family crypt Thursday. Guards found the bodies of County Paris, a kinsman of Verona's Prince Escalus; Juliet Capulet; and Romeo Montague in the Capulet family crypt and alerted Escalus and the Montague and Capulet families. Romeo and Juliet, who were secretly married Monday, both committed suicide. Paris was killed in a fight.

Details
- ✓ Deaths may end the decades-long fighting between the Montagues and Capulets
- ✓ Friends says dead teens had promising futures
- ✓ Roots of the Montague-Capulet feud
- ✓ Prince Escalus' edict against any more street fighting
- ✓ Suicide is the No. 2 killer of teenagers

Video:
- ✓ Interview with Friar Lawrence, who secretly performed Romeo and Juliet's marriage
- ✓ Interviews in their high school video year book

Poll: Should parents arrange their children's marriages?

Other recent victims of the Montague-Capulet conflict:
- ✓ Benvolio, killed by Tybalt in a street fight
- ✓ Tybalt, killed by Romeo in a street fight
- ✓ Lady Montague, died from grief after Romeo was exiled

Exercises

1. Examine a major story from a newspaper and determine its *who, what, when, where, why* and *how*.

2. Use the story from Exercise 1 and turn it into a radio news story.

3. Use the story from Exercise 1 and turn it into a TV news story. Determine what the visuals should be.

4. Use the story from Exercise 1 and turn it into a short Internet story. Break the story into smaller pieces and also recommend other sidebars for the story.

Chapter 3

GRAMMAR AND PUNCTUATION

This chapter:

- ☑ Explains the importance of proper grammar and punctuation
- ☑ Offers an overview of grammar rules
- ☑ Reviews common grammatical problems
- ☑ Offers an overview of punctuation
- ☑ Reviews common punctuation problems

Reporters with poor grammar and punctuation skills risk damaging both their reputations and the reputations of their employers. A study conducted by the American Society of Newspaper Editors found that 21 percent of adults surveyed said they find spelling and grammatical mistakes in their papers almost every day. The study also found that these errors damage newspapers' credibility. Readers believe that if reporters can't get the spelling and grammar right, then they probably can't get the facts right, either. Each misspelled word, misplaced apostrophe, garbled grammatical construction and word-usage error erodes public confidence in the news media's ability to get anything right.

While a broadcast audience won't notice poor punctuation or misspelled words — unless they're in the messages streaming at the bottom of the TV screen on the news programs — viewers and listeners do catch poor grammar and word usage. These errors can have even greater consequences for broadcast news than they do for publications. While a reader distracted by an error can continue reading a story, a distracted listener misses part of the message and cannot go back and listen to it again. If poor grammar causes too many distractions for listeners, they will go elsewhere for news.

Grammar is the system we use to relate one word to another. It provides guidelines for combining words into phrases, clauses, sentences and paragraphs to communicate ideas and information. Effective writers have a mastery of grammar.

PARTS OF SPEECH

Eight parts of that system are nouns, pronouns, verbs, adjectives, adverbs, conjunctions, prepositions and interjections.

Nouns and Pronouns. Nouns are people and other living organisms, places, things or ideas; and pronouns are noun substitutes.

The young *dog* is running in the meadow. *It* has been chasing rabbits since early this morning.

We cherish the *freedoms* guaranteed in the First Amendment. *They* protect us from government abuse.

Dog and *freedoms* are two of the nouns in these sentences. *It* is a pronoun substituting for dog, and *they* is a pronoun substituting for freedoms.

Verbs. These words explain the action or state of being of the nouns and pronouns. In the first sentence, *is running* is a verb phrase that describes what the dog is doing. In the second sentence, *cherish* describes the action of the pronoun *we*.

When we combine nouns and pronouns with verbs, we create *clauses*, which are the basic structure of communication. With the exception of interjections, all sentences must have a subject, a noun or pronoun, and a predicate verb, the verb describing the action or state of being of the subject. *The dog is running.* and *We cherish.* are complete sentences; they contain a subject and predicate verb. The subject and predicate verb in the first sentence of many news articles are often the *who* and *what* of the story.

who: dog

what: is running [in the meadow]

who: we

what: cherish [the freedoms guaranteed in the First Amendment]

The rest of the words in the sentences communicate information about the dog and what it is we cherish.

Groups of words that aren't clauses are called *phrases*. *Into the woods* is a prepositional phrase. *The little red house* is a noun phrase.

Adjectives. These words modify, or describe, nouns: the *young* dog, a *sunny* day, these *cherished* rights.

Adverbs. Adverbs modify verbs, adjectives and adverbs: *very early* this morning, the *rapidly* moving train.

Conjunctions. These connecting words join words, phrases and clauses. Some common conjunctions are and, but, yet, however and moreover.

Prepositions. These words introduce modifying phrases: These phrases always end with a noun or pronoun. The underlined words here are prepositions.

The bird flew <u>into</u> the woods, ... <u>through</u> the woods, ... <u>over</u> woods, ... <u>under</u> the bridge. Those books are <u>for</u> me. Please take a picture <u>of</u> us.

Interjections are single-word sentences that express emotion.

Ouch ! That hurt. *Damn* ! She's good.

Some Common Grammatical Problems

Grammatical rules can be tricky, and even seasoned writers sometimes are not sure of the rules and keep reference books handy. Here are some common problems writers should guard against.

Possessive Nouns and Pronouns. These are The Associated Press' guidelines for possessives in its "Stylebook and Briefing on Media Law." Most nouns become possessive by adding *apostrophe-s* to the end of the word: the *writer's* manuscript, a *newspaper's* policy. Most plural nouns become possessive by adding *s-apostrophe* to the end of the word: several writers' manuscripts; many newspapers' policies. There are many exceptions, however.

Add only an apostrophe to nouns that are plural in form but singular in meaning: mathematics' rules, measles' effects, General Motors' profits, the United States' wealth.

Treat nouns the same in singular and plural form if the meaning is singular: the Army corps' location, the lone moose's antlers.

Add *apostrophe-s* to singular common nouns ending in *s* unless the next word begins with *s*. Use only an apostrophe if the next word starts with *s*: the hostess's invitation, the hostess' seat, the witness's answer, the witness' story.

Use only an apostrophe if the word is a proper noun ending in *s*: Dickens' novels, Achilles' heel, Ladies' Home Journal.

Add only an apostrophe to plural nouns ending in *s*: the ships' fuel depot, states' rights.

For compound words, add *apostrophe-s* to the word closest to the object possessed: one major general's decision, three major generals' joint decision.

For joint possession, use a possessive form after only the last word: Mike and Mary's boat.

For individual possession, use a possessive form after both words: Mike's and Mary's boats.

Do not add an apostrophe to a word ending in *s* when it is used primarily in a descriptive sense: *citizens band radio, an Angels infielder, a writers guide.* The apostrophe usually is not needed if *for* or *by* rather than *of* would be appropriate in the longer form: a radio band for citizens, an infielder for the Angels, a guide for writers.

Use an apostrophe to make nouns before gerunds possessive. Gerunds are verbs ending in *-ing* that function as nouns.

> The surgeon general's report led to the medical profession's diagnosing life-threatening heart ailments in women at a faster rate.

Do not use apostrophes with possessive pronouns:

> The dog was returned to its owner.

It's is a contraction of *it is*. Other possessive pronouns include *mine, his, ours, yours* and *whose*.

Pronoun Cases. Besides the possessive cases, pronouns also have subjective and objective cases. The subjective case, also called nominative, is the subject of the sentence or after a form of the verb *to be*. Objective case pronouns are used after all other verbs and at the end of prepositional phrases.

Subjective Case	Objective Case
I	me
he	him
we	us
they	them
you	you
who	whom

Subjective: *He* was injured in an automobile accident.

Subjective: Police did not know who turned in the bag of money.

Subjective: It was she who was honored by the president.

Objective: Paramedics treated him at the scene.

Objective: Police did not know *whom* the money belonged to.

Objective: The president honored *her*.

You can determine whether to use who or whom by rewriting the portion of the sentence with who or who using *he/she* or *him/her* instead. If *he* or *she* is grammatically correct, use *who*; if *him* or *her* is correct, use *whom*.

For example, you would write: The money belonged to *him*. Therefore, Police did not know *whom* the money belonged to.

Pronouns Agreement. Pronouns must agree in number with the nouns they represent.

Incorrect: The rocket *barrages* took *its* toll on Israel's northern towns and farms.

Barrages is plural, but *it* is singular. The noun and pronoun do not agree in number.

Correct: The rocket *barrages* took *their* toll on the country's northern towns and farms.

Incorrect: The *audience* became unruly when *they* were told that the concert had been canceled.

Correct: The *audience* became unruly when *it* was told that the concert had been canceled.

Incorrect: *Each reporter* is required to show *their* press card.

Correct: *Each reporter* is required to show *his (or her)* press card.

Many people, particularly when speaking, make this error in the last sentence because the English language has no gender-neutral singular pronoun that refers to people. Use plural nouns and plural pronouns to avoid sexist pronouns:

Correct: All *reporters* were required to show *their* press cards.

Incorrect: If *a writer* starts a sentence with a singular noun or pronoun, *they* must use singular pronouns throughout the sentence.

Correct: If *writers* start a sentence with a singular noun or pronoun, *they* must use singular pronouns throughout the sentence.

Use *who* and *whom* to refer to people and *that* and *which* to refer to other nouns.

California has had two governors *who* were Hollywood actors.

The cougar *that* attacked the hikers was killed by trackers.

Essential and Nonessential Phrases and Clauses. Essential, or restrictive, clauses and phrases restrict the meaning of the noun to which they refer. They are needed to fully understand the meaning of the noun. Nonessential, or nonrestrictive, phrases and clauses offer additional information about the noun but are not essential for the meaning of the noun. Essential clauses or phrases are never set off by commas, whereas nonessential clauses or phrases are always set off by commas.

In the sentence, "Baboons *that live in game preserves* are not afraid of people," the essential clause "that live in game preserves" restricts the meaning of "baboons" to only those living in game preserves.

In the sentence, "Baboons, *which live in game preserves*, are not afraid of people," the nonessential clause, "which live in game preserves," tells us where baboons live, but it does not restrict the meaning of "baboon." The sentence implies that *all* baboons live in game preserves and *all* baboons are unafraid of people. Some other examples are:

The governor called legislation *that* will overhaul the state's workers' compensation system a crowning achievement of his administration.

The governor said the new law, *which* barely squeaked through the Legislature, will save both the state and businesses millions of dollars.

Verb Agreement. Singular subjects require singular verb forms, and plural subjects require plural verb forms. Subjects joined by *and* usually take a plural verb:

The *mayor and city council are* on a collision course.

But when subjects joined by "and" are meant as single units, they take a singular verb.

Bacon and eggs is his favorite breakfast.

The verb agrees with the nearest subject when subjects are joined by *or, either ... or*, or *neither ... nor*.

Neither the president nor his *aides are* likely to survive the scandal.

Neither the White House aides nor the *president is* likely to survive the scandal.

Subjects that are singular and are followed by phrases set off by commas take singular verbs. These nonessential phrases introduce groups of words that serve as conjunctions: *as well as, along with, accompanied by, in addition to* and *together with*:

The president's economic *adviser*, as well as the nation's leading tax experts, *predicts* the nation's deficit will soar.

Prepositional phrases usually have no effect on whether the verb is singular or plural:

The *board* of trustees *is scheduled* to vote on the measure Thursday.

The subject of this sentence is *board*; *of trustees* is a prepositional phrase modifying *board*.

The *board is scheduled* to vote on the measure Thursday.

When the subject of the sentence is a fraction or a word such as *half, part, some* or *plenty*, however, the correct verb is suggested by the object of the preposition that follows the subject:

Three-fourths of the *community* polled *rejects* the proposal.

Three-fourths of the *students* polled *reject* the proposal.

Some of the *money is missing*.

Some of *trees are diseased*.

"The number" takes a singular verb; "a number," which can be replaced by "many," takes a plural verb:

The *number* of co-sponsors to the Senate bill *was* 138.

A *number* of legislators *were angered* by the president's veto.

Verbs agree with their subjects even when the verbs come first:

Farther down the Mississippi *were two barges* loaded with rocks and grain.

Dependent clauses serving as a sentence's subject always take singular verbs:

That *homeowners near the landfill complained about its expansion was* no surprise to the supervisors.

Titles and plural-sounding words take singular verbs:

"Honor Among Thieves" *is* Jeffrey Archer's fictionalized account of Saddam Hussein's life.

The New York Times *has won* many Pulitzer Prizes.

Sports teams are often an exception to this rule. Although most grammar experts and sports writers agree that the sentence, "The Dodgers *are* expected to win the pennant this year," is grammatically incorrect, they also agree that common usage has made this an exception to the rule and would not write, "The Yankees *is* expected to win the pennant this year."

Units of measurement, periods of time and amounts of money require singular verbs:

Six *months is* too long to wait.

About *$100 million is* the projected cost of the building.

The *word* none requires a singular-form verb when it can be replaced with *not one* and a plural-form verb when it can be replaced by *no two* or *no amount*:

None of the students [not one of the students] failed the course.

None of the students [no two students] had the same answer for Question 5.

Verb Voice. *Voice* is the characteristic of a verb that expresses whether the subject of the verb is doing something or is having something done to it. The two types of voice are *passive* and *active*.

Active voice means the subject is an actor or agent. The subject is performing the action of the verb. The "news" is what the subject is doing.

Active *voice:* Burglars have hit several homes in the neighborhood.

Active *voice:* Military commanders removed the president from office.

Passive voice means that the subject is acted upon instead of being an actor. The subject is not performing the action of the verb. The "news" is what is happening to the subject.

Passive *voice:* Several homes in the neighborhood have been burglarized.

Passive *voice:* The president was removed from office by military commanders.

The passive voice produces sentences that contain less powerful verbs and are wordy and indirect. Good writers usually strive to write in the active voice. The passive voice, however, is preferred when the recipient of the action is more newsworthy than the performer of the action or when the *who* or *what* performing the action is unknown.

> *Passive voice:* President Kennedy was killed today by a gunman who fired on his motorcade.
>
> *Active voice:* Lee Harvey Oswald shot President Kennedy to death while the president was riding in a motorcade.

The passive voice is preferred because President Kennedy is more important than an unknown assassin.

Dangling Participles. *Participles* are verb forms sometimes used as modifiers. Participles must modify the noun or pronoun that immediately precedes or follows them. Dangling participles occur when the participial phrase modifies the wrong word.

> *Original:* Facing a crowd of hostile civilian military workers who stand to lose their jobs, his policies will not be accepted.

The participial phrase, *Facing a crowd of hostile civilian military workers who stand to lose their jobs,* should modify the subject of the sentence, which is *policies*. But a policy facing a crowd makes no sense.

> *Corrected:* Facing a crowd of hostile civilian military workers who stand to lose their jobs, the president realized his policies will not be accepted.

Now the president is facing the hostile crowd.

> *Original:* Wearing only a diaper, police found the toddler two blocks from his home.
>
> *Corrected:* Wearing only a diaper, the toddler was found by police two blocks from his home.
>
> *Written for the active voice:* Police found the toddler, who was wearing only a diaper, two blocks from his home.

Transitive and Intransitive Verbs. A transitive verb carries the action to the noun that is the object or complement (usually a noun or pronoun after the verb) of the sentence.

> John *is reading the book*.

Book is the object of the verb *reading*.

An intransitive verb does not have an object or complement.

> John *is reading*.

While most verbs are both transitive and intransitive, a few verbs are only transitive or intransitive. The most troublesome of these verbs are *lie* and *lay, sit* and *set, rise* and *raise*.

Lay is transitive, means to "put or place" and always has an object. *Lie* is intransitive, means "to recline" and does not have an object.

Present tense	Past tense	Past Participle	Present Participle
lie	lay	lain	lying
lay	laid	laid	laying

> *Transitive:* He *laid* the documents on the desk and left the room.
>
> *Intransitive:* Smith said he wanted to *lie* down and take a nap.
>
> *Transitive:* The clerk told him to *lay* his books on the counter.
>
> *Intransitive:* The cat *lay* on the window sill all morning.

Set is transitive and means "to place" and always takes an object. *Sit* is intransitive, means "to sit down" and does not take an object.

Present tense	Past tense	Past Participle	Present Participle
sit	sat	sat	sitting
set	set	set	setting

Transitive: Set the coat on the chair.
Intransitive: Sit here and wait until I get back.

Raise is transitive, means "to elevate" and always takes an object. *Rise* is intransitive, means "to ascend" and does not take an object.

Present tense	Past tense	Past Participle	Present Participle
rise	rose	risen	rising
raise	raised	raised	raised

Transitive: They *raised* the flag 10 minutes before the game began.
Intransitive: You must *rise* when the judge enters the courtroom.

PUNCTUATION

Here are refreshers on proper punctuation according to the "Associated Press Stylebook and Briefing on Media Law" and some common errors:

Apostrophes

Apostrophes indicate possession or missing letters or numbers. They also are used to form contractions and help us understand the meaning of letters or numbers that are joined but do not create words. Use apostrophes:

To show possession with nouns.

The critics praised Henrik Ibsen's "A Doll's House."

To form contractions.

"I *don't* expect that *he'll* return to the bargaining table," the mediator said.

To make plurals of a single letter.

"Mind your *p's* and *q's.*"

To indicate missing letters or numbers.

Rock *'n'* Roll has been part of the American culture for a half-century.
Several rock stars died from drug abuse in the *'60s* and *'70s.*

Colons

The colon is an announcer: It may announce statements, series, quotations or dialogue. Use colons:

To introduce statements.

At a rally Thursday, one woman carried a sign reading: "End world hunger now!"

Capitalize the first word after a colon if it is a proper noun or the start of a complete sentence.

To introduce quotations of more than one sentence.

"I've prayed for us all to come together, and it happened today," she said, adding: "When he hugged me, it was so warm. I said, 'God bless you.' I feel so much better. I have prayed for that man."

To introduce series.

Ninety percent of the world's black caviar comes from three species of sturgeon that live in the Caspian Sea: the sleek sevruga, the white osetra, and the giant beluga, the most valuable and rarest of all.

To connect two independent clauses when the second clause amplifies or explains the first.

The public got its first glimpse inside Buckingham Palace on Saturday, and the verdict was nearly unanimous: The tour was worth the admission price, but as far as homes go, the royals can keep it.

Commas

Commas indicate a short pause and are used to separate thoughts in a sentence or to divide items in a list. Use commas:

After introductory clauses, phrases or words.

When it is completed early in the next decade, the highway's capacity will more than double to 225,000 cars a day.

Although the idea was to make patrolling the community more desirable with more days off, the 12-hour shift also will increase officer accountability.

After each item in a series.

Results of a recent study showed that consumers want to use their American Express cards at Kmart, Sears and Wal-Mart.

Do not put a comma before the conjunction in a simple series like previous example, but put a comma before the concluding conjunction in a series if other conjunctions are in the sentence:

I had ham *and* eggs, coffee, orange juice, and toast for breakfast.

After *said* when introducing direct quotations or after the direct quote to introduce the attribution.

The software engineer said, "I remember when a fax machine seemed an option."
"I remember when a fax machine seemed an option," the software engineer said.

Use a colon to introduce a direct quotation longer than one sentence.

Between two independent clauses joined by a conjunction to form a single sentence.

The crew lowered the lifeboats, *and* the passengers immediately scurried into them.

To set off conjunctive adverbs (*however, moreover, nevertheless, therefore*) and other transitional expressions (*as a result, to sum up* etc.).

He noted, *for example*, that depletion of the ozone layer allows more harmful ultraviolet radiation to reach Earth. *Moreover*, higher radiation can cause increases in skin cancer and cataracts and can adversely affect crops.

To set off parenthetical expressions (*perhaps, too, also, indeed*).

The ozone depletion may, *indeed*, get worse in the next 20, 30 and 40 years, the scientist said.

To set off contrasted elements.

The older I get, the less I understand popular music.

To set off nouns used as a direct address.

Michael, bring me those papers.

To set off nonessential words, phrases or clauses.

> Scientists say that recovery will depend on the willingness of developing nations to use chlorofluorocarbon substitutes, *which may be more expensive*.

In dates, addresses, geographical names and long numbers.

> The President lives at 1600 Pennsylvania Ave., Washington, D.C.
>
> Flooding forced residents of Pajaro, Calif., to flee their homes.
>
> The Nile River is more than 4,000 miles long.
>
> Renewed negotiations to bring peace to the region were held Aug. 26, 2003, in Norway.

When the specific day is not present, do not use a comma to separate the month and year:

> The August 2003 peace accords failed to end the decades-long hostilities.

To set off participial phrases that modify some part of the independent clause. Participial phrases are modifying phrases that begin with a verb ending in *ing*.

> Hurricane-force winds struck the city Monday night, tearing roofs off buildings and uprooting trees.

Dashes

The dash is used to add drama or emphasis by creating a delay between the elements it separates. It is one of the most overworked, yet at times effective, punctuation marks. Use dashes:

To set off interruptive materials.

> The journalists — all from Nicaraguan news outlets — had been inside the house for hours.

To set off parenthetical material containing commas when the parenthetical material is in the middle of a sentence.

> High-priced ostrich products — eggs at $50 a dozen, pate en croute at $30 a pound and hot dogs at $5 to $8 apiece — are lower in fat and higher in protein than chicken, turkey or pork.

To end sentences with surprising or ironic elements.

> "Make no mistake — teaching creationism is illegal. We're going to get sued," the school board trustee said.

To separate independent clauses when added emphasis is desired.

> A mile from one of the flash points of last year's riots, a huge crowd of a different sort gathered Friday — about 3,000 inner-city residents, many in business suits with resumes in hand, were seeking hard-to-come-by work.

Most newspapers use what is an en-dash in stories. It is a dash the length of the letter *n* in 12 point type. Some Web sites also use an em-dash, which is the width of the letter *m* in 12 point type.

Ellipses

Ellipses are three periods (...) inserted in text. Do not put spaces between the periods. Spaces are needed before and after the ellipses, however. Use an ellipsis:

To alert readers that something has been omitted in quoted material.

> "There's never been anything like this ... in my recollection," he told reporters.

To suggest hesitations or pauses:

> The assemblyman said: "We'll have less access to expertise within our own staff. Who knows … ." The last period here denotes the end of the sentence.

Exclamation Points

An exclamation point adds emphasis to a clause, phrase or word. Use an exclamation point:

After an exclamatory phrase or clause.

> And now, a man-bites-mosquito story. Zzzzzzzzzzzzzz thwack!

After an emphatic interjection.

> "Wow! I can't believe I did it!" Jones said after sinking the ball into the basket from the half-court line.

After a strong command.

> Meanwhile, riot-equipped police arriving in buses had bottled up about 3,000 anti-war demonstrators chanting — "Peace Now! Peace Now!" — against the downtown lake front.

Exclamation points, like parenthetical asides in copy, should be used sparingly and almost exclusively with quoted material. Reporters' words should never get an exclamation point.

Hyphens

Whereas the dash separates words, the hyphen connects words. Use hyphens:

To punctuate compound adjectives that precede a noun unless that modifier is preceded by *very* or an adverb ending in *ly*.

> The supplementary agreements, negotiated in a round of *late-night* phone diplomacy, would establish *fact-finding* commissions and provide for trade sanctions or fines if any of the three countries fail to enforce its labor or environmental laws.

To form many prefix and suffix words.

> Bill Clinton was the first Democrat to win *re-*election in *post-*World War II America.

Consult your Associated Press stylebook *prefixes* and *suffixes* entries for general rules about hyphens with prefixes and suffixes.

After modifiers that apply to several words.

> The contest was open to *5-* and *6-year-old* children.

Use hyphens with ages when the age is followed by a noun or takes the place of a noun:

> A 16-year-old girl was killed in the crossfire.
> The race is limited to 4-year-olds.

Hyphens are not needed when the word *year* is plural:

> The shooting victim was 16 *years* old.
> Only children 4 *years* old can participate.

For combinations when the preposition *to* is omitted.

> The *San Bernardino-Los Angeles* Metrolink is the fastest way to get downtown.
> The *10-3* defeat put the team in the cellar.

Parentheses

Like dashes and commas, parentheses are marks of enclosures. Use parentheses:

To set off definitions and nonessential material.

> NASA got some good news Saturday, as the handicapped Galileo spacecraft (hampered by a jammed main antenna) explored asteroid Ida on its way to Jupiter.

To set off enumerations within a sentence.

> Although full agreement has not yet been reached, among the major elements confirmed Saturday by the government, rebel forces and U.S. officials were: (1) military withdrawal from rebel-held areas; (2) a rebel pledge not to declare independence in the areas vacated by government troops; and (3) a pledge by all parties to begin negotiating a long-term settlement.

Periods

Periods indicate the end of an independent clause or other thoughts. Use periods:

At the end of sentences that make statements, give mild commands or ask indirect questions.

> The destruction covered a broad swath from Big Sur to Orange County.

After deliberate sentence fragments.

> Right ballpark. Wrong metaphor.

To abbreviate words.

> Dec. 7, Albany, N.Y., Dr. Linus Pauling

Question Marks

Question marks indicate that the sentence is a query. Use a question mark:

After direct questions.

> Could such an approach work?

After doubtful information.

> New math plan is a plus for pupils?

Use this structure cautiously. It can imply bias and is not a substitute for attribution in a story or headline.

Quotation Marks

Quotation marks are used to denote material as accurate, word-for-word reproduction of someone else's speech or writing. Use quotation marks:

To enclose direct quotations and dialogue.

> "I'm responsible for killing 30 people with my own hands," said Adolfo Francisco Scilingo, a retired Navy commander.

To denote titles of movies, plays, songs, books and magazine articles.

> The movie "Shakespeare in Love" was inspired by Shakespeare's "Romeo and Juliet."

To identify words used in a special sense.

> Huntington Beach, Calif., calls itself "Surf City, USA."

Here are some guidelines for quotation marks:

Always place periods and commas inside the quotation mark.

> "There was no Golden Age," historian Michael Katz said.

Place semicolons and colons outside the quotation marks when they are not part of the quote.

> Some good books about journalism are Walter Cronkite's autobiography, "A Reporter's Life"; Edna Buchanan's memoir, "The Corps had a Familiar Face"; and Arnold Sawislak's satirical novel, "Dwarf Rapes Nun; Flees in UFO."

Place question marks and exclamation points inside the quotation marks if they are part of the quotation and outside the quotation marks if they are not.

> "About the time I was having these conversations with Chuck, all of a sudden from about three fashion publications I got requests for saddle shoes. I thought, 'Isn't that weird?' "
>
> "Why didn't you warn the public?" the congresswoman asked the witness.
>
> "I was trying to reason with the senator," the lobbyist told the group. "The he yelled at me, 'Go to hell!' "
>
> Who first said, "Truth is the first casualty of war"?

Do not put a quotation mark at the end of a full-sentence quote if the quotation is continued at the start of the next paragraph.

> "What's the point of going to the mall if you can't hang out?" LaDawn Smith asked. "I think that's a biased thing — they target kids they stereotype as a problem kid or kids who would be involved in gangs.
>
> "Who are those kids? Probably minority kids and boys," said Smith, who is African-American.

Put a quotation mark at the end of a partial quote even if it is followed by a full-sentence quotation at the start of the next paragraph.

> "This program, in my view, has demonstrated very well that the two sides can work together smoothly," astronaut Norman E. Thagard said, predicting that the two nations will "do many great things in space together."
>
> "Given what the costs of space exploration are these days, we need to cooperate," Thagard said at a farewell news conference with his two Russian colleagues: Mir 18 flight commander Valdimir N. Dezhurov, 32, and engineer Gennady M. Strekalov, 54.

Semicolons

Semicolons fall somewhere between the comma and the period, with more decisiveness than the first and less finality than the second. Use semicolons:

Between independent clauses when a conjunction is absent.

> Visitors to the game preserve used binoculars in a vain attempt to catch a glimpse of a cheetah; nearby, a cheetah and her cubs lay hidden in the grass watching them.

Between items in series that have commas inside the items.

> The study looked at three surgical procedures: cardiac catheterization, in which a fine tube is inserted into the heart to investigate its condition; angioplasty, in which a balloon is introduced into constricted blood vessels in an attempt to widen them and clear blockages; and coronary artery bypass surgery, in which doctors reroute blood past blocked arteries.

To separate independent clauses containing internal punctuation.

> The travelers dragged the raft out of the water and removed its rudder, benches and bolted-down containers; but it was too heavy to carry around the rapids.

Exercise 1: Parts of Speech

Label each word in the following sentences according to its part of speech.

1. The Pacific Ocean holds a year-round fascination for Southern Californians.

    The: Article

    Pacific Ocean: Noun

    holds: Verb

    a: Article /determiner

    year-round: Adjective

    fascination: Noun

    for: Conjunction

    Southern Californians: Noun

2. The lure holds despite the fact that the Pacific is sullied by sewage, strewn with debris and increasingly marked by violence.

    The: Article

    lure: Noun

    holds: Verb

    despite: prep

    the: Article

    fact: Noun

    that: Conjunction

    the: Article

    Pacific: Noun

    is: Adjective verb

    sullied: verb

    by: prep.

    sewage: Noun

    strewn: Verb

    with: Preposition

debris: Noun

and: Conjunction

increasingly: Adverb

marked: Verb

by: Prep

violence: Noun

3. Still, people keep coming back because, like the desert defines Tucson, saltwater saturates the psyche of Los Angeles.

Still: Adverb

people: Noun

keep: Verb

coming: Verb

back: Verb

because: Conj.

like: Prep

the: Article

desert: Noun

defines: Verb

Tucson: Noun

saltwater: Noun

saturates: Verb

the: Article

psyche: Noun

of: Prep

Los Angeles. Noun

Exercise 2: Problems with Pronouns

Select the correct pronoun in the following sentences.

1. The new board of directors took (its, **their**) respective places in the chamber.

2. The Mets lost (its, **their**) third game in a row.

3. (**Who**, Whom) is the best candidate?

4. (Who, **Whom**) do you wish to talk to?

5. Bill is one of those people (**who**, whom) can (**do**, does) no wrong.

6. The team members took (its, **their**) positions on the football field.

7. "How deeply have I longed to visit your land, (which, **that**) is particularly dear to me," the pope told an airport crowd.

8. Investigators said the train derailed when the engineer tried to slow it after he saw debris on the tracks, (**which**, that) had been inspected earlier that day.

9. Dozens of birds (who, whom, **that**) appeared momentarily colored the blue sky.

10. The mayor and councilman each made (his, **their**) cases to the labor committee.

11. Feminists today cheered a Canadian high court ruling (which, **that**) redefined obscenity.

12. The psychologist told parents that a child's appearance and manners reflect (his, **its**, their) upbringing.

13. No one knows (**himself**, hisself) better than (**he**, him).

14. The runaway dog was returned to (his, **its**) home.

15. The professor and his wife both lost (his, her, **their**) luggage.

Exercise 3: Problems with Verbs

Select the correct verb in the following sentences.

1. He (lay, lie) the book on the table.

2. Al Gore has (laid, lain) the groundwork for a comeback.

3. I think I'll (lie, lay) down for a while.

4. The disgraced politician has (lain, laid) low for a long time.

5. We (lay, laid) in bed all day Sunday.

6. Prices (raised, rose).

7. The firm decided to (rise, raise) its prices.

8. Don't expect your home to (raise, rise) in value during an economic downturn.

9. The bread has (risen, raised).

10. Sen. Joe Bullmoose was reluctant to (raise, rise) the issue of new taxes, but he was willing to (raise, rise) and join the fight if someone else would introduce the legislation.

11. I (sat, set) up the board for checkers.

12. Let's all (sit, set) at the table.

13. I think I'm just going to (sit, set) here for now.

14. I (sat, set) the prescription on the counter.

15. (Set, Sit) right down.

Exercise 4: Problems with Verb Agreement

Select the correct verb in the following sentences.

1. The president and the nation's governors (is, _are_) headed for a showdown on the immigration legislation.

2. A husband and father (_is_, are) what he wanted to be.

3. Neither the pliers nor the quarter-inch drill bit (_has_, have) arrived.

4. A drill, as well as 15 assorted drill bits, (_was_, were) delivered.

5. Either the president or his press secretary (is, are) will issue the statement.   _Incorrect Sentence, typo_

6. Traditional, as well as non-traditional medicine, (_is_, are) covered in the president's health package.

7. Physicians — in addition to chiropractors, podiatrists and acupuncturists — (is, _are_) expected to make more money under the president's plan.

8. The Jordanian monarch, along with the rest of Arab world, (_is_, are) hopeful that Israel will accept the pact.

9. Among the constitutional rights we cherish (is, _are_) First Amendment rights.

10. Among the constitutional rights we cherish (_is_, are) freedom of the press.

11. Agreement between the Israeli and Arab delegates on the provisions of the peace accord (_appears_, appear) likely.

12. The number of U.N. officials in Afghanistan (appear, _appears_) likely to increase.

13. A number of field officers of the U.N. high commissioner for refugees (was, _were_) sent to Jablanica to investigate the shooting.

14. That they would attack with helicopter gunships and rockets (_was_, were) unexpected.

15. That terrorists had fired on the civilians (_was_, were) deplorable.

Exercise 5: More Verb Agreement Problems

Select the correct verb in the following sentences.

1. Politics (is, are) a topic that will make one many enemies.

2. The company's board of directors (is, are) meeting Tuesday.

3. The acoustics in this board room (is, are) lousy.

4. University athletics (is, are) likely to be cut during the next fiscal year.

5. The jury (was, were) polled on (its, their) verdict.

6. None of these shirts (fit, fits).

7. Plenty of travel agents (is, are) being hit by the strike.

8. Half of the rent receipts (is, are) missing.

9. Half of the rent (is, are) missing.

10. He is one of the worst candidates who (has, have) ever spoken to the convention.

11. All of the chemicals (was, were) spilled overboard.

12. All of the building (was, were) infested with termites.

13. Three-fourths of China's professors (was, were) sent to farms during Mao Tse-tung's Cultural Revolution.

14. Two-thirds of the 35 million Americans who suffer from mild depression (is, are) women with young children.

15. Most of the team members (was, were) injured in the bus accident.

Exercise 6: Punctuation and Grammar Problems

Correct the errors in punctuation, spelling and grammar.

1. Hayes added "The tests should be completed in about two weeks. Well have a better idea then of what is killing the fish"

2. The 44 year old woman whose identity was not released was rescued late Monday and taken to Lakeside Memorial Hospital.

3. A friend and favorite companion of the president Ernest Green now a managing director of the Lehman Bros. investment bank in Washington was a major player in the full court press to raise funds for the presidents reelection.

4. "Mark always had a smile and kind word for people even when his wife was dying" the minister said in his eulogy.

5. Detroit is understandably wary about the flywheel itself; it spins at up to 55,000 revolutions per minute creating massive centrifugal forces. If it fails perhaps knocked off its axis by a collision or bad pothole the wheel can disintegrate spitting shrapnel about with deadly force.

6. The skepticism was expressed more pointedly by an attorney for the Legal Defense and Educational Fund during a three hour workshop on Los Angeles transportation issues held at the Metropolitan Transit Agncys high rise headquarters.

7. When the police the firefighters the paramedics and the coroner have left they stay on. Their job is to provide emotional first aid to families in the first few hours after a tragedy.

8. "Why leave us in suspense"? the defense attorney asked.

9. The median income in the region has been rising steadily though an increase in energy prices could hurt the areas fragile economy, and lead to lay-offs.

10. Voters in many parts of the state proved Tuesday that they were well educated and well prepared for their new tax related responsibilities.

11. "Dive"! her coach yelled.

12. The Dodgers are scrapping the cellar; they haven't won a game this season.

13. The film will focus upon Socrates' life.

14. He leaves a son Randolph Scott of Hartford, two daughters, Marilyn Marcus of Chicago and Sherri Sinnow of Los Angeles, and a brother Alfred of Detroit.

15. Mark Twain the famous author journalist had an appropriate saying that went like this The worst death is being talked to death.

Chapter 4 ⊏⊐

STYLE AND WORD USAGE

This chapter:

☑ Explains the purpose and importance of The Associated Press' "Stylebook and Briefing on Media Law" and "Broadcast News Handbook"

☑ Reviews some common style problems

☑ Discusses the importance of proper word usage

☑ Examines some common word-usage problems

Style in news writing refers to rules for such things as consistent spelling, abbreviations, numeral usage and capitalization. Dictionaries give alternative spellings for some words, and grammar books don't always agree on hyphenation rules. Is a play *canceled* or *cancelled*? and is the play performed in a *theater* or *theatre*? Foreign words, such as *Hanukkah* and *czar* can be spelled more than one way, and linguistic experts often cannot agree on the spelling of Arabic words.

Is Pennsylvania abbreviated in a newspaper or Web site as *Pa., PA* or *Penn.*? Does a candidate for public office hold a *fund raiser, fund-raiser* or *fundraiser*? Is the flight *sixteen* hours or *16* hours late?

How these words are spelled is not important as long as news outlets are consistent in what they decide is correct usage. Readers notice inconsistent spelling, abbreviations and numeral usage in a newspaper, or worse yet, in one story. These inconsistencies damage the news media's credibility as much as poor spelling and grammar do.

The Associated Press has been the arbitrator for these style decisions for decades. Copies of AP's stylebook can be found in almost every newsroom, including college newspaper offices. Additionally, many writers for public relations firms keep a stylebook handy because they know that the reporters handling their copy will have to edit the news releases to comply with AP style.

This chapter examines The Associated Press guidelines for print and broadcast news writing and explains some of the common style problems.

AP GUIDEBOOKS

"The Associated Press Stylebook and Briefing on Media Law" – commonly referred as the AP stylebook – and "Associated Press Broadcast News Handbook" are organized in alphabetical order with cross-references. Does *re-elect* really require a hyphen? Look up the word, or check the *re* entry for rules on that specific prefix or the *prefixes* entry for the general rules of prefixes. When is *pope* capitalized? Look up the word or check the *capitalization* or *religious titles* entries.

Here are some typical Associated Press entries with explanation:

AP Entries	Explanations
cabinet Capitalize references to a specific body of advisers heading executive departments for a president, king, governor, etc.: *The president-elect said he has not made his Cabinet selections.*	The entry word is always in **boldface**. Its spelling, capitalization, etc. represent the accepted form unless indicated otherwise.
The capital letter distinguishes the word from the common noun meaning cupboard, which is lowercase. See **department** for a listing of all the U.S. Cabinet departments.	The text explains the usage. Usage examples are in *italic*.
cactus, cactuses	Many entries give correct spelling, capitalization and/or abbreviations without any text explaining the usage.
cadet See **military academies**.	
Caesarean section	References to related topics are in **boldface**.
caliber The form: *.38 caliber pistol*. Follow the rules in **numerals**. See **weapons**.	
California Abbrev.: *Calif.* See **state names**.	

The main section of the AP stylebook and handbook deals with three categories of information: consistency in abbreviations and acronyms, capitalization, numerals and other areas where rules vary; general information on topics journalists frequently encounter; and proper word usage.

Consistency

The AP guidebooks are the arbitrator of correct abbreviations, addresses, capitalization, numerals, and prefixes and suffixes. The rules are often arbitrary, and some publications have their own style guides that differ from AP's. For example, while the stylebook tells print reporters to spell out "percent," some in-house stylebooks call for using the percent sign (%). The goal is to be consistent in how these terms are used. In-house stylebooks also provide guidelines on how to refer to local landmarks, people and organizations. Here is a brief explanation of some AP style rules:

Acronyms and Abbreviations

Both the "Associated Press Stylebook" and "Associated Press Broadcast News Handbook" warn against using acronyms unless you are certain that your audience will immediately understand them. Some accepted acronyms on first reference are FBI, OK, NATO, UN and US. Many other acronyms, including FEMA and FTC, are acceptable on second reference. Look up title to determine the proper usage.

Broadcast-news writers should hyphenate acronyms or otherwise indicate pronunciation so on-air reporters do not stumble over the words: F-B-I, N-A-T-0, FEE'-muh

Broadcast and print differ in their rules for abbreviations. Here are the basic rules for the two media:

Broadcast. In general, never abbreviate words. The few exceptions include courtesy titles *Mr. Mrs., Ms.* and *Dr.* when used before a name. Spell out all other titles. Capitalize formal titles only when they are before a name. Paraphrase long titles or explain them in separate sentences:

The speaker was Paul Simpson, undersecretary of state for international trade.

Or: State Department trade expert Paul Simpson said …

Months of the year, states and addresses are never abbreviated.

Print. Unlike broadcast news writing, print reporters abbreviate many titles when they are used before a name. These include *the Rev., Gov., Sen., Rep., Mr., Mrs., Ms., Dr.* and military titles. Notice that the word "the" is always used with "reverend" and that it is not capitalized. Entries for titles can be found in the stylebook under *courtesy titles, legislative titles, military titles* and *religious titles.*

Abbreviate *corporation, company, incorporated* and *limited* only when they are the last word in a company's title:

Xerox Corp., the Corporation for Public Broadcasting.

Abbreviate *Avenue, Boulevard* and *Street* and compass directions only in numbered addresses. The proper abbreviations are *Ave., Blvd.* and *St.* Do not abbreviate other designations for a roadway:

1600 E. Pennsylvania Ave.

221B Baker St.

1256 Rodeo Drive

849 W. Barkley Road

1404 N. Coast Highway

Capitalize the word and do not abbreviate it when it's part of a formal street name but does not have a specific number:

East Pennsylvania Avenue

the 1400 block of North Coast Highway

Lowercase and spell out roadway designations when they are not used with a street name or are used with more than one street name:

Massachusetts and Pennsylvania avenues.

The house is on the next street.

Always use figures for an address number:

9 Morningside Circle

149 Morningside Circle

Spell out and capitalize *First* through *Ninth* when used as street names.
Use figures with two letters for 10th and above:

7 Fifth Ave.

100 21st St.

Never abbreviate *March, April, May, June* or *July,* and abbreviate other months only when giving a specific date. Use these abbreviations: *Jan., Feb., Aug., Sept., Oct., Nov.* and *Dec.*

Thanksgiving is Nov. 20. It's always celebrated on the third Thursday of November.

Mothers Day is May 11. It's always celebrated on the second Sunday in May.

Dec. 7, 1941, is a day that will "live in infamy."

Notice that the year is set off with commas when it follows a specific date. The same rule applies when a day of the week precedes the date.

Sunday, Dec. 7, 1941, is a day that will "live in infamy."

The United States declared war on Japan, Italy and Germany in December 1941.

Never abbreviate the states Alaska, Hawaii, Idaho, Iowa, Maine, Ohio, Texas and Utah. Abbreviate the names of other states when they are preceded by a city. Do not use postal ZIP Code abbreviations for other states; use the abbreviations listed in the stylebook.

Kona, Hawaii

Carson City, Nev.

Albany is the capital of New York.

Some commonly known cities do not need to be followed by states or countries. Consult the "datelines" entry or look up the city in the guidebooks to determine if it is one of those cities.

Capitalization

The Associated Press transmits broadcast copy using upper- and lower-case characters, and the practice of writing broadcast copy in an all-uppercase format is fading. These rules of capitalization apply for both broadcast and print news media:

Avoid unnecessary capitalization. Words that should be capitalized include the following:

☑ **Sentences.** Capitalize the first word of a sentence.

☑ **Proper nouns.** Capitalize words that give a unique identification to a person, place or thing: *Robert, Sally, London, North America, World War II.*

☑ **Proper names.** Capitalize common nouns such as *east, avenue, ocean* or *party* when they are part of the name of a unique person, place or thing: *East 57th Avenue, Pacific Ocean, Republican Party.* Lowercase common nouns when they are used as plurals: *First and Main streets, Atlantic and Arctic oceans, Republican and Democratic parties.*

☑ **Popular names.** Capitalize commonly used popular names for a place even if the names are not official designations: *the Southland* for Southern California, *the South Side* of Chicago, *the Fed* for the Federal Reserve Bank, *Big Board* for the New York Stock Exchange, *the Big Easy* for New Orleans.

☑ **Derivatives.** Capitalize words derived from proper nouns that depend on the proper noun for their meaning: *Marxist, Calvinist, Christian, American, Bermuda shorts, Orwellian.* Lowercase derivatives that no longer depend on their proper noun for their meaning: *venetian blinds, quixotic adventure, french fries, narcissism, brussels sprouts.*

☑ **Compositions.** Capitalize the principal words in titles of books, movies, poems, songs, plays etc. and put quotation marks around them: *"The Agony and the Ecstasy," "A Child's Christmas in Wales."* Newspaper and magazine names do not have quotation marks: *Time magazine, the San Francisco Chronicle.*

☑ **Personal titles.** Capitalize formal titles immediately before a person's name: *Pope Pius XII, British Prime Minister Winston Churchill, Gen. Dwight D. Eisenhower, President Franklin Roosevelt.* Do not capitalize titles when they do not precede a name or when the name comes after the title: *the pope; Winston Churchill, British prime minister; Franklin Roosevelt, 32nd president of the United States.*

Do not capitalize titles that describe the occupation.

professor Harold Higgins, plant manager Mark Perez, coach John Colman.

The capitalization entry in the guidebooks refer readers to several cross references for specific types of words. These include animals, brand names, foods, heavenly bodies, holidays and holy days, and religious references.

Numerals

Numerals are numbers and can be expressed as words, figures such as Arabic numerals, or letters such as Roman numerals.

one, twelve, twenty-five; 1, 12, 25; I, XII, XXV

Rules for broadcast and print vary slightly. Both guidebooks have many separate entries for specific usage, including betting odds, dimensions, election returns, highway designations, theatrical act and scene numbers, telephone numbers, temperatures, and time of day.

Here is an overview of numeral usage:

Broadcast. Spell out numbers one through eleven, and use Arabic numerals for numbers 12 through 999. Use the words *thousand, million, billion* or *trillion* for larger numbers. Large numbers are rounded off because it is difficult to quickly count commas to say the number correctly. Broadcast-news writers also spell out single-digit numbers with million, billion and trillion as well as the words *dollars* and *percent*. A number such as *$5,987,498* would be written as *nearly six (m) million dollars.*

The words *million, billion* and *trillion* should be preceded by their first letters in parentheses to ensure they are pronounced correctly.

Use hyphens to combine the words *hundred* or *thousand* with numbers, but they are not needed when combining *million, billion* and *trillion* with numbers.

Do not use Roman numerals.

Here are some examples:

> The three (b) billion dollar budget was narrowly approved.
>
> He was fined 12-thousand dollars.
>
> The space probe's nine (m) million mile journey will take five years.
>
> A Pershing-Two missile
>
> She is three years old.
>
> 28-year-old Mabel Smith said …

Do not say, *Mabel Smith, 28, said… .* It interrupts the flow.

> About 500 supporters attended the fundraiser, while nearly one-thousand protesters rallied outside the hotel.
>
> About 15-thousand people have been killed during the five-year guerrilla war.
>
> Jack can walk two miles per hour; he walked five miles Monday.
>
> He drives five-and-one-half miles to work.
>
> The entry-way rug is three feet by 12 feet.
>
> Mayor Harold Jenkins received nearly 24-hundred votes.
>
> Jenkins received 91 percent of the vote. One of his challengers received eight point five percent of the vote, and the other challenger received one-half percent.
>
> Temperatures fell to minus 14 degrees in Fargo and to zero degrees in Billings.
>
> The game is starting late. Kickoff was scheduled for 1 p-m, and it's now 1:15 p-m.
>
> The shooting occurred shortly after midnight.

Do not write *12 midnight* or *12 noon*; it's redundant.

Print. The Associated Press' style for numbers can be confusing. In general, spell out one-digit numbers (zero through nine) and fractions less than one (one-half, as opposed to 1 1/2), and use figures for larger numbers — including numbers using the words million, billion or trillion — or numbers with fractions. This rule has many exceptions: Use figures for ages, dimensions, speeds, times of day and percents. With the exception of years, spell out numbers at the start of a sentence. Here are some examples:

> The $3 billion budget was narrowly approved.
>
> He was fined $12,000.
>
> The space probe's 9 million-mile journey will take five years.
>
> A Pershing II missile
>
> She is 3 years old.

28-year-old Mabel Smith said...

It is acceptable to write, *Mabel Smith, 28, said.*

About 500 supporters attended the fundraiser, while nearly 1,000 protesters rallied outside the hotel.

About 15,000 people have been killed during the five-year guerrilla war.

Jack can walk 2 miles per hour; he walked five miles Monday.

He drives 5 1/2 miles to work.

Some publications cannot typeset fractions. In that case, use a space to separate the whole number from the fraction or use decimals.

He drives 5 1/2 miles to work. He drives 5.5 miles to work.

The entry-way rug is three feet by 12 feet.

Mayor Harold Jenkins received nearly 2,400 votes.

Jenkins received 91 percent of the vote. One of his challengers received 8.5 percent of the vote, and the other challenger received 0.5 percent.

Use decimals for fractions in percents, and precede amounts less than one with a zero:

0.5 percent

Temperatures fell to minus 14 degrees in Fargo and to zero degrees in Billings.

The game is starting late. Kickoff was scheduled for 1 p.m., and it's now 1:15 p.m.

The shooting occurred shortly after midnight.

Do not write *12 midnight* or *12 noon*; it's redundant.

Two thousand three hundred ninety-two people voted for Mayor Harold Jenkins.

Starting sentences with large numbers, as in the last example, should be avoided. The following is an improvement:

Mayor Harold Jenkins received *2,392 votes*.

Prefixes and Suffixes

Prefixes and suffixes are morphemes, which are short sounds that have meaning, that change the words' meaning. Prefixes are at the beginning of words, and suffixes are at the end of words.

Prefixes. The rules for broadcast and print are similar. When using prefixes, the main concern is whether the word requires a hyphen. The three general rules in the guidebooks regarding the use of hyphens with prefixes are:

- ☑ Use a hyphen when the prefix is repeated: *sub-subparagraph, post-postmodern art.*

- ☑ Use a hyphen when the main word is capitalized: *ex-President Bill Clinton, pro-Syrian guerrillas.*

- ☑ Use a hyphen when the last letter of the prefix is the same vowel as the first letter of the main word: *anti-inflation, re-elect.* The two exceptions are *coordinate* and *cooperate.* This rule runs contrary to many of the first-listed spellings in "Webster's New World Dictionary." Some of the more common prefixes with separate entries in style guides are: *anti-, co-, pre-, pro-, re-, semi-* and *trans-.*

If the guidebook does not list the specific prefix or word and the three general rules don't seem to apply, refer to "Webster's New World Dictionary" to determine if a hyphen is needed. Broadcasters are also encouraged to use hyphens if they will help readability.

Suffixes. As with prefixes, the chief concern when using suffixes is whether the word requires a hyphen. Many common suffixes are listed in the style guides, including: *-down, -fold, -over, -up* and *-wise.*

Look up the suffix (not the entire word) in question in the guidebook before checking "Webster's New World Dictionary" in case it differs from the dictionary. If the word is not in the guidebook or the dictionary, make it two words if it is used as a verb and hyphenate it if it is used as a noun or adjective:

> I *walk up* two flights of stairs to my apartment.
>
> I live in a *walk-up* apartment.
>
> The Freedonian military has decided to *pull out* of southern Sylvania.
>
> The *pullout* could endanger settlements near the border.

GENERAL INFORMATION

AP's reference books are also a wealth of general information. When is snowfall considered "heavy snowfall"? What's the difference between a semiautomatic pistol and a revolver? The books contain several pages of weather terms and weapons terms. They also include descriptions of world religions and their major denominations; nobility and military ranks; explanations of the metric system; and business, earthquake, sports and Internet terms.

The books list many trademarks, which are name brands for products, so writers will know to capitalize them.

They also list all the planets and explain when to capitalize "earth"; describe foreign legislative bodies and the Seven Wonders of the World; and explain why the news media are called the Fourth Estate.

The AP stylebook for print journalism has separate sections for the business and sports terms as well as rules for punctuation. The "Broadcast News Handbook" includes business and sports terms in the main section of the book.

Word Usage

Writers who misuse words damage their credibility as much as they do when they use poor grammar. Find the word-usage problems in these sentences:

> The governor convinced the Legislature to support her tax plan.
>
> The Senate censored one of its members for calling the president a traitor.
>
> The earthquake cracked the cement freeway supports.

Convince describes a state of mind, while *persuade* involves an action. You *persuade* people *to* take action by *convincing* them *that* it is the right thing to do.

> The governor *persuaded* the Legislature *to support* her tax plan.

Censor involves removing a portion of a movie or text, while *censure* is to condemn.

> The Senate *censured* one of its members for calling the president a traitor.

Cement is a powder that is mixed with water, sand and gravel to create *concrete*.

> The earthquake cracked the *concrete* freeway supports.

Here are a few other problem words:

- ☑ **celebrant/celebrator.** A celebrant conducts a religious rite; a celebrator is having a good time.

- ☑ **complement/compliment.** Complement means to complete. Her purse and shoes complemented her dress. A compliment is praise. She received many compliments on her ensemble.

- ☑ **demolish or destroy.** Both mean something is completely done away with. An object cannot be partially destroyed.

- ☑ **majority/plurality.** Both words indicate a portion of a vote, poll or other comparison. Majority means more than 50 percent. Plurality is the largest percentage.

Janet Hughes was elected mayor by a majority of 53 percent of the votes.

Marvin Diaz was elected treasurer by a plurality of 43 percent of the votes in the three-way race. His two opponents, Robin Masters and Wanda Do, received 31 percent and 26 percent, respectively.

☑ **pardon/parole/probation.** A pardon forgives a prisoner and frees him unconditionally from prison. Parole releases a prisoner, usually provisionally, before he completes his sentence. Probation is the suspension of a prison sentence for a person who is not yet imprisoned.

☑ **principal/principle.** Principle is a doctrine or personal belief. Use principal for all other meanings. The senator invoked the principle of states rights. He stands by his principles. He is a principal investor in the project. She is the school principal. Unemployment is the principal problem plaguing the economy.

☑ **temperature/weather.** Temperatures are numbers, and numbers cannot be hot or cold. Weather is an atmospheric condition, and an atmospheric condition cannot be described in terms of numbers. High temperatures add to the fire danger. The freezing weather hampered rescuers.

☑ **whiskey/whisky.** Use *whisky* only when referring to Scotch whisky.

Exercise 1: Abbreviations and Acronyms for Print Reporters

Indicate which sentence in each group of sentences complies with the abbreviations and acronyms rules in "The Associated Press Stylebook."

1. a. General Dwight Eisenhower led the Allied invasion of Normandy, France.
    b. Police Capt. Barney Miller worked out of the 12th Precinct in New York.
    c. Detc. Harry Callahan worked for the San Francisco Police Department.
    d. Attorney Gen. John Ashcroft was appointed by President George W. Bush.

2. a. The AMA often lobbies Congress on health-care issues.
    b. The SPCA has launched a campaign alerting pet owners of the danger of leaving animals in locked cars.
    c. J. Edgar Hoover ran the Federal Bureau of Investigation for several decades.
    d. The Federal Communications Commission now allows media companies to own newspapers and TV stations in the same market.

3. a. Bill Gates lives outside Seattle, Wash.
    b. The rally is planned for 7 PM tonight.
    c. An AMTRAK passenger train has derailed near Tucson, AZ.
    d. Rev. Billy Graham has been a confidant to many presidents.

4. a. Sherlock Holmes works out of his home at 221 B. Baker Street.
    b. The White House is located at 1600 Pennsylvania Ave.
    c. Police officers sealed off the 2800 block of Harbor Blvd. while they looked for the suspect.
    d. The house 666 Mourning Widow Dr. is said to be haunted.

5. a. U.S. Steel Corporation was founded by J.P. Morgan.
    b. Shell Oil Company is part of Royal Dutch-Shell Group of Companies.
    c. Firefighters from Company C were the first emergency crew to reach the accident.
    d. The Corporation for Public Broadcasting receives funds from the National Endowment for the Arts.

6. a. The American Broadcasting Co. was once part of the National Broadcasting Co.
    b. The NRA is a strong advocate of the Second Amendment.
    c. The ACLU is a strong advocate of the First Amendment.
    d. AMVETS is a strong advocate for U.S. veterans.

7. a. Aug. is often a slow month for news.
    b. The events of Sept 11, 2001, changed U.S. foreign policy.
    c. Veterans Day, which is November 11, commemorates the end of World War I.
    d. Independence Day, which is Jul. 4, commemorates the signing of the Declaration of Independence.

8. a. Army Spc. William Knox was awarded the Congressional Medal of Honor during the Vietnam War.

   b. Navy Ens. Andrew Farragut has been assigned to the U.S.S. Missouri.

   c. Admiral James T. Kirk commanded the S.S. Enterprise.

   d. Senr. Mastr. Sgt. Miles O'Brien served aboard the Enterprise.

9. a. Senator Orin Hatch is from Utah.

   b. Representative Chris Cox is on the House Intelligence Committee.

   c. Hillary Rodham Clinton, the senator from New York, used to live in the White House.

   d. The Lt. Gov. plans to run for attorney general next year.

10. a. The Seventh Cavalry spent time at Ft. Collins in Colorado.

    b. The Mormons started their trek west from Saint Louis, Mo.

    c. Fort Lauderdale is a popular tourist destination.

    d. The United States Coast Guard was created in 1915.

11. a. The USS Trenton is currently in the Persian Gulf.

    b. Dist. Atty. Perry Mason has resigned to go into private practice.

    c. The USO entertains American troops throughout the world.

    d. Rep. senators are supporting the president's call for a missile defense shield.

12. a. The president will make his speech at 6 p.m. Eastern Standard Time.

    b. The Food and Drug Administration is responsible for ensuring that food is safe to eat.

    c. The Los Angeles Police Dept. is one of the largest in the nation.

    d. Prof. Charles Smith is an expert in scatology.

13. a. Monsg. Charles Polanski is a close friend of the president.

    b. There is a Sault Saint Marie in both Michigan and Ontario.

    c. The Rev. Charles Miniver works for a Methodist ministry.

    d. The Cayman Islds. is an expensive place to live.

14. a. The shooting took place on Main St. near Fifth Ave.

    b. The hurricane caused more than $1 billion in damage to the W. Indies.

    c. Mt. Everest claims many lives each year.

    d. The Air Force has given up its search for UFOs.

15. a. The United States still owes money to UNESCO.

    b. The Animaniacs live on the Warner Brothers studio lot.

    c. A smart politician always sends Xmas cards to campaign donors.

    d. She was sent to India by the U.N. Comm. on Health Care.

Exercise 2: Numerals for Broadcast Reporters

Use the AP "Broadcast News Handbook" to correct any problems with numerals in these sentences.

1. 55 people were killed when a Cruise 2 missile hit a bunker.

2. A 6-month-old girl was among the victims.

3. An estimated 5,000 people attended the protest.

4. A woman and her 2 children were killed when her car struck a stalled truck on Route 66.

5. Damage from the fire was estimated at $3.15 million.

6. Last night's winning lotto numbers were five, eight, 11, 22 and 43.

7. The high temperature was –7 yesterday, but it might reach 0 today.

8. More than 5,000 residents fled the island as Hurricane Nora approached.

9. The space shuttle is scheduled for liftoff in 11 days.

10. An 8-year-old girl is being hailed as a hero today.

11. Police said the gunman took $58 from the cash register and fled in a 1998 Ford Mustang.

12. The unemployment rate rose 0.8 percent last month.

13. Police found five cents and 3 paper clips in the dead man's pockets.

14. The fire consumed 15,000 acres and destroyed ten camp grounds.

15. The House narrowly approved the president's request for an additional $38.2 billion for the Pentagon.

Exercise 3: Numerals for Newspaper Reporters

Use your AP stylebook to correct any problems with numerals in these sentences.

1. 55 people were killed when a Cruise 2 missile hit a bunker.

2. A six-month-old girl was among the victims.

3. An estimated five thousand people attended the protest.

4. Henry the Eighth of England, who lived in the sixteenth century, had 6 wives.

5. The offices are at twenty-five Tenth St.

6. Authorities said the family kept 15 cats, 5 dogs, 2 pot-bellied pigs and 10 parakeets in their condominium.

7. The high temperature was –7 yesterday, but it might reach 0 today.

8. The sixties was a turbulent decade.

9. Damage from the fire will exceed $1,000,000.

10. The Great Depression in the 1930's affected economies around the world.

11. About eight percent of the rodents are infected with bubonic plague.

12. The 1st Amendment of the Constitution guarantees a free press.

13. Police found five cents and 3 paper clips in the dead man's pockets.

14. Act Two of the play is much too long.

15. Forty five people were arrested at the riot, and ten police officers were treated for injuries.

Exercise 4: Word Usage

Use your AP style guide to determine which word in parentheses is correct, and circle it.

1. He (pedals/peddles) magazines door-to-door.

2. Indiana Jones (pored/poured) over ancient Mayan tablets.

3. Ethical journalists should stand by their (principals/principles).

4. Sen. John Smelling, who dropped out of the presidential primaries in March, has (reentered/re-entered) the race.

5. The Watergate Hotel burglars (rifled/riffled) through most of the papers at the Democratic headquarters.

6. The theatrical (troop/troupe) will perform Hamlet in the campus amphitheater Friday.

7. I can't stand the hot (weather/temperatures) in Las Vegas.

8. New York City firefighters from (Company/Co.) 25 will be honored by the New York state (legislature/Legislature).

9. Plans for the inauguration ceremonies are already (under way/underway).

10. The senator said she is (eager, anxious) to debate the merits of the bill.

11. The Aluminum (Company/Co.) of America is now known as Alcoa (Incorporated/Inc.).

12. Tom Cruise is a member of Actors' Equity (Assn./Association).

13. I live at 112 Day (Ave./Avenue).

14. I live on the (100/one hundred) block of Day (Ave./Avenue).

15. Police (Det./Detective) Carl Jackson brought a thermos of coffee with him to the stakeout.

Exercise 5: Advanced Word Usage and General Information

Use your AP style guide to find any problems in these sentences.

1. Police said the murder weapon was a semi-automatic revolver.

2. The blizzard was accompanied by wind speeds of up to 25 miles per hour.

3. The concert's promoters gave windbreaker jackets to the first 25 ticket holders.

4. The company doesn't yet have a web site.

5. The Moslem holy day begins at sunset Friday.

6. He was given probation after serving two years of a three-year sentence.

7. The meteorite measured two cubic kilograms.

8. The president said he would continue to seek re-election irregardless of his loss in New Hampshire.

9. The school has banned all t-shirts with political messages on them.

10. He is a minister at the Mormon Church in Dallas, Texas.

11. The president convinced the House speaker to support the White House's education plan.

12. Iran is the only Middle Eastern country with a Sunni majority.

13. The governor insists that a bottle of catsup is always on his dining room table.

13. Thousands of celebrants gathered at Times Square to welcome the new year.

14. The fire completely destroyed the historical building.

15. U.S. forces ravished the city of Hue during the Vietnam War.

Exercise 6: Hyphenation

The asterisks (*) represent where hyphens might go in the following sentences. Remove the asterisks and make the necessary corrections to the sentences. Follow the rules in your AP style guide.

1. The president decided to shake*up his cabinet.

2. They gave her a terrific send*off.

3. The FBI stand*off lasted more than 70 days.

4. Madonna is on a world*wide tour.

5. Most race tracks have the horses run in a clock*wise direction.

6. The corporate shake*up resulted in several lay*offs.

7. It was a sell*out crowd.

8. The auto workers staged a sit*down strike.

9. The plant employees staged a walk*out.

10. The city's crime rate has grown ten*fold.

11. The vote to walk*out was unanimous.

12. The launch count*down will begin at 6 a.m.

13. Jackson is a hold*over from the last administration.

14. Let's pick*up some take*out food.

15. Hurry and chow*down and then get back to work.

Chapter 5

TOOLS FOR GOOD WRITING

This chapter:

- ☑ Explains how to create good transitions
- ☑ Shows how to eliminate wordiness
- ☑ Discusses using parallel writing structure to create a rhythm in writing
- ☑ Explains metaphors and other analogies
- ☑ Shows how to use quotes and attribution
- ☑ Explains how to write objectively
- ☑ Shows how to avoid euphemisms, slang and jargon
- ☑ Explains the difference between active and passive voice and the importance of active voice
- ☑ Explains how to show readers what is happening rather than tell them

Good writing is sometimes compared to a picture window. We see through the window what's happening in the world. We'll notice if flawed or dirty glass distorts the view, but our focus is on what we're seeing not on how clean and perfect the glass is. We take that for granted. Good writers paint pictures with words that are as clear as what we see through the window, and most people don't notice how good the writing is because they're enjoying what they see through the reporter's eyes. The reporter is *showing* them what has happened rather than simply *telling* them.

Reporters, however, do notice and appreciate good writing, and they deconstruct stories to understand how the writers crafted their stories. They look at the powerful verbs, the transitions and the clear structure.

Here are some tools they use to create powerful writing:

TRANSITIONS

Transitions are the glue that tie a story together. They connect ideas within a sentence and link the story's sentences and paragraphs to create a cohesive news story. They help the reader understand how the story's ideas connect. They also act as sign posts to alert readers to the introduction of new ideas.

The two types of transitions are *transitions of logic*, which show connections between ideas; and *transitions of thought*, in which words carry the thought from one sentence or paragraph to the next.

Transitions of Logic

Conjunctions and adverbs help show logical connections between ideas. These words or phrases are categorized as *addition, contrast, time* and *place*.

Addition. Coordinating conjunctions such as *and, also, and then* and *too* join ideas.

> Police questioned Smith again Thursday morning, *and* she *then* admitted that she kidnapped Roman.

> Sir Richard Burton was one of the first British explorers to visit Mecca. He *also* explored east Africa while searching for the source of the Nile River.

> They dragged the canoes from the river *and* carried them one mile to their cars.

Contrast. Other conjunctions use contrast to join thoughts. These include *but, and yet, however,* and *although.*

> Police searched throughout the night *but* found no sign of the boy.

> President Carter's decisions while in office have been criticized by both Democrats and Republicans. *However,* his efforts to ease world tensions and encourage democracies since leaving office have been universally praised.

> Many people believe beings from other planets have visited Earth, *although* no evidence of such visits exists.

Time. Stories are often told in chronological order. Words such as, *then, later, afterward, recently, soon* and *now* indicate a logical order in time.

> Smith *later* explained that she kidnapped Roman to get even with his parents.

> Although Davis said during the campaign that he is opposed to gun control, he *recently* said he would support banning assault rifles.

> Soldiers went through the neighborhood picking up suspects; *then* they blew up some of their homes.

Place. References to locations can also join ideas. Words that use place to join ideas include *there, where, here, beyond* and *nearby.*

> The guide showed U.N. investigators a mass grave outside the village. Dozens of shell casings from automatic rifles were lying on the ground *nearby.*

> The suspects fled through the rear entrance, *where* they were nabbed by waiting police officers.

> The wedding was held in a 12th century walled castle; *beyond* its walls, paparazzi and fans waited for a glimpse of the famous couple.

Transitions of Thought

Proper use of transitions of thought can make writing come alive. They can connect unrelated ideas so seamlessly that readers don't notice the shift in thoughts. Transitions of thought repeat words or variations of the words to carry the thought through parts of a sentence or from one sentence or paragraph to the next. The variations of the words usually are types of pronouns.

Pronouns and Possessive Pronouns. These noun substitutes often replace the previous sentence's subject.

> Proper use of transitions of thought can make writing come alive. *They* can connect unrelated ideas so seamlessly that readers don't notice the shift in thoughts.

> The president is spending the holidays at his retreat. *He* is hosting the British prime minister while he vacations, and *he* will also attend two fundraisers.

> The neighbors must be out of town. *Their* newspapers are still in the driveway.

Demonstrative Pronouns. These "pointing" words refer to a thought or thing in the previous sentence. Demonstrative pronouns include: *this, that, these* and *those.*

Some people say creationism should be included in science textbooks. *That* idea, however, is opposed by most educators and the scientific community.

The books you'll need for class are on the table. *Those* books in the box are out of date.

The money on the table has been tested for counterfeit. *This* bill is the only one that is fake.

Word Repetition. Be careful when repeating words to create transitions because too much repetition can also annoy readers. When used correctly, however, repetition is an effective tool for good writing.

From an article about an interview with actress Julia Roberts:

Lipton pointed out how *spontaneous* Roberts is as an actress. "I don't like to rehearse," Roberts explained. "I have only so many good takes inside of me." She is not so *spontaneous* when accepting a part for a movie, however.

From a radio news program's promotions for upcoming reports:

Saddam Hussein *turns* 61; the secretary of state *turns to* China; and cancer researchers look *to* new cures.

Even Rep. James Moore (R-Glendale), who usually works every weekend, *drew the line* when he refused to attend a meeting Sunday so he could take his children to the zoo. Sometimes it's easier to *draw the line* when you're the boss. Congressional staff members, caught up in the obsessive work ethic that grips Washington usually put in a full day's work on weekends.

These different types of transitions are often used together, as in this previous example, which uses contrasting transitions of ideas and a logical transition using a demonstrative pronoun:

Some people say creationism should be included in science textbooks. *That* idea, *however*, is opposed by most educators and the scientific community.

ELIMINATING WORDINESS

Shorter sentences are essential for easy comprehension. An American Press Institute study comparing story comprehension with the average number of words per sentence in newspaper stories found that 100 percent of the readers could comprehend articles that averaged eight or fewer words per sentence. Comprehension fell to 50 percent of the readers when stories averaged 29 words. Many reading-comprehension experts recommend print reporters strive for an average sentence length of 19 words, which has a comprehension rate of nearly 80 percent.

Broadcast writers must write even shorter sentences. Newspaper users can read articles at whatever speed they are comfortable with. A distracted reader can reread a paragraph. People listening to news or watching it on TV cannot play back the story if they are momentarily distracted. The writing must be simple and straightforward enough that people can follow the story while driving or preparing dinner. Broadcast news averages eight to 10 words per sentence.

The following tips will help both print and broadcast reporters write precisely:

Use specific words.

Original: The school superintendent said she will *put emphasis on* history.

Corrected: The school superintendent said she will *emphasize* history.

Original: *All of a sudden* the president stopped speaking.

Corrected: *Suddenly* the president stopped speaking.

Original: He will collect his winnings *over a period of years*.

Corrected: He will collect his winnings *over several years*.

Avoid prepositional phrases that serve as nouns. They frequently weaken the sentence because of their unnecessary wordiness.

Original: Final adoption *of the budget* is scheduled *for Tuesday*.

Corrected: The budget's final adoption is scheduled Tuesday.

Original: Sentencing *for Maxwell* was delayed *by the judge* until the Probation Department completes its psychological examination *of Maxwell.*

Corrected: Maxwell's sentencing was delayed until the Probation Department completes the defendant's psychological examination.

It's not necessary to say that the judge delayed sentencing; a judge is the only one with authority to set a sentencing date.

Avoid unnecessary verbosity. You've done your audience a favor anytime you can compress a wordy phrase by replacing a half-dozen words with one or two.

Original: The police chief said the department *had abandoned the use of* stun guns *due to the fact that* their use *many times* resulted in lawsuits.

Corrected: The police chief said the department *stopped using* stun guns *because* their use *often* resulted in lawsuits.

Original: Bill Smith, a U.N. representative, said he *will respond to the famine even before technical teams lay the groundwork for an aid program.* He said he plans to begin an emergency food airlift within days.

Corrected: *U.N. representative* Bill Smith said he plans to begin an emergency food airlift within days *instead of waiting for an aid program to be established.*

Original: The Shubert Theater is presenting "The Secret Garden" *between now and Aug. 2.*

Corrected: The Shubert Theater is presenting "The Secret Garden" *through Aug. 2.*

Original: The play was a flop *in spite of* her good performance.

Corrected: The play was a flop *despite* her good performance.

Eliminate obvious facts and unnecessary information in a story.

Original: Firefighters from Engine Co. 46, *which responded to the call,* had the fire out in 15 minutes.

Corrected: Firefighters from Engine Co. 46 had the fire out in 15 minutes.

Original: County arson investigators, *who are looking into the cause of the fire,* plan to make an announcement Monday on their findings.

Corrected: County arson investigators plan to make an announcement Monday on their findings.

Firefighters' job is to respond to fire alarms, and the arson investigators are the ones who determine the cause of fires; it's not necessary to tell this to the reader.

Watch for redundancies. The italicized words in the following sentences should be eliminated.

It was a *hot,* sultry afternoon. ("Sultry" means "hot.")

The suspect *quickly* sprinted across the yard. (Did you ever see a slow sprinter?)

The war refugees sought *a safe* haven across the border. ("Haven" is a safe place.)

Look for other words or phrases that are redundant or do not offer new information in the context of the sentence. The italicized words in these sentences are not necessary and should be eliminated:

Jason said he had begun *implementing* some of the reforms recommended by the committee.

Professor Bart Thompson has lectured in 50 countries *throughout the world.*

The project is funded by *a combination of* state and federal grants.

Print news writing: Do not summarize what someone says and then say the same thing in a direct quote.

The mayor said he would consider implementing some of the recommendations of the anti-corruption task force, but he added that he opposes an independent counsel to investigate complaints. *"I would never support an independent counsel,"* he said. "It would infringe on the autonomy of the City Council."

The first sentence in the direct quotation repeats the introductory sentence. The paragraph would read more smoothly without the quote:

The mayor said he would consider implementing some of the recommendations of the anti-corruption task force, but he added that he opposes an independent counsel to investigate complaints because "it would infringe on the autonomy of the City Council."

Broadcasters, however, often do summarize a quote before a sound bite. This gives signals to the listener that an important quote is next.

Keep the writing simple. Don't pack all the information into one sentence.

Clark, who has served in Congress for 16 years as a representative from the Texas Panhandle, said Johnson, elected this year to fill out the term of Cecil Brooks, who was killed in a plane crash in August, is too inexperienced to understand his strategy in shepherding the legislation through the House.

Turn the descriptive phrases and clauses into separate, shorter sentences for easier comprehension:

Clark said Johnson is too inexperienced to understand Clark's strategy in shepherding the legislation through the House. *Johnson was elected this year to fill out the term of Cecil Brooks, who was killed in a plane crash in August. Clark has represented the Texas Panhandle in Congress for 16 years.*

Broadcast reporters might make this four sentences: *Clark said Johnson is too inexperienced to understand Clark's strategy in shepherding the legislation through the House. Johnson was elected this year to fill out the term of Cecil Brooks. <u>Brooks was killed in a plane crash in August.</u> Clark has represented the Texas Panhandle in Congress for 16 years.*

PARALLEL STRUCTURE

Parallel structure, or parallel construction, uses consistent grammatical construction, verb tense, language and voice. *Parallelism* makes lists and sentence structure flow. Writers can create rhythm, emphasis and drama as they present ideas or action. The following sentence uses parallel structure because each item in the list begins with a verb ending in "ing":

I'm always trying to improve myself by *taking* courses, *reading* newspapers and news magazines, *being* involved with clubs on campus and *reading* good literature.

Here are some sentences that are improved by parallel structure:

Original: A reporter's typical day might consist of *meetings* with editors, *interviews* with sources and *writing* stories.

Corrected: A reporter's typical day might consist of *talking* with editors, *interviewing* sources and *writing* stories.

Original: The qualities of a good reporter include *a curiosity* about the world, *a keen sense* of observation, *writing* well and *asking* insightful probing questions.

Corrected: The qualities of a good reporter include *a curiosity* about the world, *a keen sense* of observation, *the ability* to write well and *the insight* to ask probing questions.

Here are some more examples of good parallel structure:

Heavy rains pounded Houston on Monday, leaving streets *flooded* and motorists *stranded.*

Heavy rains pounded Houston on Monday, *causing* creeks and bayous to overflow their banks, *flooding* streets and *stranding* motorists.

Heavy rains pounded Houston on Monday, *flooding* streets, *stranding* motorists and even *forcing* the Houston Astros to call off a game.

Other wording in the sentence should also use parallel structure:

Original: Zoo officials said Friday *that* the pandas were adjusting well to their new habitat and the public would be allowed to visit the exhibit in about two weeks.

The word "that" is needed after "Friday" to make clear to readers that Friday was when zoo officials made the statement rather than Friday was when the pandas were adjusting. Because "that" is needed to introduce the first clause in the compound sentence, it also should introduce the second clause:

Corrected: Zoo officials said Friday *that* the pandas were adjusting well to their new habitat and *that* the public would be allowed to visit the exhibit in about two weeks.

Parallel structure is also an effective tool for transitions within a sentence:

The writing coach said *exercising* the mind before *starting* to write is as important to a writer as *exercising* the legs before *starting* a race is to a runner.

The soldiers peered into the darkness, *listening* for the footsteps of any insurgents trying to sneak up to them, *looking* for any hostile movements in the brush, *watching* for the first flash of rifles or grenade launchers indicating they were under attack, but mostly *hoping* they would all make it safely through the night.

METAPHORS AND OTHER ANALOGIES

Analogies are words and phrases that are used in a figurative sense rather than a literal sense. Saying your love for someone is like a red rose doesn't mean that love is a flower with a thorny stem; it means that love, like a rose, is a beautiful and wondrous thing.

Metaphors and similes are types of analogies. Metaphors use ideas, often cultural or sports references, to describe something, while similes use the words *like* or *as* to compare two ideas.

Metaphor: The dictator *was a vicious shark* devouring anything that got in the way of his ambition.

Simile: The dictator *was like a vicious shark* devouring anything that got in the way of his ambition.

Analogies can create vivid, colorful writing that creates images in readers' minds. Here's how an Orange County (Calif.) Register business writer turned a routine retail-sales stories into vivid writing:

Pacific Sunwear of California has found a *warm reception* in the state for its young-men's casual fashions. The Anaheim-based retail chain said sales at stores open at least a year were up 8 percent in August, largely because of increased sales in the Golden State.

Meanwhile, things are a little *cooler* at Clothestime Inc., an Anaheim-based women's casual-clothes retailer where sales were down 15 percent for August. The company blamed the state's sluggish economy and lack of a strong fashion statement to guide women's-apparel retailers.

The writer played with the word "sun" in the company's name to describe the increased sales. Continuing the metaphor to describe a competitor's not only created colorful writing but also helped transition to discussion of a different company.

Writers often use metaphors to tighten as well as enliven their writing. The images created by the metaphors serve as a shorthand in writing and speaking:

Ross Perot *laid the foundation* of a new political party in 1988.

The House committee chairman said his hearings would *throw a spotlight* on IRS abuses.

The ambassador said the peace process would not survive the new fighting in the Occupied Territories. "We cannot put *Humpty Dumpty* back together," she said.

The professor *threw me a curve* on the test.

Noisy kids drive me *up the wall.*

His beliefs are out *in left field.*

Here's the lead for a story about an accidental death at a child-care facility:

The controversy over Carla Marie Faith's home day-care center raises two questions that strike at the *Achilles' heel* of most working moms and dads.

QUOTATIONS AND ATTRIBUTION

All news stories need sources to give credibility to the information they contain. Any information, except for general, non-controversial information and events reporters witness, should be attributed to credible people or documents. Readers and viewers need to know where the information comes from to help them assign importance to it.

For example, a story about NASA's Martian probe sending its first images from the Red Planet would not need attribution for when the rover landed, descriptions of the images, the cost of mission or background on previous missions. An explanation of what the images signify and the scientists' reactions would need attribution.

Let's look at part of a story about a county board of supervisors' public hearing and approval for a housing project:

Greenwood developer Jack Hachmeister said, "The 450-home Greenwood housing tract is a good compromise between fulfilling the needs of homebuyers and protecting the environment."

Reporters and readers would be skeptical of a developer claiming that a business venture would help the environment. Good reporters would find other sources, credible people with no financial stake in the project, to add balance to the story:

"I agree," Sierra Club President Jenell Smith said. "The project protects the most pristine portions of Greenwood Valley from future development."

Other sources in this story might be county supervisors and other county officials, and other speakers at the meeting. The general information about the project that is part of the public record would not need attribution.

It would be possible for the reporter to write this story without attribution by reporting only what she heard and saw at the meeting: that the county Board of Supervisors approved 450 homes in Greenwood Valley. The story, however, would not be good journalism because the reporter is not putting the story in perspective. Even when the reporter is an eyewitness to a trial, conflict or government action, she needs to talk to experts and participants to explain the *how* and *why* of the story.

Single-source stories are a basically news releases, and reporters who write them are little more than stenographers for the politicians, government agencies or other special interests that provided the information. The only stories that don't need multiple sources are short items such as meeting announcements, secondary city government stories, short "police log" stories or other brief announcements.

USING QUOTATIONS

Reporters use quotes sparingly and for emphasis. They use quotes for colorful statements, strong statements of opinion or for quotes from authoritative statements. Most of a source's comments are paraphrased for clarity and brevity.

Broadcast reporters seldom quote a source. They introduce speakers and use their voices for the sound bites. Reporters need to work with a source, particularly someone who is not accustomed to being interviewed, to get the succinct comments they need for their reports. While they don't tell the speakers what to say, they will ask the same question more than once to give the speaker the opportunity to better phrase his response.

Print reporters also must be careful to put quotation marks (" ") only around words that are direct quotes, which are the exact words the speaker uses. If you change the wording, remove the quotation marks.

> Original: "The wounded soldiers were treated with first aid at the scene and then evacuated from the site to a hospital in Basra for further treatment of their wounds," a military spokesman said.

> Better: A military spokesman said the wounded soldiers were given first aid at the scene and then flown to Basra for additional treatment.

Notice that the paraphrased version is several words shorter.

The AP stylebook tells reporters to never alter quotations even to correct minor grammatical errors or word usage. It recommends that writers either paraphrase an awkward quote or ask the speaker to clarify. It also discourages the use of mispronounced words like "gonna" and "ain't" that convey regional dialects or poor education. Making someone sound uneducated is disrespectful and demeaning.

The Los Angeles Times, in a 2001 story on then-Sen. Strom Thurmond's failing health and who might replace him in the Senate, quoted a woman from his home state:

> But in places such as Mims' Corner Store in Edgefield, which looks just as it should with corncob pipes dangling from the wall, buckets of seeds on the floor and dusty old men sipping Bud and watching "The Price Is Right," such conversation draws some hard looks.

> "It ain't nice to speculate on another man's demise," explained Louise Mims, the generously cut proprietor. "And Strom ain't going anywhere anyway. Y'all just wasting your time."

The descriptions of the store and woman and her mispronounced words in the quotes say as much about the reporter as it does about Edgefield, S.C. People looking for bias in the news media would say the reporter is an elitist out of touch with the people he interviews.

Partial Quotes. While it is always better to use complete sentences for direct quotes to avoid taking the speaker's words out of context, reporters sometimes use partial quotes, which are sentence fragments, for clarity and brevity:

> Original: "We're going to, my boys are going to whip their ass on the court tomorrow night," Blades coach Mark Philips said.

> Better: The Blades "are going to whip their ass," coach Mark Philips said.

Orphan Quotes. Orphan quotes are one or two words in quotation marks. Use orphan quotes only when you want to make it clear that the words are the speaker's and not the reporter's.

> Bailey said he didn't believe peace between Sylvania and Freedonia was possible because he did not trust "Freedonian scum."

SOURCES

Reporters should be wary of using unidentified sources. Identifying sources and explaining their authority on the subject give the story credibility. Using several sources gives the story depth. Using sources on both sides of the issue gives the story balance.

> Original: The suspect pointed his gun at the police officer before the officer shot him, a spokesman said.

> Better: The suspect pointed his gun at the police officer before the officer shot him, police Sgt. Joe Thusrby said.

> The manager, Juan Valdez, said he believed the officer saved both their lives. "If he hadn't fired, I'm sure the robber would have shot both us," said Valdez, who was standing behind the counter and witnessed the shooting.

News stories have three types of sources:

☑ **Primary sources.** People directly involved in the event, such as members of Congress, community activists, or crime or accident victims.

☑ **Secondary sources.** People who witnessed or have knowledge of the event but are not directly involved. These secondary sources are witnesses to crimes or accidents or other events and people who spoke to witnesses immediately after a news-making event. Secondary sources' comments give the story color and imagery. Reporters are sometimes secondary sources.

☑ **Expert sources.** People who have expertise in the topic and can explain the background and give the story perspective. These sources might be Wall Street analysts discussing a proposed merger, fall in stock prices etc.; political analysts discussing an upcoming election or why a candidate won; or a university biologist known as an expert on the environment discussing the potential impact of a road project.

Attribution

Types of Attribution. Three types of attribution are *on the record, on background* and *anonymous*. Some information reporters receive is also *off the record*.

On the record identifies sources of information. Most sources are on the record because identifying sources and explaining their background give stories credibility. Audiences want to know if sources have a stake in the issue that the reporter is writing about.

Some sources, particularly in government, want to help reporters understand complex issues, but the sources do not want to be part of the story. They brief reporters on background about the history of the issue or its political ramifications. Reporters use background information to explain the *how* and *why* of the story and use other, named sources for the *story's who, what, when* and *where*. Reporters might describe an on-background source, for example, as *an official in the Chancellor's Office* said in a background briefing that ... .

Some sources want to help reporters get vital information but do not want their names used, and reporters refer to sources as anonymous. The most famous anonymous source in recent years was the so-called Deep Throat, who helped Carl Bernstein and Bob Woodward uncover the Watergate scandal for the Washington Post. Reporters use anonymous sources sparingly, if at all, because a story without named sources has little credibility. Careful reporters find other sources who will corroborate the information on the record. Using anonymous sources can also have legal ramifications. Reporters and their employers sued for libel will have difficulty defending themselves if they cannot identify the source of the information, and reporters have been jailed for refusing to identify sources.

Sometimes sources want to share information with reporters to help them understand the story, but they do not want their names or the information made public. Reporters need to make it clear to sources that anything they say is on the record unless reporters and sources agree at the onset of the interview that what is said is background or off the record. A source can go off the record during an interview, but he must tell this to the reporter before he gives the information, not after the reporter already has it. Reporters sometimes ask sources if they can use what the source tells them if they get the information from other named sources.

Attribution Words. *Said* is usually the best word for attribution. It is neutral and doesn't imply any opinion about the statement or its source. Avoid words such as *contended* or *claimed*. They imply that the reporter doesn't believe the statement.

Be careful how you use these attribution words:

☑ *According to*. Use this attribution to refer to non-human sources:

According to a State Department report, ... *According* to a New York Times article, ...

☑ *Explained*. Make sure the speaker actually is explaining, not simply saying, something

☑ *Stated*. Use this only for documents and formal announcements; everything else is said.

The report *stated* that crime is down 8 percent in county.
The presidential directive *stated* that all refugees would be granted asylum.

☑ *Added.* Don't use *added* as an alternative for *said.* Use it only when the statement adds something to a previous statement:

Smith said three of the victims were treated and released at Mercy Hospital, *adding* that one person was kept overnight for observation.

☑ *Admitted.* Avoid using *admitted*; it implies that the speaker was caught in a lie or confessed to a crime. Use it only in that context:

Pete Rose admits in his autobiography that he lied when he said he did not bet on sports.

☑ *Asked.* Use this word only when the speaker asks a question:

"Why didn't the police step in and stop them?" *asked* Joanne Drew, who witnessed the gang attack in the park.

☑ *Think or believe.* Avoid these words. You are not a mind reader; you only know what people say, not what they think.

Poor: Lee *believes* that taxes were already too high.

Better: Lee *said he believes* that taxes were already too high. Lee *said* taxes were already too high. Lee *argued* that taxes were already too high.

☑ *Say vs. said.* Reporters writing hard-news stories prefer *said.* The events they are writing about are in the past. They must also be careful to avoid arbitrarily switching between *say* and *said* in the same story. Feature writers often prefer *say* because it is both timeless and it gives a sense of immediacy:

Stephen Hawking *says* the universe can be defined in one mathematical equation.

Say — and the use of the present tense — is often preferred in feature writing:

"The universe can be defined in one mathematical equation," Stephen Hawking *says* as he nervously circles the room in his motorized wheelchair.

Said is specific; it connotes a point in time:

Linus Pauling *says* taking large doses of vitamin C daily prevents cancer. Vitamin C "is an inexpensive way of staying healthy," he *said* in an interview Tuesday.

Attribution Placement. Broadcast reporters usually introduce the speaker or attribution before airing the video or audio sound bite or reading the paraphrased information.

Reporter: Sandra Perez is the organizer of the event. Cut to video and sound on tape of Perez speaking.

Print reporters usually start with the quote and insert the attribution for a new speaker at the first logical pause in the quote:

"Running for president was the right decision," Riley said. "While we couldn't raise the money needed to stay in the race to the end, we have changed the agenda of the frontrunners."

The only time print needs to put the attribution before the speaker is when a new speaker is introduced.

"Running for president was the right decision," Riley said. "While we couldn't raise the money needed to stay in the race to the end, we have changed the agenda of the frontrunners."
Republican frontrunner Sen. John Golds praised Riley. "I'm sorry she lost in the marketplace of fundraising instead of the marketplace of ideas."

Put the word "said" after the speaker's name unless a dependent phrase or clause follows the name:

"I want Tom Cruise to star in my next film," Martin said. (not said Martin.)

"I want Tom Cruise to star in my next film," said Martin, who has worked with Cruise on two other movies.

OBJECTIVITY AND FAIRNESS

Reporters for the mass media in the United States strive for objectivity and fairness in their writing. Their job is to give both sides of the issue and let their readers and listeners draw their own conclusions.

While most reporters do not slant stories to favor one side, they sometimes accidentally word news in ways that color or show bias. Here are some pitfalls to guard against:

Adjectives and Adverbs

Avoid these modifying words if they express opinion, even if the opinion is shared by many other people.

Original: Two pedestrians were killed in a tragic accident Wednesday.

Describe what happened and who the victims were and let the audience determine whether the deaths were a tragedy.

Corrected: Two pedestrians were killed in an accident Wednesday.

Original: Tickets to the concerts are only $50.

Fifty dollars is a lot of money if you don't have $50 to spend on concert tickets.

Corrected: Tickets to the concerts are $50.

Original: Fullerton firefighter John Perez is a hero today for saving a child trapped in a burning car.

Describe what occurred and let the readers or viewers decide if he is a hero, or let someone else call him a hero.

Corrected: Fullerton firefighter John Perez is being hailed as a hero today after he saved a child trapped in a burning car.

Crime Stories

Do not declare someone guilty of a crime before a jury does. Stories that accuse people of crimes need careful attribution.

Original: Centerville police arrested a drunk driver who struck and killed two pedestrians.

Who says the driver had been drinking? The reporter is condemning the motorist without offering evidence or attribution to support the claim.

Corrected: Centerville police arrested a suspected drunken driver who they said struck and killed two pedestrians.

Sexism and Stereotyping

What's wrong with these sentences?

Secret Service agents are always ready to use their bodies to shield from harm the man they are assigned to protect.

A police officer is allowed to carry a concealed weapon even when he is off duty.

Both sentences are sexist. The writer assumes that only men need Secret Service protection or work as police officers. Use the plural form of nouns and pronouns to avoid sexism:

Secret Service agents are always ready to use their bodies to shield from harm people they are assigned to protect.

Police officers are allowed to carry a concealed weapon even when they are off duty.

Be wary of gender specific words when discussing people in general. Find the gender-neutral equivalent:

    policeman = police officer
    mailman = mail carrier
    councilman = council member
    workman = worker
    newsman = reporter

However, don't get carried away with political correctness and make up words to avoid sexism:

    chairperson = chair
    spokesperson = representative
    fireperson = firefighter

Use gender-specific words when referring to one individual whose sex is known to you:

    An Exxon spokeswoman said the company would issue a statement later today.
    "We won't have any comment until we get the Coast Guard's report this afternoon," Lee White told a news conference this morning.

Identifying Women and Minorities

Mention someone's race, age or ethnic background only when it is relevant to the story. Some instances where this is appropriate include when writing about the first woman or minority elected to high office or breaking another societal barrier, and describing a missing person or a crime suspect. Descriptions of crime suspects should be specific enough that they are useful in spotting someone. Reporting that a robbery suspect is a male Hispanic, mid-20s, 5 feet 9 inches and 155 pounds is useless because too many people fit that description. All the writer is doing is perpetuating fear of minorities. Don't use descriptions unless they include distinguishing marks or other information unique to that person.

EUPHEMISMS, SLANG AND JARGON

News writiers want to use clear, precise, specific words. Nonspecific, broad and euphemistic words and phrases or jargon are detours to avoid saying directly what we mean.

Euphemisms. Examples of euphemisms include using "economically non-affluent" for poor people, "passed away" for dead, "cultural group concept" for apartheid and "ethnic cleansing" for genocide. During the Gulf War, the Pentagon referred to "target-rich environments" and avoided mentioning that the targets were people on the ground.

Jargon. Reporters covering a beat for any length of time tend to pick up a lot of their sources' technical jargon, and that jargon sometimes makes its way into copy. Here are some examples:

    Original: The county is looking for ways to *mitigate detour traffic* while the highway improvements are under way.
    Corrected: The county is looking for ways to *ease traffic congestion* on the detour route while the highway improvements are under way.
    Original: A Los Angeles man was killed Monday in a *car rollover* on Highway 71 in Chino.
    Corrected: A Los Angeles man was killed Monday when his *car rolled over* on Highway 71 in Chino.
    Corrected: Police took a *male suspect*, 18, into custody.
    Corrected: Police took an 18-year-old man into custody.

Eliminate slang and clichés — those wasted, stale phrases — and replace them with clearer details:

    Original: The couple said they had been *ripped off.*

Corrected: The couple said they were *robbed* by two masked men.

Original: The fighter *tipped the scales* at 210 pounds.

Corrected: The fighter *weighed* 210 pounds.

Slang. Every generation creates its own slang, a code only their peers can understand. Journalists for the mainstream mass media must never forget that the majority of their viewers and readers are older and often more conservative than they are. These people may have never heard the slang used by many 20-year-olds. At best, some slang might puzzle readers; at worst, it might offend them. Limit your vocabulary to words that are in Webster's New World Dictionary.

ACTIVE AND PASSIVE VOICE

One technique for sharp leads is to use the *active voice*. Sentences in the active voice are shorter and their verbs are livelier than those written in the *passive voice*. In the active voice, the subject of a sentence performs the action of the verb:

John Coltrane plays tenor saxophone in the band.

John Coltrane is the subject of this sentence, and Coltrane does the action of the verb *plays*. The sentence also has a direct object, *saxophone*, which is the noun after the verb that the verb acts on. This sentence structure, subject-verb-object, Coltrane-plays-saxophone, is a clear, direct writing style that generally is preferred by reporters in all media.

In the passive voice, the sentence's subject doesn't perform the verb's action; it is a passive player that is acted upon:

The tenor saxophone was played by John Coltrane.

The focus now is on the saxophone rather than on the musician. This passive version is clumsy and stilted. All the life has been drained from the sentence. The active version is dynamic; it is direct with a faster pace and a strong, unencumbered verb.

Passive voice: A child who accidentally fell into the lowland gorilla's habitat at the Bronx Zoo on Sunday was rescued by one of the gorillas.

Active voice: A lowland gorilla rescued a child Sunday who accidentally fell into the gorilla's habitat at the Bronx Zoo.

Passive voice: Five houses were engulfed by a fast-moving brush fire Thursday near Loveland, Colo.

Active voice: A fast-moving brush fire engulfed five houses Thursday near Loveland, Colo.

In the first active-voice sentence, the subject-verb-object is *gorilla-rescued-child*. In the second sentence, the subject-verb-object is *fire-engulfed-houses*.

Use the passive voice only when the receiver of the action is more important than the performer of the action:

John Wilkes Booth assassinated President Lincoln at Ford Theater last night.

A hangman executed John Wilkes Booth today for assassinating President Lincoln.

In both of these active-voice sentences, the receivers of the action, Lincoln and Booth, are much more important than the performers of the action, Booth and the hangman.

The passive voice is preferred in both of these sentences:

President Lincoln was assassinated at Ford Theater last night.

John Wilkes Booth was hanged today for assassinating President Lincoln.

The information in these lead sentences are now arranged in the order of their importance.

Show, Don't Tell

Careful writers paint pictures with words. They use their writing skills to *show* their audience what is happening rather than simply *tell* them. Describing what happened is a passive experience for readers. Showing what happened involves reader and lets the readers experience the event and draw their own conclusions.

Let's examine the first few sentences of a brush fire story by Kevin O'Hanlon for The Associated Press:

> POOLVILLE, Texas — Linda Dixon stood ankle-deep in the ashes looking for bits and pieces of her life. She wasn't having much luck.
> "There's nothing left. Nothing," she said, her face ruddy and covered with soot from digging in 90-degree heat.
> Dixon's small wood-frame ranch house was one of 65 homes destroyed by raging grass fires that continued to spread Thursday in Parker and Wise counties in north Texas.

A less skillful or more rushed writer would have written:

> Raging grass fires that have destroyed 65 homes in two Texas counties continued to spread Thursday in north Texas.

The second version tells that fires are destroying homes in Texas, while O'Hanlon's version takes us to Texas and lets us experience the fire through the eyes of one of its victims. These phrases, "ankle-deep in the ashes looking for bits and pieces of her life" and "her face ruddy and covered with soot from digging in 90-degree heat" show us what's happening and lets us experience with the woman.

Let's look at this feature story on a long-haul trucker published in the Philadelphia Inquirer Magazine:

> It is 10:15 on a Sunday morning, cheerless and chilling. Rod Stewart is singing above the static on AM radio. The CB radio is squawking but getting no attention from the truck driver, 39-year-old Steve Daffron, who is working his way through Chattanooga church traffic toward Interstate 24, air brakes hissing, gears groaning. It is the beginning of another 12-hour workday for Steve, a 6-foot-1, 256-point former college fullback and one the few truck drivers in the world with a college degree.

Like the article about the fires, this story is showing what Daffron is experiencing through the careful use of strong verbs and vivid adjectives: a "cheerless and chilling" Sunday morning, "air brakes hissing, gears groaning."

Use Strong Verbs. Look for verbs that that show action and avoid using adverbs to prop up weak verbs:

Original: A man with a gun told the woman to give him all her money.

Corrected: A gunman demanded all the woman's money.

Original: The accident victim was transported to the hospital.

Corrected: The accident victim was rushed to the hospital.

Original: Clarence came suddenly through the door.

Corrected: Clarence burst through the door.

Original: I am very tired.

Corrected: I am exhausted.

Original: Lynn said she is very happy with the verdict.

Corrected: Lynn said she is ecstatic with the verdict.

Original: He walked aimlessly through the park.

Corrected: He wandered through the park.

Eliminate Vague Modifiers. These include such words as *a lot, kind of, perhaps, quite, really, somewhat, sort of* and *very*. Again, look for specific words that connote an extreme condition.

Original: The speaker looks *very tired.*

Corrected: The speaker looks *exhausted.*

Original: The defendant appeared *extremely happy* about the verdict.

Corrected: The defendant appeared *ecstatic* about the verdict.

Original: The hikers were really hungry.

Corrected: The hikers were famished.

Exercise 1: Transitions

Use transitions to connect or combine these short sentences.

1. The dog is barking. It hears a strange noise outside.

2. Congress voted to lower taxes. It did not eliminate the highest tax bracket.

3. Police burst into the room. They ordered everyone to lie on the floor.

4. The wolves are beginning to prowl. The wolves must be looking for prey.

5. They unloaded everything from the trailer. The car still couldn't tow it up the hill.

6. They searched for five hours and found the hiking trail they had wandered away from.

7. The coins in frames are not for sale. The coins in the display case are for sale.

8. Abraham Lincoln is remembered for leading the nation through its greatest crisis. Lincoln ended slavery.

9. Some people say that photos of astronauts on the moon are all faked. Most scientists laugh at that notion.

10. Traffic was backed up for five miles. The cause was a jackknifed truck.

Exercise 2: Eliminating Opinion

Rewrite the following sentences to eliminate any opinion or bias.

1. This talented 14-year-old has many exciting opportunities.

2. Fortunately, none of the injuries was life threatening.

3. Carl's Jr. is donating 10 cents to the Make a Wish Foundation for each of the delicious burgers purchased next week.

4. The acclaimed magician Dr. Presto will present his hilarious show Tuesday evening in Carter Auditorium.

5. Bartock, who makes exceptional handcrafted jewelry, once again will offer his fine work to buyers at the county fair.

6. The conference will be in Maui, Hawaii, which is the perfect location for learning and relaxation.

7. Billings, a petite blonde who has two grandchildren, will be sworn into office Jan. 16.

8. Police have arrested an illegal alien who stole a woman's purse in Central Park.
   man/woman

9. The Open Hearth Soup Kitchen, which does a terrific job of feeding the poor, now wants to open a homeless shelter for these unfortunate victims of government policies.

10. An African-American has been named CEO of the North American Broadcasting System.

Exercise 3: Quotes and Attribution

Properly attribute the following quotations for a newspaper.

1. on first reference to John Conners, president of Acme Robotics Inc.: "Our robots are designed to serve mankind. They would never run amok and try to take over the world."

2. on second reference in the story to NASA scientist William Martinez: "All the evidence shows that Mars once had oceans. That means Mars could have supported life. I don't know what the life forms would have looked like."

3. from the Web site of the Society of Professional Journalists' Greater Los Angeles Chapter: "SPJ is dedicated to the belief that quality and responsible journalism are the foundations of a free and informed society."

4. from a news release distributed to reporters by the White House: "The president categorically denies that he helped Acme Robotics win the government contract. He didn't ask anyone about it, and no one brought it to his attention."

5. on first reference to Greenville Police Chief Sarah Chou: "We have two suspects in custody. They both match the descriptions given by witnesses."

6. on second reference to Greenville Police Chief Sarah Chou: "We have two suspects in custody. They both match the descriptions given by witnesses."

7. from a news conference with Gen. George Glenn: "We, uh, my men were ambushed, gunned down, while trying to help, providing food and water, to these people. The attackers were thugs who deserve no mercy."

Exercise 4: Avoiding Euphemisms, Slang, Jargon and Cliches

Rewrite these sentences to eliminate any euphemisms, slang and jargon.

1. Johnson, who was 95, passed away in his sleep Monday night.

2. The NCAA is looking into allegations that coaches are doping their players to build their strength.

3. The news is broadcast 24-7, though it's not updated very often.

4. Police nabbed two homies who were allegedly packing heat.

5. 'Tis the season for family get togethers.

6. The company plans to outsource 200 manufacturing jobs.

7. The elderly man was scammed out of his life savings.

8. Police took a female suspect, 14, into custody and transported her to juvenile authorities.

9. He's making a mountain from a mole hill with his parking ticket.

10. The searched turned up 12 grams of coke and a pound of pot.

Exercise 5: Active and Passive Voice

Indicate whether the following story leads are in the active or passive voice.

1. ATHENS, Greece (CNN) — Search-and-rescue teams worked through the night to cut through mountains of broken concrete slabs, hoping to find scores of people believed trapped by a strong earthquake that struck the Greek capital on Tuesday.

2. BELFAST, Northern Ireland (AP) — Former U.S. Sen. George Mitchell spent a second difficult day Tuesday trying to repair the 1998 peace accord as Northern Ireland received a grim reminder of one of its most horrible events.

3. RICHLAND, Iowa (Reuters) — Investigators tried Tuesday to find the cause of an explosion that destroyed a house in southeartern Iowa, killing at least seven people and injuring six others.

4. NEW YORK (AP) — Thousands of acres in New York City have been sprayed with insecticide after more people were suspected of being infected with St. Louis Encephalitis, a virus spread by mosquitoes.

5. JERUSALEM — Setting a landmark in Israel's decades-old conflict between democracy and security, between respecting human rights and protecting citizens from terrorism, the Supreme Court on Monday banned the use of torture in interrogations.

6. ALBUQUERQUE, New Mexico (AP) — The state's top prison and law enforcement officials announced an investigation Monday into why a privately run prison didn't notify state police about a riot in which a guard was stabbed to death.

7. WASHINGTON — Two sources — an administration official and a congressional aide — say they have been informed Attorney General Janet Reno has offered Republican former Sen. John Danforth the job of heading an independent inquiry into the government's use of force at the fiery end of the Branch Davidian standoff in Waco, Texas.

8. EUREKA, Calif. (Reuters) — A dredging vessel spilled hundreds of gallons of oil into the waters outside northern California's Humboldt Bay but appears to have avoided causing serious environmental damage, officials said Tuesday.

9. PORT SAID, Egypt (CNN) — Egyptian President Hosni Mubarak was slightly injured Monday in Port Said by a knife-wielding man who was then shot dead by security police.

10. BERLIN (AP) — Despite losing in two state elections, Chancellor Gerhard Schroeder pledged to push ahead with unpopular cuts to generous social benefits.

WRITING SUMMARY LEADS

This chapter:

- ☑ Explains the importance of writing the leads that draw the audience into the story
- ☑ Shows how the first sentence sets a story's tone
- ☑ Explains the difference between active and passive voice and the importance of active voice
- ☑ Shows how to prioritize the *who, what, when, where, why* and *how* and determine which should be included in the lead
- ☑ Explains when and how to use attribution in the lead
- ☑ Explains how to handle leads for stories that have multiple topics
- ☑ Explains how to localize the lead

While journalists can take several approaches to how they report the news, the *summary lead* (pronounced "leed" and sometimes spelled "lede") is a time-tested approach to explaining an important, hard-news story in just a few words. It is one of the news writers' essential tools. As its name implies, the summary lead is the first sentence of the story that gives readers and listeners a quick overview of what is to follow. It tells them why the story is newsworthy by quickly explaining *what* happened and *who* was involved.

The summary lead is used in all media — print, broadcast and the Web — but while print and broadcast writers have other ways of telling the news, Web reporters prefer the summary lead because it conveys the information in the least amount of words. People who get their news from the Internet tend to skim stories, and a summary lead followed by the most important information can tell the story in three or four paragraphs. Keep in mind, though, that studies show that people on Web sites will read long stories in their entirety if the stories are well written and compelling.

In broadcast news, anchors report some shorter stories, those around a minute or less, in their entirety. They also present some story leads and then introduce field reporters who provide the rest of the story. Reporters write suggested leads in these instances, but news programs' producers are in charge of the anchors' copy to ensure it flows with the other stories.

A good summary lead must get to the point of the story as soon as possible. That first sentence must be concise and direct and must entice the reader into continuing with the story. Strong verbs and adjectives are the reporter's best tools for luring the reader into the story.

The lead should be between about 20 and 30 words for newspapers, 25 or fewer for the Web sites and even shorter for broadcast news. A short lead on a compelling story can have a greater impact on the reader:

DALLAS — President John Fitzgerald Kennedy was shot and killed by an assassin today.

If you count the president's name as one word, Tom Wicker's lead for the New York Times is only nine words. His short sentence, however, was for many readers like a knife through the heart.

Let's deconstruct the newspaper's lead for the story about Romeo and Juliet's double suicide in Chapter 2:

VERONA — The bodies of three teenagers from the city's prominent families were found in a family crypt Thursday in what authorities say was a slaying and double suicide.

This 28-word sentence tells us that three children from prominent families were found dead in a cemetery, but it doesn't tell us *who* they were, *what* exactly happened, *how* they died or *why* this tragedy occurred. (We do have the *when* and *where*, however: in Verona on Thursday.) The sentence is a brief summary of what happened. It tells us just enough to pique our interest and draw us into the story. We want to know who these children were and how their bodies came be in such a macabre location.

Writers have to keep several things in mind when they craft their leads. Here are some tips on creating sharp, effective leads:

SETTING THE TONE

The lead sets the story's *tone*, or emotion, and signals to readers how serious the story is. An amusing story can have a light-hearted tone. Let's look at this broadcast story read by the anchor, for example:

Hillview Principal George Ramos has something to cluck about today. Ramos agreed to spend the day in a bird costume if his students raised five hundred dollars for a field trip to the Natural History Museum.

Even stories about potential tragedies can be treated lightly, providing they have happy endings. Here's another short broadcast story read by the anchor:

A beeping pager summoned police and fire fighters to the post office today. The postmaster called authorities after a worker heard a ticking noise inside a package.

Police evacuated the buildings on the four hundred block of Main Street while they waited for the bomb squad to arrive. The bomb squad used a portable X-ray machine to see what was in the package, and they discovered the pager. We don't know who the caller was trying to reach, but he certainly got everyone's attention.

While reporters for newspapers or Web sites would have used the word *whom* in the last sentence, broadcast reporters probably would have intentionally made the grammatical error. *Whom* can sound formal and stilted and could distract the listener from the message. Reporters for print and the Web, however, should use proper grammar. Their words will be part of the public record for decades, and they want to be remembered for using them correctly.

These two examples share the news characteristic of *uniqueness*, and good writers look for the unusual and ironic when reporting about the day's events. In a story about a decorated police officer who was fired for refusing to comply with department grooming standards, a newspaper reporter wrote:

Last year Porterville police officer Jay Sloan was a hero; today he is unemployed because his sideburns are too long.

A story about an elderly woman's problems with Social Security Administration led with an impossibility:

An 81-year-old Fullerton woman was told Thursday that the reason she has not received her Social Security checks for the past four months was that she is dead.

Barbara Jordan, a retired teacher, said officials told her that four months ago her check was returned with the word "deceased" written on the envelope.

This type of wry humor makes stories lively and interesting, but always remember to stay within the bounds of good taste. Stories dealing with death, abortion, religious practices and other sensitive or controversial topics should not be reported in a humorous or ironical manner because they will offend some readers.

ACTIVE VOICE

Using the active voice is one technique for showing rather than telling what happened. The active voice helps readers and listeners mentally see what has taken place. With the active voice, the *who* element of the lead is performing the action of the *what* element, which is often followed by a direct object that explains more of the *what* element.

> Police arrested two men Monday night who they said were breaking into cars in the campus parking lot.

Police, the *who* element, are performing the *what* element, arresting two men. It is difficult to picture events in the passive voice, and the lead becomes wordier:

> Two men were arrested by police Monday night after the officers spotted them allegedly breaking into cars in the campus parking lot.

Use the passive voice only when the focus is on the receiver of the action rather than on the performer of the action.

> More than 2,000 people in Honduras were killed when a mudslide destroyed their hillside shanty town Tuesday night.

The focus in this sentence is on the deaths rather than mudslide. The active voice would shift the focus away from the deaths:

> A mudslide in Honduras destroyed a hillside shanty town Tuesday night, killing more than 2,000 people.

CHOOSING THE LEAD'S NEWS ELEMENTS

Many people only read a newspaper's headlines and lead sentences, so reporters writing summary leads need to get to the point of the story immediately. They need to tell readers as quickly as possible why this story is important and what information is the most timely and relevant.

The six elements of news found in most news reports in all media are *who, what, when, where, why* and *how*. The summary lead contains the story's most important news elements, although the specific details of those story elements aren't always in that first sentence, as we saw in the lead of the Romeo and Juliet story. All six elements are almost never in the lead sentence because the sentence would be too long and awkward. The most common elements in the lead are *who* and *what*, followed by *when* and *where*. In the story about the deaths of Romeo and Juliet:

> *Who:* Three teenagers
> *What:* were found dead
> *When:* Thursday
> *Where:* in a crypt in Verona.

Before starting to write, identify the essential aspects of the story and the latest information; that is, determine which of the five *W's* and the *H* are the most important and which information is the most recent. These are the facts that make up the first sentence. For example, if a reporter was writing about the sinking of the ocean liner Titanic, the lead would not start at the beginning of the ill-fated voyage. The story would not begin with:

The luxury liner Titanic left England three days ago on her maiden voyage to New York. The first two days were uneventful, except for the fact that a young couple met and fell in love.

Last night, however, was very eventful. The ship hit an iceberg off Cape Race, Newfoundland, and sank at 2:27 a.m. today, killing 1,517 of the 2,223 people aboard.

The hypothetical reporter writing this recap of events in chronological order did not prioritize the story's news elements. The most important elements in this story are *who*: the Titanic passengers and crew; *what*: died; *how*: they drowned; and *why*: the ship sank after hitting an iceberg. The *when* and *where* should also be in the lead, but they are secondary elements.

The lead also needs to convey the *magnitude* of the story. Magnitude, the scope or size of what happened, is one of the characteristics of news. If a small fishing boat with three people aboard struck an iceberg and sank with all hands, the story would not be front-page news on two continents. The large number of deaths and the prominence of some of the passengers gave the story greater impact and made the disaster front-page news.

A more appropriate newspaper lead for this story would be:

More than 1,500 people aboard the ocean liner Titanic drowned early today when the ship struck an iceberg and sank off the coast of Newfoundland.

The luxury liner, which was making its maiden voyage from England to New York, hit the iceberg shortly before midnight Sunday and disappeared near Cape Race at 2:27 a.m., the Coast Guard reported. Of the 2,223 people aboard the great ship, only 706 survived. They were rescued by the liner Carpathia a few hours later and taken to New York.

Notice that the first sentence does not give the exact time of the disaster or any information about survivors. Don't weigh down leads with too many details. Keep them short and interesting. Remember, the lead is a summary of what occurred. The details are in the second paragraph or later in the story.

Assuming the technology existed, broadcast news outlets would have reported the sinking and deaths hours earlier when the Carpathia wired the news to authorities. TV and radio reports at the time the newspaper are printed would *update* the story and emphasize what's happening now.

Survivors of the sunken ocean liner Titanic are safe in New York and receiving medical attention this afternoon. Authorities are questioning them and trying to figure why the ship struck the iceberg. It was on its maiden voyage from England to New York.

The 700 survivors spent several hours in lifeboats before they were rescued. More than 15-hundred others drowned after the Titanic sank early this morning off the coast of Newfoundland.

Here's reporter Joanne Drew at New York Harbor with the details.

Since broadcast stories are shorter than print stories, the exact location of the accident and the name of the ship that picked up the survivors are eliminated from the first few sentences.

The *Who* Element

The *who* and *what* story elements are the most important parts of a news story, including this Titanic story, and are included in the lead. In the Titanic story, the lead did not name any one victim because so many people were involved. The *magnitude* of the story made it newsworthy, not the *prominence* of some of the victims.

The *who* element in many other stories, however, might only involve one person, and whether that person is identified by name and how much background information on the person is included in the lead depends on the person's prominence. For example:

U. S. President Abraham Lincoln is remembered as the man who led the nation through its greatest crisis.

We all know, or should know, who Lincoln was, and to describe him as "United States president" looks silly. Simply state:

Abraham Lincoln is remembered as the man who led the nation through its greatest crisis.

Other names in the news are known to many readers, but not to all, and some explanation of who they are is needed to help identify them:

> Jerry Brown easily won re-election as Oakland's mayor Tuesday.
>
> Neil Armstrong will be autographing his new memoir at a fund-raiser for the Children's Science Museum this afternoon.

While many readers may remember Jerry Brown as California's idiosyncratic former governor and Neil Armstrong as the first man on the moon, others may not, or they may have to search their memories to identify these people. Clear communication involves giving the reader all the necessary information to understand the story.

A greater explanation of the *who* needs to be included in the leads:

> Jerry Brown, the former governor of California and erstwhile presidential candidate, easily won Oakland's mayoral election Tuesday.
>
> Former astronaut Neil Armstrong, who was the first man to walk on the moon, will be autographing his new memoir at a fund-raiser for the Children's Science Museum this afternoon.

Broadcast journalists should avoid the dependent clauses in these sentences:

> Former California Governor and erstwhile presidential candidate Jerry Brown easily won Oakland's mayoral election Tuesday.
>
> Former astronaut Neil Armstrong will be autographing his new memoir at a fund-raiser for the Children's Science Museum this afternoon. Armstrong was the first man to walk on the moon.

Sometimes the *who* of the story is completely unknown to the public, and using the person's name would only clutter the lead.

> Michael Taylor was killed and Karen Taylor was seriously injured when a pickup struck their car Monday night in Marysville.

We don't know who these people are. Are they husband and wife? brother and sister? We need to put the *who* of the story in a context people can relate to. We accomplish this by using short descriptions of the people to identify them in the lead and including their names later in the story:

> A 4-year-old boy was killed and his mother was seriously injured when a pickup struck their car Monday night in Marysville.
>
> Michael Taylor suffered internal injuries and was pronounced dead at the scene. His mother, Karen Taylor, 28, was taken to Marysville Community Hospital, where she was listed in serious condition with multiple rib fractures and a punctured lung, a police spokesman said.

Another example:

> An environmental lawyer has filed an injunction to block construction of a golf course near Caspers National Forest.
>
> Lynn Logan, who is seeking the injunction on behalf of the group Save The Wilderness, said the golf course would encroach on the habitat of the endangered bluebottle butterfly.

If these story leads were for broadcast news, we would rewrite the compound sentences and eliminate the dependent clauses:

> A 4-year-old boy was killed and his mother was seriously injured when their car was struck by a pickup Monday night in Marysville.
>
> Michael Taylor suffered internal injuries and was pronounced dead at the scene. His 28-year-old mother, Karen Taylor, was taken to Marysville Community Hospital. A police spokesman said she is in serious condition with multiple rib fractures and a punctured lung.
>
> An environmental lawyer has filed an injunction to block construction of a golf course near Caspers National Forest.

Lynn Logan is seeking the injunction on behalf of the group Save The Wilderness. She says the golf course would encroach on the habitat of the endangered bluebottle butterfly.

The *What* Element

The *what* element is the predicate verb in the first sentence. Every story has a *what* element, otherwise there would be nothing to report because nothing happened. The verb is the action. Make sure the most important aspect or aspects of the *what* are in the lead. Also make sure the lead includes what *really* happened. For example:

The Mayberry City Council met Tuesday night.

A four-hour standoff ended peacefully in Mayberry early Tuesday evening.

The council did meet, and a standoff did end, but readers don't know what happened at the meeting or in the standoff. Don't state the obvious, that the council met, and don't make the reader wonder what really happened. Tell readers what happened as completely and interestingly as you can in a few words:

The Mayberry City Council voted Tuesday night to install parking meters on Main Street.

A four-hour standoff ended peacefully in Mayberry early Tuesday evening after a man in Central Park brandishing a .22 caliber pistol surrendered to police.

The *When* Element

The *when* element is often in the first sentence if the story is timely, but it is seldom a major element and should not be at the beginning of the sentence. Compare how the information in these sentences is prioritized:

Early this morning a hippopotamus escaped from the Safari Land.

A hippopotamus escaped from the Safari Land *early this morning*.

Obviously, the second sentence gives the information in order of importance. The missing hippo is more important than the time of day it escaped.

It is not necessary to give the time element in the lead if the story is not current. Reporters don't always have up-to-date information on events happening in some countries, and they cannot always stay current with every local court action or political maneuvering. Sometimes information comes to light long after the event occurred. In these cases, move the time element farther down in the story:

Acme Inc. has agreed to pay two former employees $1.5 million each to settle a sexual harassment lawsuit.

The settlement, filed with the court last week, also requires the company to pay all legal costs and to institute a new training program for its managers.

The second sentence is fine for a newspaper or a Web site, but a broadcast-news writer would break it into two separate thoughts:

The settlement also requires the company to pay all legal costs and to institute a new training program for its managers. It was filed with the court last week.

Here's another example of a broadcast story:

Anchor:
Senate Majority Leader Scott Bowman is quietly putting together an informal committee to explore a run for the presidency next year. Here is reporter Ramon Garcia with the story.

Garcia: [stand-up in front of Capitol building]

Sources close to the Republican leader say Bowman held separate meetings with GOP strategists Carmen Manson and James Burman last month. A member of Bowman's staff also said Tuesday that the senator has been holding meetings with his top campaign contributors. The staff member wished to remain anonymous. ...

Here's the newspaper version:

Senate Majority Leader Scott Bowman is quietly putting together an informal committee to explore a run for the presidency next year, sources close to the Republican leader say. Bowman held separate meetings with GOP strategists Carmen Manson and James Burman last month. A member of Bowman's staff, who wished to remain anonymous, also said Tuesday that the senator has been holding meetings with his top campaign contributors. ...

Be careful not to juxtapose the day of the week and another proper noun, such as someone's name. Running these capitalized nouns together can confuse the reader:

Original: Morgan Johnson Tuesday pitched a perfect game as the Indians beat the Yankees, 3-0.

Corrected: Morgan Johnson *on Tuesday* pitched a perfect game as the Indians beat the Yankees, 3-0.

Even better: Morgan Johnson pitched a perfect game Tuesday as the Indians beat the Yankees, 3-0.

Make sure the reader knows which event the time element refers to. Sentences reporting a statement by someone often need the word *that* to clarify the action. For example:

Original: President Taylor said Tuesday he is sending an envoy to Freedonia to try to get the peace talks back on track.

Did the president make the statement Tuesday, or did he send the envoy Tuesday? It's impossible to determine from the wording of this sentence. Inserting the word *that* sheds light on the sentence's meaning:

Corrected: President Taylor said Tuesday *that* he is sending an envoy to Freedonia to try to get the peace talks back on track.

Corrected: President Taylor said *that* Tuesday he is sending an envoy to Freedonia to try to get the peace talks back on track.

The first sentence now makes it clear that the president made the statement Tuesday. The second sentence tells us that the envoy is leaving Tuesday.

The *Where* Element

The *where* element of the story often is important enough to include in the lead, although the *who* and *what* usually have a higher priority.

A newspaper story's *dateline* — the first word in all capitalized letters indicating where the story was written — often serves as the where element:

WASHINGTON — President Bush signed legislation Tuesday giving tax breaks to parents who send their children to private schools.

Broadcast stories don't have datelines. Writers weave the where element into the story.

Today in Washington, President Bush signed legislation giving tax breaks to parents who send their children to private schools.

The city or country where the events occur can also be used to modify the *who* of the story:

A *Los Angeles* Superior Court judge today refused to block implementation of California's anti-bilingual education initiative.

You can also use the location in a prepositional phrase in the sentence:

President Reagan was shot this afternoon as he was getting into his limousine *outside a Washington, D.C., hotel.*

A 4-year-boy was killed and his mother was seriously injured when their car was struck by a pickup Monday night *in Marysville.*

Writers for the Web must make sure that readers understand where the events they are reporting about occurred. Assume people around the world are accessing the site, and these visitors might not know the region. If the Web site is for a local news outlet, the home page should include the city and state. Readers will understand that news categorized as "local" is from that region.

The *Why* and *How* Elements

These two news elements, which explain the story and take it beyond the headline, are often too complex to include in the lead. Sometimes, however, a short phrase in the lead can introduce the *why* or *how* of the story. This is particularly useful for print reporters, who use longer sentences than broadcast reporters.

> More than 1,500 people aboard the ocean liner Titanic drowned early today *when the ship struck an iceberg and sank off the coast of Newfoundland.*
>
> Fox Entertainment, *seeking to boost ratings by bucking broadcasting tradition*, said Monday that it will introduce new TV shows throughout the year rather than only in the fall.
>
> Stock prices rose Wednesday *after Fed Chairman Alan Greenspan told the House Banking Committee that he didn't anticipate any increase in interest rates this year.*

Notice that the *why* or *how* is often a short prepositional phrase after the sentence's verb.

ATTRIBUTION

Most of the examples of leads in this chapter do not have *attribution*; that is, the source of the information, in the lead. Putting the attribution in the lead increases its wordiness without offering any additional important information. The attribution can go in the second or third sentence of the story. Newspaper reporters usually put the attribution at the end of the sentence, while broadcast reporters put it at the beginning of the sentence.

The attribution is needed in the lead, however, if the lead is sensational or potentially libelous.

> *Print:* President Nixon plans to resign Friday and will leave the White House, congressional sources said today.
>
> *Broadcast:* Congressional sources say President Nixon plans to resign Friday and will leave the White House.
>
> *Print:* A Tustin man apparently distraught over his impending divorce went to his wife's place of employment Wednesday and gunned down the 27-year-old woman and two of her co-workers, police said.
>
> *Broadcast:* A Tustin man went to his wife's work Wednesday and gunned down the 27-year-old woman and two of her co-workers. Police say James Lee apparently was distraught over his impending divorce.

Notice that even when attribution is needed in the lead, it is not necessary to name the source or give his or her credentials and title. That information can go later in the story in order to keep the lead as tight as possible.

DOUBLE-ELEMENT LEADS

Double-element leads, also called *shotgun* or *umbrella leads*, contain multiple whos and/or whats on the same topic. This allows the writer to combine related stories into one story.

Double-element leads can be tricky to write because a greater amount of information has to be woven into the first paragraph in a clear and concise manner. They should be no longer than a conventional summary lead.

Let's take a look at two versions of a story about the Pentagon revising rules on relationships among military personnel. The first version, written by an Associated Press reporter, is a single-element lead, followed by a second paragraph introducing a new, related story.

WASHINGTON — Although adultery is "unacceptable conduct," military commanders shouldn't seek criminal charges unless behavior disrupts the armed forces, according to new Pentagon guidelines released Wednesday.

At the same time, Defense Secretary William Cohen ordered a prohibition of close or intimate contact between officers and enlisted troops throughout the 1.4 million strong military, issuing stricter rules on personal relationships as more women join the military.

This conventional summary lead has separate paragraphs dealing with the two aspects of the military's revised policy. A reader skimming the paper, reading headlines or the stories' leads, might not read as far as the second paragraph and would not learn about the policy regarding officers and enlisted personnel. A Los Angeles Times reporter writing about the same guideline revisions combined the two ideas into one double-element lead:

WASHINGTON — The Pentagon on Wednesday issued new rules on personal relationships that will outlaw many Army romances and end some friendships, while upholding controversial sanctions against adultery throughout the services.

Neither of the topics in the Los Angeles Times' lead has as many details in the lead as the Associated Press version, but the two summaries are clear enough to let the reader know what is going on.

A reporter for the Orange County Register, writing about the last, turbulent day of the state legislative session, crafted a double-element that drew the reader into the story:

SACRAMENTO — The chaotic Assembly enters the final hours of the legislative year today mired in partisan wrangling after embittered and embattled Speaker Doris Allen handed her leadership post to Republican Brian Setencich.

Notice how smoothly the two thoughts in this 32-word sentence flow together: The legislative year is ending and the Assembly speaker is giving up her leadership post. The colorful adjectives lure the reader into the story to determine why the Assembly is *chaotic* and the speaker is *embittered* and *embattled*.

When using double-element leads, make sure each element is explained, even if only briefly, in the next one or two paragraphs. Don't force the reader to wade through six or eight paragraphs on one topic before you begin to explain the second topic.

Here's an example of a broadcast shotgun lead:

Forest fires continue to spread across parts of New Mexico, Arizona and California. The fires have destroyed more than 50 thousand acres of timberland in California and another 50 thousand acres in Arizona and New Mexico. A beetle infestation has killed or damaged the trees in Arizona and New Mexico. And the two-month drought has turned forests in the Southwest into tinder boxes.

LOCALIZING THE LEAD

Since *proximity* is an important characteristic of news, a story that includes local people, organizations or issues is often more newsworthy than a story on a similar topic that lacks a local angle. *Localizing* a story originating from the state capital; Washington, D.C.; or elsewhere in the world puts the story in a context that readers can more closely relate to.

A news outlet's wire editors, who monitor dispatches sent to the newsroom from news services around the world, are always on the lookout for local names that can turn a national or world story into a local story. They carefully read state and national and international stories to determine if local agencies or projects are receiving funds. The editors always check the hometowns of accident or disaster victims to determine if local residents were involved.

Reporters then rewrite the stories to include the local angle in the lead and to insert additional details and local reaction in the body of the story.

Sometimes including a local angle in the lead of a national story takes little effort. In a Los Angeles Times story updating settlement talks in a lawsuit against tobacco companies filed by several states, a phrase localizing the issue was added to the lead:

Negotiators for the major tobacco manufacturers and more than 40 state attorneys general, *including Dan Lungren of California*, completed a second day of talks Tuesday aimed at reaching a settlement that could resolve massive suits against the industry.

The Los Angeles Times also tweaked the lead of an international story, the announcement of Nobel Prize winners, to emphasize the local angle:

Three Americans, *including a UCLA pharmacologist*, were awarded the Nobel Prize for Physiology and Medicine on Monday for their discovery that nitric oxide — a common gas better known as an air pollutant — transmits signals within the human body.

Often, however, localizing a story involves more work than simply rewriting the lead. Once reporters realize that a nonlocal story has a local angle, they need to gather the information to turn it into a local story. This is how the Orange County Register reported an arrest in connection with the slaying of comedian Bill Cosby's son, Ennis Cosby, after an alert wire editor realized that a murder suspect had attended school in the area:

From staff and news-service reports
    LOS ANGELES — A Russian-born teen who attended Los Alamitos schools gunned down Bill Cosby's son in a random robbery attempt, police said Thursday.
    Those who knew Mikail Markhasev, who left Los Alamitos High at the end of his sophomore year, recalled him as quiet and reserved. He attended McAuliffe Middle School and Los Alamitos High School from 1992 through 1995. He came to the United States eight years ago.
    Police Chief Willie L. Williams on Thursday confirmed that Markhasev's arrest came after a tipster went to the National Enquirer in hopes of claiming a $100,000 reward.

Exercise 1: Active and Passive Voice

Rewrite these sentences so that they are in the active voice (subject-verb-object).

1. The advertising campaign is being run by the vice president for external affairs.

2. A man with a gun was arrested by police on suspicion of robbing a gas station.

3. "Slaughterhouse-Five" was written by Kurt Vonnegut Jr.

4. The ship was under the command of Katherine Janeway.

5. The city's $32 million budget was unveiled by Mayor Kenneth Haskins.

6. The First National Bank on First Street was robbed by two women with guns.

7. A man was injured in Barstow when a meteorite pierced his foot.

8. The meeting was attended by all the faculty members.

9. An 18-year-old man's 10-year prison sentence for shoplifting a sports coat was overturned by the state appeals court.

10. A home run and a single were hit by catcher Mike Ellis in the bottom of the ninth inning.

Exercise 2: Correcting Summary Leads

These sentences are summary leads for stories for newspapers and Web sites. Correct any problems with structure or style.

1. Tuesday, someone shot at a police officer as he was assisting a motorist on the Roosevelt Expressway.

2. President Bush says he is sending Secretary of State Colin Powell to the Philippines to discuss terrorism issues. Bush made his announcement yesterday (Tuesday).

3. Michael Johnson was killed early today (Sunday) when his car hit a bridge support on Interstate 80. Police say Johnson was going at least 90 mph. Johnson, 28, is a police officer but was off duty at the time.

4. Martin Chang was walking his dog on the Palm Drive yesterday (Thursday) evening. They walked about two blocks when the dog, named Chuck, got excited about something in a pile of leaves. Chang thought it was a squirrel and dropped the leash so Chuck could chase it. Chuck dug in the leaves and uncovered a headless corpse. Martin called the police on his cell phone.

5. Palmview Mayor Matthew Denny said Friday he will attend the National Mayors Conference in Kansas City, Mo.

6. Janet Bowles left her home six months ago determined to swim in the Pacific Ocean. She finally got her feet wet yesterday (Sunday) after walking more than 2,000 miles from Dayton, Ohio.

7. Student body elections were held yesterday (Tuesday) at Argon State College. 200 students voted. 3,000 students are enrolled at the college. Helen Davis was elected student body president. She received 102 votes in the three-way election.

8. Wednesday night a village near Lima, Peru was covered by a mud slide. Most of the homes were damaged or destroyed, and at least 50 people were killed.

9. Yesterday (Friday) city officials honored Juan Rameriz. He was given a medal by Fire Chief Albert Benny. Rameriz was honored for saving a woman in a car accident. He pulled her from a burning car and put out the flames on her clothes.

10. Early this morning (Sunday) a Mark Holmes was arrested by police in a coin-operated laundry. Holmes was nude. Holmes told officers he had spilled beer all over himself and needed to wash his clothes. Police covered him in a blanket while his clothes finished drying. Police were summoned by a woman in the laundry who called them.

Name: Amber Nelson-Thorneycroft   Date: 02/5/09

Exercise 3: Correcting Summary Leads

These sentences are summary leads for broadcast stories. Rewrite them to correct any problems with structure or style. Assume the anchor will read the entire story.

1. A trial was ordered today (Tuesday) for Dennis Drummond. He is accused of killing a man in a bar fight. Drummond, 23, is a bookkeeper. The judge said there was enough evidence to bound him over for trial. The trial will start next month. Drummond could get up to 11 years in prison if convicted.

    A trial was ordered today for a 23 year old bookkeeper accused of killing a man in a bar fight

    A trial was ordered today for Dennis Drummond, 23. Drummond is facing up to 11 years for killing a man in a bar fight

2. Firefighters were summoned to the 700 block of Elm St. today. Two boys, ages 8 and 9, were climbing in a neighbor's oak tree and couldn't get down. The neighbor called the fire department. Firefighters used a ladder to get them out of the tree.

    Firefighters had to be summoned today to the 700 block of Elm St. where two boys ages 8 and 9 had gotten stuck in a tree

3. Last night (Friday) the Acme Manufacturing Co. plant was destroyed in a fire. The fire caused $4 million in damage. Officials think it was deliberately set. An arson investigation has started.

    Friday night the Acme manufacturing was destroyed in a fire believed to have been caused by Arson

4. A lawsuit was filed against the Harbor City yesterday (Thursday) by Mel Conney. Conney works for the city. He is a tree trimmer. He says in his lawsuit that he hurt his back when he fell off a ladder. He says the ladder was defective. City Manager Marjorie Henderson refused to comment.

    City manager Marjorie Henson refused to comment on the lawsuit filed against Harbor City by a former city tree trimmer claiming he hurt his back as a result of a defective ladder

5. Paul Lee was deer hunting in Angeles National Forest yesterday (Sunday) when he shot himself in the leg. Lee, 25, was with three friends. He shot himself when he fell out of a tree. His friends took him to Angeles Hospital. He is listed in good condition.

6. Paul Robertson disappeared at State Beach this afternoon (Sunday). Robertson, 12, was with his family for a day at the beach and disappeared while body surfing. Lifeguards are continuing to look for him.

7. Martin Chang was walking his dog on the Palm Drive yesterday (Thursday) evening. They walked about two blocks when the dog, named Chuck, got excited about something in a pile of leaves. Chang thought it was a squirrel and dropped the leash so Chuck could chase it. Chuck dug in the leaves and uncovered a headless corpse. Martin called the police on his cell phone.

8. Over the Labor Day weekend, about 150 people were rescued by lifeguards at Gulf Shores. That's 50 more than last year. Chief Lifeguard Lynn Cook said the unusually hot weather brought more people than usual to the beach and Hurricane Georges in the Caribbean made swimming in the ocean more dangerous.

9. Early this morning (Sunday) a Mark Holmes was arrested by police in a coin-operated laundry. Holmes was nude. Holmes told police he had spilled beer all over himself and needed to wash his clothes. Police covered him in a blanket while his clothes finished drying. Police were summoned by a woman in the laundry mat who called them.

10. No one was injured this morning (Thursday), but the Mayfield Freeway was closed for two hours in both directions after a tractor-trailer rig hauling diesel fuel jackknifed and crashed into the center divider, spilling fuel over lanes in the both directions.

Exercise 4: Emphasizing the *Why* or *How*

Use a summary lead to write short newspaper stories based on these notes. Include the why or how element in the leads.

A. **Meeting canceled**

Today is Wednesday. Write a short story for Thursday's edition based on these notes taken during a phone conversation today with the Cedar Springs city manager's secretary, Rose Wood:

Wood:

The city Traffic and Parking Commission's regularly scheduled meeting for tomorrow night has been called off.

It was canceled because of the death of the commission chairman's wife.

She died of cancer.

Her name is Jane Austin.

Jane Austin died this morning.

The chairman is Steve Austin.

Jane Austin was 48.

The commission's next regular meeting is two weeks from tomorrow at 7 p.m.

B. **Satellite fails**

Today is Sunday. Write a short story for Monday's paper based on the following information. Your source is the U.S. Space Command at the Johnson Space Center in Houston.

U.S. Space Command:

A NASA Earth observation satellite burned up in the atmosphere.

It happened Sunday.

The satellite was out of control.

The satellite was over the Atlantic Ocean off the coast of Antarctica when it burned up.

The satellite was called a Lewis spacecraft.

The satellite was supposed to demonstrate advanced Earth-imaging technology.

The technology was for scientific and commercial purposes.

The satellite was going 17,000 mph when it burned up.

The satellite started tumbling out of control days after it was launched in August.

Exercise 5: Car Accident

Write summary leads from the following story notes for both broadcast and print news outlets. Make sure the lead contains the most unusual or ironic aspect of the story. <u>Do not write the entire story; write only the lead.</u>

Today is Saturday. You are a reporter in Springville, Mont. Write summary leads for a newspaper story and a broadcast story based on your conversation with Springville police Sgt. Phil Marcus. Here are your notes:

A car accident happened at 6 p.m. last night on Highway 180 just north of town.

The car veered off the highway and into heavy brush on the edge of the road.

The car was a 2000 Honda Civic.

The driver was Brian Bates, 45, of Springville.

No one else was in the car.

Bates wearing seatbelt.

Bates not injured.

Car scratched but not seriously damaged.

Bates told police he was driving south at 60 mph.

Bates told police a red pickup passed him going very fast.

Bates told police a man in the back of the truck stood up.

Bates told police man was naked.

Bates told police man threw his underwear at Bates.

Bates told police underwear hit the windshield.

Bates told police it momentarily blocked Bates's view.

Bates told police he got flustered and swerved.

Bates told police car went off road.

Underwear blue Fruit of the Loom jockey shorts, size 38.

Police looking for red pickup.

Driver might be charged with leaving scene of accident.

Exercise 6: Suspect Dies

You are a police reporter in Newport Beach. These are your notes of telephone conversations Friday with Newport Beach Police Department Sgt. John Thursby, police detective Bob Martinez and a representative from the coroner's office. Both Thursby and Martinez witnessed events. The only direct quotes are in quotation marks.

Write a summary lead for a broadcast story to air Friday evening and for a newspaper story for Saturday's edition.

Thursby:

John James Johnson was arrested early Friday morning.

He was arrested on suspicion of drug sales.

He was arrested in his hotel room.

He was staying at the Hartford Hotel in Newport Beach.

Just after being handcuffed by police, he went over the balcony of his room

He was killed instantly by the fall.

Johnson was 27.

He was from Arizona

Johnson's room was on the 10th floor.

The incident occurred at 1:30 a.m.

Johnson had been staying at the hotel for about 1 week.

Police had gone to his room to arrest him after undercover officers had gone to his room earlier Thursday night.

They purchased 3 ounces of cocaine from Johnson while in his hotel room.

They returned around 1:15 a.m. and arrested him.

After handcuffing him, the investigators told him to sit in a chair.

He complied with the order.

A few minutes later, while authorities were searching the room, he jumped up, sprinted through an opening in the sliding glass door, onto the three-foot-wide balcony and went over the railing.

Police don't know if he intended to commit suicide or lost his footing while trying to escape authorities.

Martinez:

"The momentum of the body and the speed of his run, carried his body to the balcony railing, where he lost his balance and tumbled over the railing."

Coroner's spokesman:

Autopsy on Johnson is planned next week.

Hartford Hotel representatives would not comment on the death.

Chapter 7

Basic News Writing – The Inverted Pyramid

This chapter:

- ☑ Discusses the background and advantages of inverted pyramid style of news writing
- ☑ Explains the structure of the inverted pyramid
- ☑ Shows how to organize information and quotes in the inverted pyramid style

The inverted pyramid style of news writing has been an integral part of journalism since the 19th century. It's thought to have been first used during the Civil War, when reporters for the first time were sending their dispatches via the telegraph. The news stories had to be concise because reporters were charged by the word to send dispatches. They also had to make sure the most important information was at the top of the story in case the telegraph lines were cut or the military commandeered the telegraph. Reporters started putting the most important information at the top of the story, starting with a summary lead, and organized the rest of the story in descending order of importance.

The basic structure of stories written in the inverted pyramid style is the summary lead, which gives the most important and latest information. The second and third paragraphs add details to what is written in the lead. The body of the story gives more details, supported by attribution and quotes from sources. The story's *how* and *why* elements are usually in the body of the story. The information is organized by the importance of the information, starting with the most important information. People stop reading the story when they're satisfied that they have enough information on the topic, so inverted pyramid stories simply end. The stories don't have a summary statement or use other devices for closure.

People spend on average less than 30 minutes each day reading their newspapers, and the inverted pyramid helps readers to get through their papers quickly. People can get a variety of information by reading only the headlines and deck heads and the first few paragraphs of the stories. Another advantage of the inverted pyramid is that it provides the most important infor-

Summary lead
Most important
Important
Somewhat important
Not important
trivial

mation right away, which is what many people want with hard-news stories. Wire services still rely on the inverted pyramid for most of their stories so their clients, the news media, can cut the stories from the bottom to fit their individual needs on length.

Many stories written for the Internet also are written in this style because it helps readers quickly scan Web sites. Some Web sites send alerts on breaking news to subscribers or post news bulletins on their sites. These are always summary leads soon followed by stories in the inverted pyramid.

Many of the broadcast stories we see and hear are written in the inverted pyramid style because of broadcast news's brevity. With short stories, the TV or radio anchor will read all of a story; with longer stories, the anchor provides the summary lead and introduces the reporter, who relates the rest of the story.

One of the disadvantages of this style is that — while it can easily report the story's *who, what, when* and *where* — people are discouraged from reading far enough into the story to get the complete *why* and *how*. Also, since the summary lead capsulizes what's in the story, the information sometimes is repeated in the body of the story.

Another disadvantage is that reporters are locked into a formula in which there are no surprises in the story — everything is in the lead — and reporters are discouraged from experimenting with their writing.

Let's dissect this newspaper account of a police-chase story written in the inverted pyramid:

Four people were arrested early Saturday after a car chase through Azusa in which authorities said they found a loaded rifle in the suspects' vehicle.

The summary lead explains *who* (four people), *what* (were arrested), *when* (early Saturday), *where* (Azusa) and *why* (a loaded rifle was found in the car after a chase). The lead doesn't identify the suspects or give the exact time and location of the chase. That will be in the body of the story. The lead needs attribution ("authorities said") because it accuses people of committing crimes.

The chase started at 1:57 a.m. at 11th Street and San Gabriel Avenue when police tried to stop a 1999 Hyundai after hearing a firearm may be in the car, Lt. Frank Chavez said.

The second paragraph gives the exact time and location of the chase. The 33-word sentence also describes the car, explains why police wanted to stop the car and identifies the source for the story.

Before officers could stop the car, two women somehow got out of the vehicle and later were arrested while hiding at a resident's home, police said.

About six blocks from where the chase started, two boys got out of the car and were also arrested.

Police believe there may be a fifth suspect, as the car was found abandoned in an alley near Dalton and Alameda avenues.

Officers recovered a loaded rifle from the vehicle, Chavez said.

The third, fourth and fifth paragraphs offer more details about the chase and arrests.

The sixth paragraph repeats the information about the rifle. Information in a summary lead is sometimes repeated in the story.

Adriana Molina, 22, of Pasadena is being held on $20,000 bail, and Patricia Patalloh, 20, of San Gabriel is being held on $50,000 bail.

The two boys are 14 and 17 years old, and bail was not set for them.

The four are being held at Azusa jail on suspicion of possession of stolen items and handling a firearm, Chavez said.

The last three paragraphs identify the suspects and explain what's happening to them.

The broadcast version of the story would stress what's happening now, and the lead would be in the present tense. This report is a little over a minute long and would be read by the anchor:

> Four people are in custody today after they led police on an early morning car chase through the streets of Azusa. Police found a loaded rifle in the suspects' car when they were finally caught.
> Police Lieutenant Frank Chavez says police were tipped that a firearm might be inside the 1999 Hyundai. The chase began at Eleventh Street and San Gabriel Avenue.
> Chavez says two women and two teenage boys are in custody. They all managed to get out of the car and were all captured.
> The car was found abandoned in an alley near Dalton and Alameda avenues. Chavez says there may be a fifth suspect who was driving the car.
> Twenty-two-year-old Cathy Molina of Pasadena is being held on 20-thousand dollars bail and 20-year-old Carmen Chan of San Gabriel is being held on 50-thousand dollars bail.
> The two boys are 14 and 17 years old, and bail was not set for them.
> Chavez says all four are being held at Azusa jail on suspicion of possession of stolen items and handling a firearm.

The exact time of the chase is omitted to simplify the story for broadcast. Attribution goes at the beginning of the sentence in broadcast stories.

If the newspaper and TV station share a Web site or each other's resources, the print story would be on the Web site with a link to the video report. It could also have links to previous crime stories based on FBI statistics as well as stories about problems with guns or youth crimes in the city.

This newspaper's report of a NASA probe landing on Mars is much longer than the previous story and includes information on other, related topics. The inverted pyramid style would allow editors to easily cut it from the bottom:

LA CANADA FLINTRIDGE — NASA's Opportunity Mars rover safely landed on Martian soil Saturday night, about 6,600 miles from its identical twin, the Spirit rover, which touched down Jan. 3.

The summary provides the who (NASA's Mars rover), what (landed safely), when (Saturday night) and where (Mars). It also mentions the first rover.

"We're on Mars, everybody," shouted Rob Manning, manager of the entry, descent and landing team of the Mars mission.

The quote is a reaction to the lead and shows the ground crew's emotions.

The mission control room at JPL erupted in jubilation just after 9 p.m. as the series of confirming signals indicating Opportunity's safe touchdown rolled in rapidly.

The third paragraph gives more reaction to the lead and details of the *when* element.

Gov. Arnold Schwarzenegger, former Vice President Al Gore and Rep. Adam Schiff, D-Pasadena, joined in the celebration, shaking hands with the scientists and engineers.

The fourth paragraph identifies VIPs who were also at the Jet Propulsion Laboratory for the landing.

NASA administrator Sean O'Keefe and several others in the control room wore the same clothing they wore for Spirit's landing, showing superstitious support for the same perfect landing they saw earlier this month.

While this information is not important and could easily be cut, it adds color and human interest to the story.

"It's far better to be lucky than good, but the harder we work the luckier we seem to get," O'Keefe said later at a news conference.

Team members warned earlier Saturday that it was possible that there would be no communication that night from Opportunity.

Opportunity's landing came on the same day scientists declared the Spirit rover's condition improved from critical to serious, following problems that began Wednesday morning.

Those working to determine the source of Spirit's difficulty have a theory that explains many of its abnormal behaviors, said Pete Theisinger, the project manager. They believe the problem is likely to lie in the vehicle's memory that stores information overnight or the software that communicates with that memory, he said.

The team is uncertain what the consequences of the problem will be, but Charles Elachi, JPL director, said he is "completely confident without any hesitation" that they will get the rover working again. The scientists are not going to rush the healing process, though.

Theisinger added that "I think we're probably like three weeks away from driving."

The work on Spirit is not expected to delay getting Opportunity off the lander and onto the ground. It took Spirit 12 days to complete that process.

During its journey to the Red Planet, the second rover traveled about 280 million miles, about 20 million fewer than Spirit, due to the varying distance between Earth and Mars.

Opportunity blazed through the Martian atmosphere at speeds in excess of 12,000 mph. About six minutes later, it began a series of topsy-turvy bounces on the surface of Mars. Protected by a honeycomb-like network of airbags, the rover was designed to rebound as high as a four-story building on initial impact.

NASA, which has poured $820 million and more than three years of intensive planning into the Mars Exploration Rovers mission, launched Opportunity on July 7. Spirit's launch vehicle blasted off on June 10.

The quote in the sixth paragraph expands on the previous paragraph.

This paragraph explains why no scientific data were sent by the rover. It also serves as a transition to the next paragraph.

The eighth paragraph changes topics to discuss the other Martian rover, Spirit, which was briefly mentioned in the lead. Starting the sentence with "Opportunity," which was the last word in the previous paragraph, creates a smooth transition to the new topic.

The ninth paragraph describes NASA's problems with Spirit.

The next paragraph offers more information on Spirit and concludes with a quote on the rover's prognosis. The reporter used the partial quote because it expresses the speaker's thoughts so well. The phrase "completely confident without any hesitation" must be in quotes so readers will know that the reporter is not expressing an opinion.

The attribution is used before the quote here so readers will know that someone other than Elachi is speaking.

Paragraph 12 transitions back to Opportunity. The writer named both rovers in the first sentence in order to ease readers through the transition.

The 13th and 14th paragraphs describe Opportunity's journey to and landing on Mars.

This paragraph is background information. It and the following three paragraphs could be cut from the story.

Mission controllers scheduled Opportunity's launch for a later date in part to allow the team time to apply corrections gleaned from Spirit's experiences.

JPL scientists used part of that time to create a reproduction of the first rover's landing using the data Spirit sent back to Earth. Based on what they observed, the entry, descent and landing team reprogrammed the parachute on Opportunity's lander to deploy one second earlier than Spirit's did.

This gave the lander more leeway to slow down as it streamed through the thinner-than-expected Martian atmosphere.

As with Spirit's landing site, scientists chose Meridiani Planum largely because it holds promise of revealing scientific secrets that might help piece together the history of water, and possibly life, on Mars.

Unlike Gusev Crater, which was chosen because it appeared to be an ancient lake bed, scientists were interested in Opportunity's landing site because it falls in an Oklahoma-size patch of the mineral gray hematite.

Hematite, which contains high amounts of iron, usually forms in the presence of liquid water. Since life requires liquid water, scientists designed the Opportunity mission to analyze the rocks "to determine whether liquid water was around in the past when these rocks formed and whether that past environment was favorable to life," said Joy Crisp, a JPL project scientist.

Two-thirds of the 30-odd missions to Mars, including intensive efforts by the Soviets in the 1960s and '70s, have ended in failure.

In a sobering reminder of what could go wrong, the European Space Agency's Beagle 2 has not been heard from since its scheduled landing Dec. 24.

A Japanese spacecraft, Nozomi, attempted to reach orbit around Mars but was declared lost earlier in December.

The 16th paragraph explains how the launch dates reported in the previous paragraph were chosen.

These two paragraphs explain in more detail about the corrections mentioned in the previous paragraph.

The 19th paragraph moves logically from preparations for the landing to landing site.

These two paragraphs give more details on the landing site and why it was chosen.

The story changes topics in the 21st paragraph and discusses previous missions to Mars. The writer should have used a transition here, perhaps starting the paragraph with "Scientists have speculated for decades on whether life exists or once existed on Mars, and the rovers are the latest missions to look for answers. Two-thirds of the 30-odd missions…"

The last two paragraphs recount the latest failed Mars missions.

This story can easily be cut from the bottom. The fate of previous missions is the least important part of the story. The choice for the landing site is also expendable, as is the update on Spirit in this story.

The 730-word story uses only five quotes, and two of those are partial quotes. Reporters paraphrase sources to tighten and clarify their statements. Direct, word-for-word quotes are used only when the speaker's words are concise and add color the story.

If this story were written for broadcast, the writer would lead with what is happening now instead of what happened Saturday. Broadcast news always stresses immediacy, and the lead usually is in the present tense. Here's how a TV station might report a 90-second version of the story:

ANCHOR:
They're celebrating at the Jet Propulsion Laboratory today after NASA's Opportunity rover safely landed on Martian soil. Here's reporter Brad Smith with the story.
B-ROLL FOOTAGE OF ENGINEERS AND VIPS CHEERING INSIDE THE JPL MISSION CON-TROL ROOM
VOICE OVER OF SMITH:
Cheers broke out in the mission control room Saturday after Opportunity sent signals indicating a safe touchdown. Governor Arnold Schwarzenegger, former Vice President Al Gore and Pasadena Congressman Adam Schiff were on hand to join the celebration.
Opportunity landed about 66 hundred miles from where its sister probe Spirit rover touched down earlier this month.
NASA administrator Sean O'Keefe and several others are wearing the same clothing they wore for Spirit's landing. They thought the clothes that brought them luck last time might work again.
SOUND ON TAPE: SEAN
"It's far better to be lucky than good, but the harder we work the luckier we seem to get."
SMITH STANDUP:
It will be a few days before Opportunity leaves its lander and starts exploring.
The Martian rover is in an area that scientists think once contained water. Water is essential for life to exist, and NASA wants to know if there really was water here and perhaps some life forms.
NASA scientists also say they might have found the problem with the ailing Spirit rover. Spirit stopped sending data Wednesday, and engineers believe the problem is in memory or communications software. They say they'll get Spirit working again.
This is Brad Smith reporting from Pasadena.

The only quote here is with the speaker on camera. Broadcasters usually paraphrase sources unless they have the voice and image of the speaker on tape. Notice that "said" is replaced with "says" to give the story more immediacy.

Besides the print and broadcast stories, the Web page could also have links to NASA's Web site on the Spirit rover and the photos that Spirit has transmitted to NASA, other pertinent NASA Web sites, a detailed update on Spirit's repairs, stories about previous Martian probes, a poll on people's attitudes to spending money on space exploration and even a movie-industry Web site describing and offering for sale fictional encounters with the Red Planet.

Here is a national story that a Southern California reporter localized by interviewing local sources:

Fast food chains could not be held liable for consumers' super-sized waistlines under legislation the House passed overwhelmingly Wednesday.

Health experts in Los Angeles County, where more than half the adult population is either overweight or obese, blasted the legislation nicknamed the "cheeseburger bill," claiming it makes food companies less accountable to the public.

But supporters called the bill vote a victory for personal responsibility and a first step in putting the brakes on abusive class-action lawsuits.

"I believe we need to get back to the old-fashioned principles of personal accountability and common sense, and get away from this new culture where everybody tries to play the victim and blame others for problems," said the bill's author, Rep. Ric Keller, R-Fla.

The national obesity epidemic, added Rep. David Dreier, R- Glendora, in a statement "can be contained if we take more steps to improve our own health through exercise and a balanced diet.

"Suing corporations won't make anyone healthier. But bringing the issue to the forefront will," Dreier said.

Officially known as the Personal Responsibility in Food Consumption Act, the legislation split the Los Angeles congressional delegation along party lines.

While 55 Democrats broke with their party to vote in favor of the bill, none was from Southern California. Rep. Ron Paul of Texas was the only Republican to vote against it.

Rep. Grace Napolitano, D-Santa Fe Springs, blasted the legislation as an unnecessary protection of the multibillion-dollar food industry.

"We as consumers need to make responsible health choices about what we eat," Napolitano said in a statement. But the legislation, she said, "is not about helping people make more nutritious choices. It is about providing the fast-food industry with an unfair advantage by giving them a level of liability protection that has not been granted to any other industry."

The article begins with a summary lead about legislation approved in Washington, D.C. The lead has two whos and whats:
Who: fast-food industry
What: is protected from liable lawsuits
Who: the House of Representatives
What: voted to protect the fast-food industry from lawsuits

Important secondary details that were not included in the lead.

Source 1: author of the bill

Source 2: reaction from a local congressman

These are secondary facts.

Source 3: reaction from a local congresswoman.

The congressional debate came a day after the government said eating too much could soon replace smoking as the No. 1 preventable cause of death in America. Two out of three adults and 9 million children are overweight and obese, the report said.

According to a 2003 Los Angeles County Department of Health Services survey, 55 percent of the county's adult population is either overweight or obese.

These are secondary facts.

Source 4: Los Angeles County Department of Health Services

Yet, while obesity is widely recognized as an enormous health problem in the United States, fast food companies and several lawmakers said Wednesday that people need to use some common sense before super-sizing their orders or topping them off with an extra order of greasy fries.

Dr. Bill McCarthy, an adjunct associate professor of psychology at UCLA's School of Public Health, rejected bill supporters' arguments that overeating is purely a matter of taking responsibility for what one eats.

Source 5: UCLA public health professor

"Our grandparents were quite successful at being thin, and we're not. Does that mean that we have an epidemic of irresponsibility?" McCarthy asked.

He noted that fast food restaurants and cafeterias provide one out of every three meals eaten in America today.

Notice the the attribution here is "asked." McCarthy is being quoted asking a question.

While suing fast food companies is not the solution to solving obesity, McCarthy maintained that it is one important tool along with demanding to have the calorie and fat content of fast food prominently displayed for potential consumers.

"If you want to enhance personal responsibility, I would think an important way of doing that is to increase people's knowledge about what they're eating,' he said.

Last year a federal court dismissed lawsuits by two New York teenagers who alleged that McDonald's failed to supply enough nutritional information and misled consumers about the nutritional value of its food.

Name:	Date:

Exercise 1: Train Accident

You are a police reporter for the Springfield Report. Today is Sunday. These are your notes from a telephone conversation regarding a story you will write for Monday's edition of the newspaper. The story is based on a phone conversation with the Casper County Sheriff's Department media relations officer, Sgt. Barbara Nguyen. Write the story in the inverted pyramid style. Make sure your story complies with the rules of grammar, punctuation, spelling and AP style. Keep in mind that these are hastily written notes that may not comply with those rules.

1. 16-year-old Michael Jones was killed when he was struck by a freight train.

He lived at 112 Day Avenue, Springfield.

2. Jones was walking west on the main Santa Fe tracks when struck.

He was near the intersection of Belquist Ave. and Brando Road.

He was hit from behind.

Apparently didn't hear train or its whistle.

It happened at about 3:20 p.m. Saturday.

The train had 40 cars.

It was traveling at 45 mph.

The engineer applied the brakes when he saw Jones.

The train stopped about a mile from the scene of the accident.

Investigators for the National Transportation and Safety Board are also looking into the accident.

Exercise 2: Train Hits Teen

You also freelance for a local TV station. Use your notes from Exercise 1 to write a short broadcast story to be read by the anchor.

What else would you put on your Web site for this story?

Exercise 3: New Principal

You are a reporter for the Mayfield Daily Report. Today is Friday. Write a story for Saturday's edition based on a news release faxed to you today by Carmen Ortega-Clarke, superintendent of the Mayfield Unified School District, and your telephone conversation with John Hawksworth. Write the story in the inverted pyramid style. The only direct quotes are in quotation marks. Make sure your story complies with the rules of grammar, punctuation, spelling and AP style. Keep in mind that these are hastily written notes that may not comply with those rules.

Fax:

A new principal has been named for Mayfield High School.

The principal's name is John Hawksworth.

Hawksworth is 34 years old.

The principal's salary is $67,000 annually.

Hawksworth is currently assistant principal at Springfield High School, in the next county.

He's been assistant principal there for five years.

Prior to that he was a science teacher at Springfield High.

Hawksworth has a master's degree in education from the University of Arizona.

He has a bachelor of science degree from Illinois State University.

Hawksworth:

Is originally from Mayfield.

He graduated from North Mayfield High School 15 years ago.

He also attended Mayfield High, but was expelled at the beginning of his senior year.

He was expelled for leading a campus demonstration.

The demonstration was against the principal.

The students wanted the principal fired because he canceled the football program.

The principal canceled the football program because of budget cuts.

"I still think that principal was wrong. Canceling football hurt the school, but I don't know what I'd do today to a kid who led a demonstration against me."

Exercise 4: New Principal

You also freelance for a local TV station. Use your notes from Exercise 3 to write a short broadcast story to be aired Friday evening and read by the anchor.

What else would you put on your Web site for this story?

Exercise 5: Car Accident

Today is Saturday. You are a reporter in Springville, Mont. Write a news story for Sunday's edition in the inverted pyramid style based on your conversation with Springville police Sgt. Phil Marcus. Make sure your story complies with the rules of grammar, punctuation, spelling and AP style. Keep in mind that these are hastily written notes that may not comply with those rules.

Here are your notes:

Car accident at 6 p.m. last night on Highway 180 just north of town.

Car veered off the highway and into heavy brush on the edge of the road.

2000 Honda Civic.

Driver: Brian Bates, 45, of Springville.

No one else in the car.

Bates wearing seatbelt.

Bates not injured.

Front of car dented and scratched but not seriously damaged.

Bates told police he was driving south at 60 mph.

A red pickup passed him going very fast.

A man in the back of the truck stood up.

Bates told police man was naked.

Man threw his underwear at Bates.

Underwear hit the windshield.

It momentarily blocked Bates' view.

He got flustered and swerved.

Car went off road.

Underwear blue Fruit of the Loom jockey shorts, size 38.

Police looking for red pickup.

Pickup driver might be charged with leaving scene of accident.

Exercise 6: Car Accident

You also freelance for a local TV station. Use your notes from Exercise 5 to write a short broadcast story to be aired Saturday evening and read by the anchor.

What else would you put on your Web site for this story?

Exercise 7: Barge Accident

You are a reporter for The Athens (N.Y.) Examiner, a small daily paper in New York State. Today is Wednesday. Write a news story for Thursday morning's edition based on the following notes from your interview with Coast Guard Petty Officer Charles Snyder; and David Harris, the supervisor of the Upstate New York Water District. Write the story in the inverted pyramid style. The only direct quotes are in quotation marks. Make sure your story complies with the rules of grammar, punctuation, spelling and AP style. Keep in mind that these are hastily written notes that may not comply with those rules.

Charles Snyder:

There has been an accident involving a barge.

The barge was on the Hudson River.

Was just south of Athens.

Transporting fuel oil to Albany.

Carrying more than 2 million gallons of oil.

Barge hit a rock.

Happened today.

Accident occurred at about 2 p.m.

Barge was traveling north.

Rock was part of a jagged ledge just under the surface of the river.

Barge's point of origin was New York Harbor.

Destination was Albany.

Rock tore a hole in the barge's oil tanks.

Some of the oil leaked into the water.

The hole in the barge was just below the water line.

"We do not yet know how much oil escaped. It does not look like a major spill, however."

Athens and several other cities in the area take drinking water from reservoirs.

Reservoirs get water from the Hudson River.

David Harris:

Upstate New York Water District supplies water to the area and is in charge of the reservoir.

Does not know whether the spill would affect the water supply.

"We'll have a better idea what's going on after we take samples down river from the spill."

Barge is owned by the Howell Fuel Co.

Howell is based in Newark, N.J.

Exercise 8: Barge Accident

You also freelance for a local TV station. Use your notes from Exercise 7 to write a short broadcast story to be aired Saturday evening and read by the anchor.

What else would you put on your Web site for this story?

Exercise 9: Suspect Dies

You are a police reporter in Newport Beach. These are your notes from telephone conversations Friday with Newport Beach Police Department Sgt. John Thursby, police detective Bob Martinez and a representative from the coroner's office. Both Thursby and Martinez witnessed events. The only direct quotes are in quotation marks. Write a newspaper story for Saturday's edition. Make sure your story complies with the rules of grammar, punctuation, spelling and AP style. Keep in mind that these are hastily written notes that may not comply with those rules.

Thursby:

John James Johnson was arrested early Friday morning.

Arrested on suspicion of drug sales.

In his hotel room.

Was staying at the Hartford Hotel in Newport Beach.

Just after being handcuffed by police, he went over the balcony of his room.

Killed instantly by the fall.

Johnson was 27.

From Arizona.

Johnson's room was on the 10th floor.

Incident occurred at 1:30 a.m.

Had been staying at the hotel for about 1 week.

Police had gone to his room to arrest him after undercover officers had gone to his room earlier Thursday night.

They purchased 3 ounces of cocaine from Johnson while in his hotel room.

They returned around 1:15 a.m. and arrested him.

After handcuffing him, the investigators told him to sit in a chair.

He complied.

Few minutes later, while authorities were searching the room, he jumped up, sprinted through an opening in the sliding glass door, onto the three-foot-wide balcony and went over the railing.

Police don't know if he intended to commit suicide or lost his footing while trying to escape authorities.

Martinez:

"The momentum of the body and the speed of his run carried his body to the balcony railing, where he lost his balance and tumbled over the railing."

Coroner's spokesman:

Autopsy on Johnson is planned next week.

Hartford Hotel representatives would not comment.

Exercise 10: Suspect Dies

You also freelance for a local TV station. Use your notes from Exercise 9 to write a short broadcast story to be aired Friday evening and read by the anchor.

What else would you put on your Web site for this story?

Exercise 11: Council Candidate

You are a reporter for the Oroville Gazette. Today is Monday, Jan. 14. Write a story in the inverted pyramid style for Tuesday's edition based on your conversations today with Harry Song, City Council members Janet Bowles and Mark Carpenter, and Oroville City Clerk Hyram Johnson. Other information is from the newspaper's morgue. The only direct quotes are in quotation marks. Make sure your story complies with the rules of grammar, punctuation, spelling and AP style. Keep in mind that these are hastily written notes that may not comply with those rules.

Song:

Plans to run for the City Council.

Picked up candidacy papers from the City Clerk's Office today.

"The city has been stagnating for years. I remember when every building was always freshly painted and the merchants knew everyone's name and everyone knew their names. Now the megastores are moving in outside the city limits, and businesses in the city are slowly dying. We need to revitalize the downtown area to bring the shoppers back and rebuild our tax base."

Plans to use his own money to finance his campaign.

"I don't be beholden to any special-interest groups."

Information from your files:

The City Council election is March 2.

Two council members' terms expire in March: Janet Bowles and Mark Carpenter.

Song, 51, is a lifelong Oroville resident.

He owns Song's Hardware and Building Supplies on Sutter Street.

The business was founded by his father 42 years ago.

His father, who is dead, was Herbert Song.

Herbert Song committed suicide 25 years ago.

Harry Song is 5 feet, 9 inches tall and weighs 220 pounds.

He is bald.

He has been married to Mabel Song for 26 years.

Has two children: Matthew Song, 24, and Maureen Song, 19.

Matthew senior at Northwestern State University.

Maureen has problems with drugs and drifts around the state from job to job.

Has been arrested twice for shoplifting.

Maureen has an illegitimate son, Zappa, who is 3.

Zappa lives with Harry and Mabel Song.

Johnson:

Confirms that Song picked up candidacy papers.

No one else has picked up papers or indicated to him that he or she plans to run for office.

Deadline to pick up papers is Feb. 10.

Must be returned by Feb. 17.

Information from your files:

Bowles is completing her second term on the council.

Carpenter was elected to the council six years ago in a special election called after Councilman Cliff Harper died.

Carpenter was re-elected to a full four-year term four years ago.

Bowles:

Has not decided if she will run for a second term.

"When I first ran for City Council eight years ago, I set a series of goals that I wanted for the city. Most of those have been met, and I need to decide if I want to continue."

Carpenter:

Has not decided if he will run.

Exercise 12: Council Candidate

You also freelance for a local TV station. Use your notes from Exercise 11 to write a short broadcast story to be aired Monday evening. The anchor will introduce you, and you will do the on-air reporting. You have your interview with Song on tape.

What else would you put on your Web site for this story?

| Name: | Date: |

Exercise 13: Missing Child

You are a reporter for The Weedpatch Dispatch, a small, community daily newspaper in Central California. Today is Thursday. Write a story for Friday's edition based on the following notes. Your sources are Weedpatch police Sgt. Vincent Slutzske and Mary Chavez. The only direct quotes are in quotation marks. Make sure your story complies with the rules of grammar, punctuation, spelling and AP style. Keep in mind that these are hastily written notes that may not comply with those rules.

Slutzke:

Roman Chavez is 4 years old.

He was missing over night (Wednesday night).

Roman's parents are John and Mary Chavez.

Weedpatch police found Roman today at 12:30 p.m.

He was unharmed.

He was found at the home of Yolanda Luxenberg.

Luxenberg is 21 years old.

Luxenberg is a friend of Roman's baby sitter, Pailynn Routt.

She's 19.

"Roman was unharmed and in good spirits. He was playing with Luxenberg's dog and didn't want to leave."

Roman disappeared from the home of his parents.

Routt lives with her divorced mother

Routt's mother's name is Lynette Routt.

Lynette is age 37.

The Chavezes live at 10050 Cielo Drive.

Roman disappeared while Pailynn Routt was baby-sitting him last night.

Said she fell asleep while watching television.

Said when she woke up she assumed Roman was still in bed.

Routt watching TV when the parents returned home at 10 p.m.

Roman was not in the house.

Police and others searched for the boy throughout the night.

Searchers went door-to-door.

About 20 volunteers last night searched the woods near the Chavez home.

Thought Roman might have wandered there from the house.

This morning they questioned Routt again.

"Something about her story didn't smell right."

Routt said she lied last night.

Said she had taken Roman.

Took Roman to Luxenberg's house last night while she was baby-sitting.

Police retrieved the boy from Luxenberg's house.

Luxenberg said she didn't know that Roman's parents didn't know where he was.

Said Routt told her Chavezes knew where Roman was.

Routt said she told Luxenberg that she had an emergency at home.

Told Luxenberg she would return for Roman later in the evening or in the morning.

Routt told police that she was mad at the Chavezes.

Was mad because they said her boyfriend could not come over while she baby-sat.

Police will give their report to the district attorney's office for any further action.

Routt said she concocted the kidnapping to get even with the Chavezes.

Mary Chavez:

She and her husband happy to have Roman back.

She doesn't wish Routt any ill will.

"Pailynn is a good girl. She just got upset. She loves Roman and would never let anything happen to him."

Exercise 14: Missing Child

You also freelance for a local TV station. Use your notes from Exercise 13 to write a short broadcast story to be aired Friday evening and read by the anchor.

What else would you put on your Web site for this story?

Exercise 15: Expressway Baby

You are a reporter for the Southside Chicago Daily Mail. Today is Tuesday. Write a story in the inverted pyramid style for Wednesday's morning edition based on your conversation with Dade County Sheriff's Department Sgt. Marvin Jones; Isabel Lee, 22; John Perez, a truck driver for United Parcel Service; and Martha Penkingcarn, spokeswoman for Southside Community Hospital, whom you spoke to Tuesday evening. The only direct quotes are in quotation marks. Make sure your story complies with the rules of grammar, punctuation, spelling and AP style. Keep in mind that these are hastily written notes that may not comply with those rules.

Jones:

Mary Robbins gave birth to a baby Tuesday afternoon.

Was on her way to Southside Community Hospital when baby was born.

Baby was born on the Expressway.

Mary's sister Isabel Lee was driving her to the hospital.

When Mary and her sister were 5 miles from the hospital, a truck a few cars in front of them jack-knifed, blocking all eastbound traffic.

Traffic was heavy because the afternoon rush hour had started.

All vehicles came to a halt.

Paramedics, driving on the westbound lane's left shoulder, arrived few minutes after baby was born.

Mother and child were transported to hospital.

Lee:

Is 22 years old.

The baby, a girl, weighed 8 pounds, 3 ounces.

The baby, named Jessica, is Mary's first child.

Mary, 25, married to John Robbins.

Went into labor at 4:45 p.m. at her home.

Lee was there to drive her to the hospital.

The hospital, Southside Community Hospital, 15 miles east of Mary's home.

Usually takes about 20 minutes to drive from house to hospital.

Most of the drive is on Southside Expressway.

Lee couldn't change lanes because of the stalled traffic after the accident.

Car was trapped in the No. 2 lane (the second lane from the left).

They were still trapped at 5:20.

Mary's contractions only seconds apart.

Lee asked the driver of the van next to her for help.

That driver was Perez.

Perez:

Was making his last delivery of the day.

45 years old.

Radioed his dispatcher and asked her to call paramedics.

Has worked for UPS for 15 years.

Drove a truck cross country for five years before joining UPS.

Assisted in the birth of his two children and attended Lamaze classes.

Unfolded a blanket in the back of his delivery van.

He and Lee helped Mary walk from the car to the van and lie down.

With Perez and Lee assisting, Mary gave birth at 5:35.

"I've been a driver for 20 years, and before today the biggest emergency I encountered was a lady with a flat tire. This is a day I'll never forget."

Penkingcarn:

Both mother and daughter were resting and were in good health.

Exercise 16: Expressway Baby

You also freelance for a local TV station. Use your notes from Exercise 13 to write a broadcast story to be aired Friday evening. The anchor will read the lead and introduce you. You will do your standup in front of the hospital, and you have taped an interview with Perez.

What else would you put on your Web site for this story?

Chapter 8

BEYOND THE SUMMARY LEAD AND INVERTED PYRAMID

This chapter:

- ☑ Offers alternatives to the summary lead
- ☑ Shows story structures that differ from the inverted pyramid
- ☑ Offers examples of news stories written in various styles and formats

The summary lead and the inverted pyramid are the standards for reporting news stories. They are the bread and butter of most traditional media outlets. Occasionally, reporters will incorporate other types of leads and story structures when writing news stories. These provide variety to the audience and help maintain reader and viewer interest.

This chapter examines some of the variations on the standard news format by presenting some alternative leads and story structures you can experiment with once you've mastered the basics of writing news stories. Chapter 12, Feature Article Writing, will offer some additional options that are appropriate when crafting feature stories.

ALTERNATIVE LEADS

There are several types of leads that can be used in place of the classic summary lead when writing for print, broadcast and online media. Some build suspense gradually to grab reader interest, while others use feature-oriented writing techniques to capture the attention of the audience. What's important to remember when using an alternative lead is to ensure that the news becomes clear to the audience within the first few paragraphs or sentences in the case of broadcast writing. Readers and viewers have come to expect to be told the news up front, and they may not have the patience to go looking for it if it is buried inside a story. Here are some options for writing news leads.

Blind Leads

A blind lead introduces a news item in the opening paragraph of a story but leaves out crucial details such as names or titles. These follow in the second or third paragraph to fill in the blanks. Blind leads are used to avoid bombarding readers with too many details at once. They work well when writing about unfamiliar people or government agencies. Here's an example:

> The newly elected mayor of San Francisco made history today by appointing the city's first female fire chief.

This brief lead presents two characters who may be unknown to some readers and therefore doesn't identify them in the opening sentence. A follow-up paragraph reveals their identities and includes additional details:

> Mayor Gavin Newsom named Joanne Hayes-White to take the helm of San Francisco's 1,800-member fire department. She is a 14-year veteran of the department.

Delayed Leads

The delayed lead backs into the news by using a short anecdote or narrative to set the scene for what is to come in a print or online article. This opening is followed by a paragraph called the nut graph, which explains the focus of the story. Sometimes in a story with a delayed lead, the headline will be used to announce the news to readers so they don't have to wade through the first few paragraphs to find out what the news is, particularly in online writing.

The delayed lead works well for news features as in the following example from the San Gabriel Valley Tribune, which uses an anecdotal delayed lead, telling a short story that eases the audience into the main point of the article. As you can see, this example ends with a transitional paragraph that will move readers from the lead into the remainder of the story.

> The former tomboy answered the phone, and it was Mom. Even across the miles, she could easily visualize mother shaking her head as she spoke.
> "It's just amazing," Mom said. "You are the only person — forget girl — that I ever knew who wanted to buy a baseball team. And you were 9."
> Jamie McCourt doesn't remember those ambitions as a young girl growing up in Baltimore, though she hardly doubts the story's validity.
> "I loved, loved baseball," McCourt said. "I would drag my dad to Orioles games, would always keep score."
> Now, 41 years after announcing that goal to her mother, her young dream has become striking reality. Last week, her husband, Frank McCourt, was approved by Major League Baseball as the new owner of the Dodgers.

Another approach to the delayed lead is to use a narrative opening. This is a brief chronology of events that recounts the details of an incident as they occurred, building up to a nut graph that reveals the news. Here's an example from the Los Angeles Times:

> One of the first issues to confront the first Congress in 1789 was how members ought to address the new president, George Washington.
> The more regal Senate wanted to give him a title, suggesting "elective majesty" and "serene highness," among others. The more populist House wanted no part of such honorifics. To resolve their differences, each side appointed representatives to a conference committee, which settled on the title members use to this day: Mr. President.
> The House and Senate have been using conference committees to resolve their differences ever since. But now, as a result of a 50-50 split between Republicans and Democrats, the Senate finds itself stalemated over the device that is supposed to break stalemates.

Although it has become a popular way of presenting the news, the delayed lead should be used with care so as not to minimize the significance of the story or the dignity of the story's subjects. It is not the best option to use when reporting about accident victims, situations involving deaths or other sensitive topics.

Throwaway Lead

The broadcast version of the delayed lead is called a throwaway lead. Its purpose is the same — to slowly draw the audience into the story before announcing the news. The throwaway lead is written so that the beginning can easily be cut if necessary to accommodate time constraints if other breaking news takes precedent. Here's an example:

Chicago residents are stocking up on staples like bread and milk to prepare for another round of bad weather. A new snowstorm moving in from Canada is expected to hit the Lake Michigan area by early morning. This is the third major storm to affect the region since January first. Weather forecasters predict the storm will dump ten to twelve inches of snow on the area before moving south.

As you can see, the first sentence of the lead could easily be "thrown away" without affecting the remainder of the story.

Umbrella Lead

The umbrella lead is used in broadcast writing to introduce several news stories that share an over-arching theme. It is useful when talking about issues that have the same basic premise but may affect different populations, such as when reporting the weather. Consider the following example:

A new snowstorm moving in from Canada is expected to hit the Lake Michigan area by early morning.
And in the Pacific Northwest, Seattle residents are bracing for a blizzard that is expected to dump over 15 inches of snow on the city.

Since the theme of both stories is an oncoming snowstorm, the umbrella lead presents both topics with a single opening rather than spending time introducing each one separately. The story can then go on to give details about the impact the snowstorms could have on the two separate locations.

Question Lead

On the surface, the question lead seems as though it should be one of the easier leads to write. The basic premise is simple enough — ask a question in the opening paragraph, then use subsequent paragraphs to answer it.

In reality, however, the question lead can be very tricky to write and should be used sparingly. The challenge of the question lead is to come up with a question that will engage readers and viewers and not lose them after the first line. For example, consider the following question lead about the opening of an exhibit at a local natural history museum:

Have you ever wondered how snakes shed their skin?

If the answer is "no," readers and viewers have no incentive to remain interested in the story beyond the opening question, even though what follows may include other details about the exhibit and what it encompasses besides snakes.

If you do come up with a question lead that has mass appeal, be sure to answer the question in the first few paragraphs or sentences of the story. When writing a news story, you don't want to keep the audience hanging too long.

Quote Lead

The quote lead is another one that appears to be an easy way to begin a news story because it involves using a quotation from one of your sources to grab the attention of the audience. In most cases, though, readers and viewers want context for quotations before reading or hearing them. As a result, editors generally discourage writers from using quote leads. This is especially true in broadcast writing where a quotation may not make sense to the audience without an explanation of who said it or what it meant. Broadcasters also usually tend to use speaker voice, which makes it even more difficult to understand the context.

Once in a while you may run across a quote that perfectly captures the essence of the story you are reporting. But as with the question lead, if the quote does not have mass appeal for your readers or viewers, you may lose them before they ever get into the story. Therefore, in most situations it's best to present the news by using another lead format and use the enticing quote later in the story.

ALTERNATIVE STORY STRUCTURES

As explained in Chapter 7, the inverted pyramid is the standard story structure used in news writing, and if you scan the front section of a newspaper, you will likely find that the majority of stories rely on this structure when reporting hard news. In the past, more creative approaches to writing have been relegated to the feature sections of newspapers or even to the business or sports pages.

But in recent years news media have begun expanding their repertoires of story structures for all aspects of the news. This adds variety to the news offerings and in some cases may be more appropriate for the kinds of stories being reported. Sometimes readers prefer to learn about the events of a story in the sequence in which they occurred, or they want some closure to stories rather than simply having them end. Here are some alternative story structures that can be used when writing news.

Narrative

The narrative format often uses a personal approach to news writing because it starts out with a short anecdote, or recounting, of an incident that draws readers into the story and helps them connect with the topic being discussed on an emotional or personal level. The opening may introduce a character or tell a story about something that has happened that readers may be able to relate to themselves, as in the following example from San Gabriel Valley Tribune reporter Tracy Garcia:

> When 72-year-old Don Chin went looking a few years ago for a way to stay in shape, he thought about joining a fitness club, but most seemed too crowded, too expensive and required signing a long-term contract, he said.
>
> Then Chin, a Hacienda Heights resident, discovered Rio Hondo College's Fitness Center, a 6,000-square-foot, on-campus facility with more than 100 exercise machines and a full-time fitness instructor. And the cost, just $18 per semester, is a fraction of what many private clubs charge for membership.
>
> "It's a great deal; I can afford it," Chin said, working out on the center's equipment. "And everyone here, all the teachers, they're really nice. They taught me everything I needed to know at the beginning. So now I can choose what exercises I want to do."

Immediately following this opening anecdote is a nut graph (or, in this case, graphs) that summarizes the main point of the article so that the audience can clearly see the intended news interest of the story. This serves as a transition to the rest of the article.

> An average of 400 people work out at the Fitness Center each day, nearly 35 percent of them 55 or older, college officials said.
>
> The center has stationary bikes, treadmills, cross-country skiing machines, rowing machines, stair steppers, weight-training machines, two Super Circuit training systems that combine weight training with aerobic activity and a stretching area with stability balls and foam rollers.
>
> The center's director, Rod Porter, said it may well be the community's best kept secret, and he encourages people to spread the word.

Following this transition, the story can go on to discuss a broader topic that may or may not include the character or incident in the lead that was used to hook the readers. This part of the story should include facts and quotes that convey the bulk of the news:

> "The more the better," Porter said. "Unlike some of the bigger clubs, this center is user friendly."
>
> "Here we teach them circuit training and what they need to know about the equipment so they feel comfortable using it," he added. "It benefits them a lot better."
>
> New members to the Fitness Center must register for a one-unit, one-semester course called, "Lifelong Fitness Laboratory."

After a one-time mandatory orientation session and a two-hour health and fitness assessment from the faculty, students can make unlimited visits to the center throughout the semester. But everyone who enrolls must complete at least 45 hours of exercise at the center to pass the class.

Students can register for the course only four times, Porter said. After that, their membership is classified by the college as "community service" and their fee is doubled.

But even at $36, it's still far less expensive than many private gyms, Porter said.

For Rosemead resident Becky Chacon, the best part about working out at the Fitness Center isn't the low cost or the friendly staff.

"It's that you don't have to dress like a hoochie-mama to be here," Chacon said. "It's like the instructor told us — we're not here to impress. This is what the doctors say we need to do to be healthy."

Circle

The circle format is similar to the narrative style of news writing, but it provides a sense of closure to the audience that most print news stories omit. A typical news story is written in a way that allows the ending to be cut by a copy editor to account for space constraints if necessary. There is no clearly delineated ending to indicate closure to the reader.

The circle format deliberately provides closure by tying the ending of the story back to its beginning, bringing the story full circle. This technique is similar to the story structure used in feature article writing, as Chapter 12 will explain.

In the previous example, for instance, the story about the Rio Hondo College fitness center begins with an anecdote about Don Chin's search for the perfect workout facility and ends with a quote from Becky Chacon, another center patron unrelated to Chin. In fact, after the story's beginning, Chin is never mentioned in the article again.

If this article had been written in a circle format, instead of wrapping up with Chacon's quote, the story's conclusion would return to Chin and might include an ending similar to the following:

Chin is grateful that his search for an affordable fitness center led him to Rio Hondo College. "I'm happy with the facility because the cost is so reasonable. Best of all, there's no extended contract to sign. I can renew my membership each semester and don't have to make a long-term commitment."

The circle format is also appropriate for broadcast stories that incorporate sound bites and need closure to wrap up the story. For example, here's how a broadcast version of the fitness story might be presented. The segment begins with a comment from the news anchor:

About 400 people a day work out at the Rio Hondo College Fitness Center, but director Rod Porter thinks it may be the best kept secret in town.

This opening would be followed by a sound bite from Porter talking about what the center offers and why it's such a good value for the money. Following his remarks, the piece could include a sound bite from Chin explaining how his quest for an affordable workout facility led him to Rio Hondo. Then cut back to the news anchor, who wraps up the story:

The low cost makes the Rio Hondo fitness center appealing to many local residents and students of all ages. College officials report that nearly 35 percent of those who use the facilities are 55 or older.

This ties the story back to the beginning, which started out by saying how many people use the fitness center. The ending explains who they are.

Hourglass

The hourglass format combines elements of the inverted pyramid with a chronological storytelling approach to the news. It is frequently used when reporting crime stories or sports news where readers may be interested in a play-by-play account of what happened.

A typical hourglass story begins with a summary lead that presents the most important elements in inverted pyramid style, as in the following example.

> Spokane police arrested a teenager attempting to start a fire in a dumpster behind a local high school early Monday morning. The 17-year-old Greenacres resident was caught with a propane torch behind Lewis Valley High School around 3:15 a.m.

Following this initial news statement, the article includes a turnaround sentence or paragraph that indicates the format of the story is about to change as the pyramid flips upside down. This is similar to how an hourglass tapers off from broad to narrow, then changes its shape in the middle and begins to widen again. The following sentence serves as the transition for this story.

> A woman living across the street from the high school alerted police to the teen's whereabouts.

The remainder of the story includes an explanation of how the details of the incident unfolded in chronological order.

> "I was awakened by some noise behind the house, looked out my window and saw a flickering, bright light. Since it was three in the morning I knew something wasn't right, so I called the police," said Greta Hart.
> Officers arrived on the scene shortly afterwards and caught the teen trying to ignite a cardboard box with a propane torch. They arrested him and took him to the Spokane jail, where he is presently being held.
> The name of the suspect has not been released because he is a minor.
> An investigation is pending, according to Spokane police Sgt. Phillip Larson.

Exercise 1: Delayed Leads

Write a delayed lead for a news story based on the facts about the baby born on the expressway in Exercise 15 of Chapter 7. Then write a throwaway lead for a broadcast version of the story.

Exercise 2: Writing Blind Leads

You are a reporter for the Santa Rosa Press-Democrat. Write a blind lead for a news story using the following facts:

Professor Ida Kutler has received a $500,000 grant from the American Beverage Association to research how consumers make decisions when ordering coffee at Starbucks.

She is a business professor at Sonoma State University in Rohnert Park, Calif.

The American Beverage Association is a trade association whose members include more than 500 manufacturers and retailers of hot and cold beverages nationwide.

Kutler is the author of a book called, "Hurry Up and Choose: The Art of Decision Making."

Exercise 3: Writing Umbrella Leads

Write an umbrella lead that could be used to cover both of the topics listed below for a TV newscast.

Jackie Long is a 21-year-old woman who won $80 million in the Illinois Powerball Lottery. She is a college student at Northwestern University in Chicago.

An 86-year-old grandmother hit a $90 million Megabucks jackpot at Bally's Casino in Reno, Nev. It is the largest single jackpot won at the casino since 1999. The woman, Loretta Wolff, is a retired librarian.

Exercise 4: Writing a Narrative Story

Write a news story in narrative format using the following information:

An 86-year-old grandmother hit a $90 million Megabucks jackpot at Bally's Casino in Reno, Nev.

It is the largest single jackpot won at the casino since 1999.

The woman, Loretta Wolff, is a retired librarian.

She has two children and five grandchildren.

She was in Reno celebrating her birthday with her two daughters, Joan Wolff and Barbara Powers.

Every year she and her daughters do something different to celebrate her birthday. Last year they took a cruise to Mexico.

Loretta had never been to Reno before. She always dreamed of going to Reno or Las Vegas.

Her daughter Joan was competing in a bowling tournament in Reno, so they combined the tournament with Loretta's birthday celebration.

Loretta worked for 30 years as a reference librarian at the San Antonio Public Library in Texas. She retired in 1984.

Loretta:

   "I've never won anything before in my life, not even a church raffle."

   "I don't know yet what I'll do with all the money. Maybe I'll go to Las Vegas next."

Barbara:

   "I saw all this commotion across the room and went to see what the fuss was about. When I got there, I saw two dozen people crowded around a slot machine, and at the center of the crowd was my mother."

Exercise 5: Writing for Broadcast

Write a broadcast version of the story from Exercise 4 using the circle format.

Exercise 6: Writing in the Hourglass Format

Write a news story in hourglass format using the following information:

20 people were displaced from a Florida nursing home as a result of a fire.

Two elderly women were taken to Price Memorial Hospital and treated for smoke inhalation.

Fire consumed three-fourths of the home.

The fire started in the kitchen of the home as dinner was being prepared.

The owner called 911.

There were no fatalities.

Firefighters arrived on the scene at 5:10 p.m.

Residents are temporarily being housed at the Daytona Holiday Inn.

The two-story nursing home is located at 1741 W. Lomita Ave., in Daytona.

The exact cause of the fire is unknown.

Source of information: Daytona fire investigator Kevin Campbell.

Chapter 9

GATHERING INFORMATION

This chapter:

  ☑ Explains the importance of research

  ☑ Discusses research sources

  ☑ Explains how to use the Internet when conducting research

If you were going to buy a car, it's unlikely that you would simply go to your neighborhood car dealership and purchase the first car you saw on the lot. Instead, you would think about why you needed the car and what you planned to use it for. You might ask your friends what kinds of cars they drive, how they like them and where they bought them.

Once you'd determined the kind of car you wanted, perhaps you would get a copy of Consumer Reports to see how it was rated. You would begin to investigate the cost of the car and how much this cost might vary with the addition of accessories and upgrades. Maybe you would visit some car dealerships, talk to an auto broker, or surf the Internet to see if you could find a decent price online.

By the time you finally bought the car, you most likely would have learned a great deal about the whole process of purchasing an automobile as well as about the car itself. So the next time one of your friends asked you about your car and where and how you bought it, you could speak knowledgeably based on your own research.

Research is equally important when writing for all forms of media. Just as you want to have some background knowledge before making a major purchase, you want to have a thorough grasp of your topic before beginning to write about it. In news writing, research consists of gathering background information about a topic to the point that reporters feel comfortable enough to convey this information to readers and viewers in terms they will understand. Doing sufficient research can make the writing process flow smoothly, for when a reporter has done good research, the story should come together with ease.

This chapter will discuss the process of gathering information through documents and online sources, while the following chapter will explain how to gather information by interviewing human sources.

TYPES OF SOURCES

In today's multimedia world, many computer-savvy budding journalists automatically think of the Internet as the first place to go to conduct research. A young reporter may instinctively turn to an Internet search engine such as Google or Yahoo because of the vast amount of information that can be obtained through these sources.

But while an Internet search engine can be an invaluable resource, it is just the tip of the iceberg when it comes to gathering information for a news story. A great deal of material can also be gathered through public records and documents, reference books, databases and corporate publications. And while many of these can be accessed through the Internet, it's important for reporters to know where to look for the most relevant, up-to-date information to help them write their stories. Following is an overview of the types of research sources that are available to reporters.

PUBLIC DOCUMENTS

A wide range of documents are considered public records and are available to reporters to use as part of their research. These can be helpful when trying to determine whether someone owns property, has any driving violations or has ever been married or divorced, for example.

Many states have "sunshine laws," which spell out the kinds of records that are required to be accessible for inspection by the public. It's advisable for reporters to know their state sunshine laws in the event that they are refused access to documents that should be available under these laws. In most cases an agency may not willingly volunteer public documents to reporters but, if required by law, should cooperate and provide them when asked.

Here are some of the types of documents that may be considered public records:

police logs	tax returns
election returns	city council meeting minutes
property deeds	drivers' licenses
court transcripts	government agency reports
marriage licenses	divorce proceedings

REFERENCE BOOKS AND MATERIALS

There are a number of reference books and materials that should be standard fixtures in a reporter's repertoire of sources. Some of them, such as telephone or ZIP code directories, are fairly common, while others may be more specialized. Many of the following reference materials are also available online.

Almanacs

Almanacs contain facts and statistics on just about everything from A to Z. They include information on weather, agriculture, geography, politics and a host of other topics. Almanacs are useful volumes for reporters to keep on their desks for handy reference.

Telephone Directories

These can be extremely useful to reporters trying to locate a source or find an address for a person or business. Reverse, or criss-cross, directories list entries by address and telephone number, which can be of assistance when trying to track down the name of someone who lives at a specific address. Telephone directories also frequently include the phone numbers of government agencies, as well as information about local communities.

Employee and Other Directories

Many organizations publish directories of their employees, which list names, titles, and phone and office numbers. Some of these are available online through company Web sites. Other directories that may be helpful to reporters include ZIP code directories and academic directories listing the specialty areas of faculty members who may be useful as expert interview sources.

Reader's Guide to Periodicals

This is an index of articles published in English-language popular magazines dating back to 1890. Entries are sorted by subject and author, and article topics encompass fiction, nonfiction, poetry and reviews of artistic works. An online version of the guide is available for a fee and includes citations and abstracts dating from 1983.

Who's Who in America

This publication features short biographies of thousands of prominent American men and women. Entries discuss individual achievements, career accomplishments, educational backgrounds etc. An online Who's Who database is also available. Other versions of the publication include "Who's Who" in specialized fields such as medicine, law, politics and education.

Maps

Maps can help reporters find their way to remote locations or navigate the shortest route to the site of a breaking news story. Beyond traditional paper maps, several Web sites such as Mapquest (www.mapquest.com) and Yahoo Maps (maps.yahoo.com) offer online mapping services. It's possible to obtain detailed driving directions from these sites as well.

News Databases

Before beginning work on a story, you may want to find out what others have already written about your topic. This will provide some background knowledge about the subject and help you determine how to make your story different from what's already been done.

There are a variety of news databases that allow reporters to access articles and television transcripts from media outlets all over the world. Many of these databases offer the full text of these articles and transcripts, presenting the stories as they appeared in their original form. While some of these databases can be accessed for free, most are available for a subscriber's fee. If you are employed by a news media outlet, it's possible that this fee will be paid for by your employer.

Lexis-Nexis — www.lexisnexis.com. This subscription database contains information from national and regional newspapers, broadcast outlets, legal and medical publications, business journals, and wire services. It includes the full text of articles and transcripts, as well as Congressional and legal documents. More than 5,600 news outlets are available through this database.

Proquest Newsstand — www.proquest.com. This is a collection of articles from major U.S. newspapers, with information available from 1986 to the present. More than 350 publications are represented. The database has a detailed index, which includes information on companies and their products. This is a subscription database.

Expanded Academic ASAP — www.galegroup.com. More than 3,000 articles from academic journals and general interest magazines are contained in this subscription database. About half of the articles include the full text, while the remainder provide abstracts or detailed citations. Some entries also contain images included in the original publications.

Ethnic NewsWatch — www.proquest.com. This subscription database features articles from 240 newspapers, magazines and journals representing the ethnic and minority press. The collection includes articles in both English and Spanish and can be sorted by ethnic group and/or article type. Some of the publications represented address topics not typically covered by the mainstream press.

Alternative Press Watch — www.proquest.com. Articles from alternative media are included in this subscription database, offering viewpoints that may challenge the coverage featured in more traditional media. The database includes alternative weekly newspapers as well as special topic magazines and journals addressing issues such as civil rights, feminism, environmentalism, spirituality and disability rights.

Factiva.com — www.factiva.com. A combination of what was formerly two business databases, Factiva.com includes information from Dow Jones Interactive and Reuters Business Briefing. It provides access to business publications and news wires, company reports and Web sites from more than 100 companies, with information available in over 20 languages.

Wall Street Journal Online — www.wsj.com. Full-text coverage of articles from the country's top business newspaper are contained in this subscription database. An in-depth index allows for searching by companies, people, products and geographic location. Articles date from 1984 to the present, and each article includes a 75-word abstract.

CQ Researcher — www.cqpress.com. A spin-off of the Congressional Quarterly government publication, this subscription database features in-depth reports prepared by journalists on political and social issues. Some reports include accompanying maps, tables and charts. Information is published 44 times a year and is also available in print format.

PR Newswire — www.prnewswire.com and **BusinessWire** — www.bizwire.com. These services enable companies to post corporate news releases online as a means of keeping the media and the public updated about their activities. The databases include announcements about breaking news, new products, investor information etc. This information can be accessed for free.

Fact and Statistical Databases

Suppose you were working on a story about the unveiling of a new roller coaster at the local theme park and you wanted to weave some interesting facts and statistics into your story. When did the first roller coaster make its debut? How fast is the world's speediest coaster? Which U.S. theme park has the most roller coasters? To gather this information, you could consult one of a number of fact and statistical databases, which include a compilation of data that can you can use to add substance to your story.

FactSearch — www.oclc.org. This subscription database specializes in statistical information related to public policy, environmental, health and political issues. The information is drawn from more than 1,000 sources and includes material dating from 1984. It's updated every three months and is available on a subscription basis.

Encyclopedia Britannica Online — www.britannica.com. An electronic version of the popular encyclopedia, this subscription database allows users to search for information by entering words, phrases or questions on an assortment of topics. The database encompasses more than 73,000 articles, including information from journals and magazines. Information is available at www.eb.com.

MSN Encarta — www.encarta.msn.com. Another encyclopedia option, this database is available through the Internet and offers access to more than 4,500 sources of facts and figures. A more advanced version of the database containing over 60,000 articles is available to users for a fee.

Government Resources

Many federal government agencies have Web sites that include detailed information about their purpose and the services they provide to the public. In addition, many of these sites include links to databases that contain government reports, public policies, legislative activities, press releases, phone directories and downloadable consumer publications

STAT-USA — home.stat-usa.gov. This database is sponsored by the U.S. Department of Commerce and offers access to data related to U.S. economic indicators, international market research reports, and other business, economic and trade-related information.

FedStats — www.fedstats.gov. This central clearinghouse database offers links to statistical information from more than 100 government agencies. Information can be accessed by topic or agency.

The White House — www.whitehouse.gov. The White House Web site includes the text of presidential speeches, transcripts of radio broadcasts, press briefings, proclamations and executive orders. Information is also available about administrative nominations and appointments, as well as recent presidential actions.

Federal Bureau of Investigation — www.fbi.gov. The FBI Web site includes links to reports on topics such as terrorism, civil rights, cyberspace piracy and street violence. Press releases and transcripts from the agency's weekly Web chats are accessible through the site's press room, along with congressional testimony and text of speeches from FBI administrators.

Central Intelligence Agency — www.cia.gov. The CIA Web site features links to reports on safety and security, Congressional testimony of agency personnel, and a special section on the war on terrorism. Also included on the site is a downloadable version of "The World Factbook," which features factual and statistical information about countries throughout the world.

Food and Drug Administration — www.fda.gov. The FDA regulates food, drugs, animal drugs, medical devices and cosmetic products. The organization's Web site includes information on recently approved products, recalls, Congressional testimony and upcoming meetings, as well as the full text of recent speeches by given by FDA representatives.

Federal Trade Commission — www.ftc.gov. The FTC works to prevent unfair business practices, consumer fraud and deceptive trade activities. A variety of consumer publications on topics such as health and fitness, travel, and e-commerce can be downloaded from the organization's Web site. Information from recent commission hearings is also available.

Federal Communications Commission — www.fcc.gov. The FCC regulates television, radio, cable and satellite communication. The Web site includes links to annual reports, budgets, current regulations and the organization's long-term strategic plan. Information about FCC codes and policies are also available.

Census Bureau — www.census.gov. The Census Bureau collects statistical information related to the U.S. population. Based on data gathered from Census 2000, this Web site features information about population estimates, housing trends, demographic projections and income tabulations.

Library of Congress — www.loc.gov. The Library of Congress is the world's largest library and serves as the research branch of Congress. The library's Web site offers access to the current text of pending Congressional legislation, as well as illustrated guides of some of the facility's special collections.

Corporate Publications

A reporter working on a story about a specific organization may want to obtain some background information about the company's activities and the products and services it offers the public. Often this information is readily available from the organization's public relations department. A number of organizations with Web sites post some of this information online and sometimes identify a link on their sites specifically targeted to the media where reporters can access these materials.

Press Releases. Many organizations regularly publish press releases about their activities, products and services. These releases contain information that can be used to generate story ideas for reporters.

Keep in mind that there may be some bias built into these releases because they are intended to promote the organization issuing them. Nevertheless, press releases can be useful places to start when working on a story because they may alert reporters to activities they might otherwise not know about. A reporter can start with the basic facts contained in a press release and build on them with further research. Reporters can search for press releases at PR Newswire and BusinessWire.

Annual Reports. Many companies also issue annual reports detailing their financial activities for the year. These can be useful for reporters working on stories that require the inclusion of information about an organization's financial status. Annual reports also may include background information about a company, an overview of products and services, and names and biographies of key personnel.

Miscellaneous Publications. Other corporate publications that may be of use to reporters conducting research include employee newsletters, shareholder communications, press kits, fact sheets and company magazines.

CONDUCTING RESEARCH ON THE INTERNET

As noted in the previous section, there are many research options that go beyond Internet search engines. But there's no denying that the Internet is a powerful tool and, when used correctly, can help reporters gather information quickly, efficiently and effectively. The key to using the Internet for research is to understand where to go to get this information and to take steps to ensure that the information gathered is accurate and up-to-date.

Using Search Engines and Subject Directories. Search engines and subject directories help reporters navigate a pathway through the vast amount of information available on the Internet. With a search engine such as Google or AltaVista, users type a word or phrase into an on-screen box. The engine then searches the World Wide Web and provides links to sites that relate to the entered words.

Reporters can hone their searches by including phrases such as "and," "or," "not" or "but" to limit the number of links returned. For example, when trying to obtain information related to Albany, Ga., a reporter could type in the phrase "Albany and Georgia" in quotation marks to avoid getting information on cities called Albany in other states such as New York or California.

Subject directories such as Yahoo sort information into categories that can be divided into subcategories. This is useful when searching for something specific. For example, when trying to obtain a list of recent Academy Award winners, a reporter could start by clicking on a category called, "Entertainment," then click on "Awards," then on "Movies and Films," then on "Academy Awards," and then on the listing of the most recent awards. Although this might sound cumbersome, it is actually faster than typing the phrase "Academy Awards" into a search engine and ending up with thousands of entries to sort through.

Here is a list of search engines and subject directories that are useful for reporters conducting research on the Internet:

Search Engines
    All the Web — www.alltheWeb.com
    Alta Vista — www.altavista.com
    Ask Jeeves — www.ask.com
    Excite — www.excite.com
    Google — www.google.com
    Hotbot — www.hotbot.com
    Teoma — www.teoma.com
    Vivisimo — www.vivisimo.com

Subject Directories
    About — www.about.com
    Academic Info — www.academicinfo.net
    Looksmart — www.looksmart.com
    Yahoo — www.yahoo.com

Verifying the Accuracy of Online Information. A reporter's credibility is crucial, so it's important not to make the mistake of assuming that anything found on the Internet is legitimate and can be used in a story.

Some Web sites may be biased because they have been created by individuals or organizations advocating a particular political stance or cause. There are precautions that can be taken to avoid being duped into using information in your story that is not 100 percent accurate and legitimate.

Web sites that end in .com, for example, are considered commercial sites and may be used by organizations to sell products or services. While these may well include accurate material, it's always best to view the information found on these sites with a skeptic's eye. More objective information is likely to be found on government sites that end in .gov or the sites of nonprofit organizations that end in .org.

No matter where or how information is found on the Internet, it's always a good idea for reporters to seek out a second source to try to verify the information. This can be accomplished by locating an organization's phone number on the Web site and calling someone there directly or by verifying facts with an impartial outside source who may be able to confirm the information found online.

Finally, reporters need to make sure the information they obtain from the Internet is up-to-date. This can be achieved by checking to see when a Web site was last updated, or if no date is given, e-mailing the Web master and asking how recently information was posted to the site. This can eliminate the possibility of including information in a story that may no longer be valid because it is out of date.

Exercise 1: Open Records

Find out if your state has a sunshine or public records law. If it does, explain what the law includes as far as access to public records and documents.

Exercise 2: Public Records

You are writing a story about a parole hearing for a man who was sentenced to prison two years ago on a reckless driving conviction. The 25-year-old man struck a 3-year-old girl who was riding a tricycle. A witness noted that the man had been driving erratically and ultimately veered onto the sidewalk where the girl was riding her bike. The youngster lost both her legs in the accident.

List the public records or documents that you will need to gather background information for your story.

Exercise 3: Addresses and Maps

You've been assigned to cover a story at the local school district headquarters. Locate the address of the building and then get driving directions from your home from an online mapping program. List both the address and the directions.

Exercise 4: Campus Resources

Find out whether your college or university has access to any of the news databases discussed in this chapter. Choose a topic from the following list and search for six articles related to this topic using one of these databases. Include full citation information for each story found.

Trends in online journalism

Pros and cons of LASIK surgery

Hazards of roller coasters

Tips for opening a restaurant

Impact of chain stores on small businesses

Exercise 5: Statistics

Use a fact or statistical database to answer the following questions and explain where you found this information.

How high is the world's tallest mountain?

Where is it located?

How many hamburgers did Americans consume last year?

What's the world's most visited theme park?

What is an aardvark and what is its native country?

What percentage of the world's surface is land?

When was the sewing machine invented?

Exercise 6: Government Web Sites –

Look at five of the government agency Web sites discussed in this chapter. Make a list of resources on each site that might be helpful to reporters doing research on the agency's activities and explain why this information would be of use to them.

Exercise 7: Company Web Sites

Choose a company and visit the organization's Web site to find an online press release. Explain how you would use this press release to write a story for a local newspaper. Include ideas for building on the information contained in the press release and other sources you would consult before writing the story.

Name:	Date:

Exercise 8: Search Engines

Type the name of your favorite musical group into the search engines listed in this chapter. Compare the results. Then write a brief overview of the similarities and differences you found when using the various engines to search for the same information.

 *Chapter 10* ⅠⅠ

INTERVIEWING

This chapter:

☑ Explains the difference between on-the-spot and planned interviews

☑ Explains preparation for an interview

☑ Discusses development of effective interview questions

☑ Shows the steps involved in the interview process

☑ Discusses the importance of listening

☑ Discusses the pros and cons of taking notes vs. using recording devices

☑ Examines the ethical challenges of interviewing

Interviewing is the backbone of effective media writing. Whether writing for print, broadcast or online media, reporters rely on interviews to provide details that build on their own research and knowledge about a subject.

When writing news stories, reporters incorporate interviews into their work to give perspective to their writing. An eyewitness at a crime scene can provide first-hand details about what happened. The relatives of an accident victim can speak from the heart about their loved one. Quotations obtained during interviews can add color to a story, offering readers and viewers a sense of what happened from those who were there.

Interviews are also widely used in feature writing. What would a personality profile be, for example, without direct quotations from the subject of the story? Or a how-to piece without information from an expert source? Interviews provide feature writers with rich information from outside sources, which they can use to bring their stories to life for the audience.

Interviews are a key part of the research process when preparing public relations materials. A public relations writer for a hospital, for instance, might be assigned to publicize a new surgical procedure being performed by one of the hospital's physicians. By interviewing the doctor who will conduct the surgery, the writer can gather technical details about the procedure and then use the information obtained during the interview to put together a news release for the media or an article for the employee newsletter.

Interviewing can sometimes be intimidating to fledgling writers. But like playing the piano or speaking another language, it is a skill that can be learned and improved upon with practice. The art of interviewing relies on learning the basics and fine-tuning them with each subsequent interview.

203

TYPES OF INTERVIEWS

Reporters generally use two types of interviews when writing for the media — on-the-spot and planned. The on-the-spot interview is used when covering breaking news. For instance, a fire breaks out at a local restaurant, and your TV station sends you to cover it. At the scene, you interview several key witnesses, including one of the restaurant's waitresses and a customer who had been eating breakfast and was forced to evacuate when the fire broke out. You might also talk to a police officer on the scene or to the fire chief to find out the suspected cause of the blaze.

In another breaking-news scenario, a government official gives a press conference at a local airport about the latest changes in airport security procedures. Your newspaper sends you to talk to the official after the press conference as well as to get some comments from airline passengers who could be affected by the changes.

The goal of the on-the-spot interview is to gather information that can shed light on and add depth to the 5ws of a story. The on-the-spot interview is spontaneous and often requires reporters to think quickly on their feet. In most cases, on-the-spot interviews are likely to be brief, as reporters may want to talk to several people at the scene of an event to get a variety of comments on a subject rather than concentrate on getting an in-depth perspective from a single source.

A planned interview can be scheduled ahead of time, giving the writer more time for preparation and research. A second-day story on the restaurant fire, for instance, might focus on the investigation into the cause of the blaze and could include interviews with fire officials and the restaurant's owner. Since there would be a time lapse between the fire and the follow-up story the next day, the reporter would have an opportunity to think about which sources to interview and what kinds of questions to ask.

Feature writers and public relations practitioners frequently incorporate planned interviews into their work since their deadlines may not be as immediate as those of news reporters. This gives them more time to determine the most appropriate sources to interview for their stories.

While much of this chapter will concentrate on techniques for conducting planned interviews, many of the methods discussed can also be applied to on-the-spot interviews. In most cases the basic steps involved in conducting an effective interview will be the same regardless of the type of story. The primary difference is that the on-the-spot reporter working under deadline pressure will not always have the luxury of selecting interview subjects as deliberately as someone conducting a planned interview.

PREPARING FOR THE INTERVIEW

Selecting Sources

An effective interview begins with preparation. The first step is to choose sources who will enhance your story and offer insight into your topic. The best way to do this is to select people who are experts about the subject you are writing about or who are intimately connected with the story in some way. Think about the angle or approach of your story and select sources who can substantiate this approach with their personal knowledge and observations about the topic.

When writing about a leadership change at a local clothing manufacturer, for example, speak to someone who can explain the reasons for the change and talk about the qualifications of the new leader. This might be a member of the organization's board of directors, someone involved in the hiring process or industry analysts. If you were doing a piece for the school paper on a student who won a prestigious scholarship, some logical sources to interview would be the student, teachers who had taught the student and family members who could share their personal knowledge about the individual's personality, character and educational goals.

Arranging the Interview

The next step is to contact the source to set up the interview. Explain the purpose of your story and your interest in interviewing the person you have contacted. Ask the source when he or she might be available for an interview. If at all feasible within the parameters of your deadline, try to be as flexible as possible to accommodate the source's schedule when setting up the interview.

Give the person an approximate idea of how long the interview will last — 15 minutes, half an hour etc. Sometimes a source might hesitate at doing a long interview and want to restrict you to a short time frame. In that case, if the person is adamant about keeping it brief, try to work within the source's request even if you were hoping for a longer interview. Often, what starts out as a 15-minute interview can go much longer once you get there and begin talking. People tend to relax and open up once they realize the interview is not as threatening as it initially appears.

Arrange to meet at a place that is convenient for both of you — the person's home or workplace or a public location such as a coffeeshop or restaurant. If you are planning a telephone interview, try to arrange to call the person at a place where he or she won't be easily distracted. Setting up a phone interview with someone who wants to answer your questions while driving to work, for example, is probably not the best idea.

Doing Background Research

Before the interview, take time to do your homework. Learn as much as you can about the person you will be interviewing and the subject you will be writing about. This up-front preparation can save you valuable time at the interview because you won't need to spend time asking questions about items you might have been able to find out about ahead of time on the Internet or through other research sources.

Doing background research also works well to show your interview subject you are interested in and somewhat knowledgeable about the topic at hand. For instance, let's say you were writing a story about the local Society for Prevention of Cruelty to Animals, which was in danger of being shut down because of lack of funding. When preparing to write the story, you arrange to interview the SPCA director about the reasons for the potential closing. In doing research, you learn that half of the organization's funding comes from government grants. At the interview, you say to the director, "I understand that 50 percent of your funding comes from the government. Where does the other 50 percent come from?" This shows the director that you have taken the time to learn something about the SPCA, and it is likely to get the person to open up and answer the question.

Sometimes it's tempting to skip the background research step of the interview process, especially when feeling pressured for time. Some beginning writers will try to postpone the research step until after they have conducted the interview. However, be aware that this approach can backfire. A young reporter for a university alumni magazine in North Carolina once conducted a telephone interview with a well-known poet who was based in San Francisco. It had taken her several attempts to reach the individual, but she was finally able to make contact and set up the interview.

Everything was going well until the poet asked the reporter what she thought of his writing. She told him she hadn't had time to read any of his work before the interview but that she planned to do so afterwards. But at that point it was too late. The poet became irritated, scolded her for being unprepared and abruptly ended the interview before the reporter had gotten through all her questions. What she learned the hard way was that it's much better to be prepared up front rather than risk losing the interview and jeopardizing the story.

Developing Interview Questions

As a beginning media writer, it's always a good idea to go into an interview with a prepared list of questions that reflect the focus of your story and are designed to encourage the person you're interviewing to talk to you. When you put together this list of questions, think about the angle of your story and what you are hoping to learn from the interviewee to help develop this angle. If you are seeking specific information about a topic, you want to make sure you ask all the relevant questions during the interview. That way when you are ready to write, you will have all the material you need from the source to enable you to put the story together with ease.

In a live broadcast interview, you probably will not have the opportunity to compose a long list of questions ahead of time. Instead, jot down some key points you want to cover and then see how the interview develops from there.

The two types of interview questions are closed-ended and open-ended. Closed-ended questions are those seeking specific answers that don't require much elaboration. "Where were you born?" Philadelphia. "What is your favorite color?" Blue. "How many siblings do you have?" One. While they can be useful, close-ended questions are limiting and should make up only a small part of your interview questions. Instead, concentrate on open-ended questions, those that cover broad topics and invite the source to speak freely about the subjects you put forth.

For example, "Can you tell me about your college experience and how it led to your career as an architect?" is likely to get the source to tell you a story rather than to give a one or two word answer. A good open-ended question should inspire the interviewee to talk at length and many times will elicit answers to some of the close-ended questions you have prepared before you even ask them.

When putting together your question list, you want to combine an assortment of questions that are fairly easy or lightweight for the source to answer with questions that may be more difficult or sensitive in nature. It's always best to start the interview with the easier questions to break the ice and then build up to the more challenging ones. This will put your source at ease and help create a sense of trust between you. Then, as the interview progresses, you can ask the more intricate and challenging questions once this sense of trust has been established.

Don't be afraid to take risks with your questions. Sometimes beginning reporters are reluctant to ask difficult or delicate questions because they don't want to offend the source or because they don't think the person is likely to answer them. The best way to find out what kinds of questions your source will answer is simply to ask them. You may be surprised by how much people are willing to reveal during an interview. But if you never ask, you may miss out on an opportunity to gather some valuable information. In the event that a source does refuse to answer one of your questions, don't be concerned — just move on to the next one. You may be able to rephrase the question and ask it again later on in the interview and get the person to respond.

As part of your list of questions, at the end of the interview be sure to verify the spelling of your source's name and his or her exact title. You should also double-check contact information in case you need to follow up with any additional questions after the interview is over.

CONDUCTING THE INTERVIEW

Once you've set up the interview, done some background research and put together a list of questions, you're ready to begin. On the day of the interview, give yourself plenty of time to get where you're going to avoid being late. Dress appropriately for the setting. For example, if you're interviewing someone in a business setting, wear business clothes. If you're interviewing a citrus grower in his Florida orange grove, wear more casual clothing.

When you arrive at the interview, introduce yourself and make some small talk to help your interviewee feel comfortable. Settle in to the spot where you'll be conducting the interview, and get out your note pad or tape recorder. If you do elect to use a tape recorder, be sure to ask the source's permission before turning it on.

Guiding the Discussion

Ideally, an interview should flow like a good conversation. Even though you are asking questions and your source is answering them, if handled properly the interview should not feel like an interrogation. Your goal is to gently ease your source into a conversation about your topic as you navigate through your list of questions. The best way to do this is to begin with a broad, open-ended question that will jumpstart the conversation and encourage the source to begin talking freely right from the onset.

In general, people enjoy talking about themselves, especially when asked to discuss their work or their areas of expertise. Even those who are initially reluctant to participate in an interview will generally relax and open up once they realize they have an attentive audience. Your job as the audience is to encourage your interview subjects to provide interesting and pertinent information that could enhance your story.

Listening for Information

In order to facilitate this flowing conversation, in addition to asking questions, one of your main responsibilities is to listen carefully to the answers given by your source. It's all too easy to get caught up in your notetaking or in worrying about whether your questions are all being answered, to the point that you may not be listening as attentively as you should to what the source is saying. You want to pay close attention to the answers and listen for clues that may lead you to ask follow-up questions that are not part of your original list.

For example, let's say you are interviewing a woman who owns a travel agency for a story you're working on about female entrepreneurs. When you ask her how she started her business, she says she was motivated to open the agency while recuperating from a car accident three years earlier. At this point you can choose to go on to your next question, or you can follow up on what she's just told you by asking, "Can you tell me about the accident and how it led you to start thinking about opening your own business?" This is likely to result in an anecdote, which will provide depth to your story.

During the interview you also want to listen for comments that will work as effective direct quotations or sound bites for your story. Not everything your source will say will be worthy of repeating to your audience, but some remarks may be ideal for characterizing the essence of your story. You want to listen carefully during the interview to ensure you don't miss a usable quote that might be interspersed with less relevant comments.

Keep in mind that your prepared list of questions is simply a guide to help you maneuver through the interview. Don't be afraid to stray from your list as the interview progresses if the source offers information that touches upon topics you haven't thought of and that can potentially take your story in a new and different direction. Just be careful not to let your source lead you so far astray that when you attempt to put the pieces together, you realize that while you have an abundance of fascinating information, you don't have enough of what you need to write your story.

DEALING WITH INTERVIEW CHALLENGES

While most people are very accommodating during interviews and are willing to answer your questions, occasionally you will encounter the difficult or challenging interviewee. This might be someone who is not readily forthcoming with information or someone who has been burned by the media in a previous interview and is distrustful of your motives and reluctant to talk to you. A difficult interviewee can be especially challenging if you are seeking a sound bite for a television interview, since the person's resistance may be reflected by negative body language as well as by a reluctance to speak.

The best way to approach the challenging interview source is to act as professionally as possible — be polite, gracious and agreeable while trying to encourage the person to talk to you. You might interject some information about yourself into the conversation as a means of trying to connect with the source on a personal level. Tell a brief story that relates to one of your questions and see if the individual will respond in kind.

Explain to the source why his or her information is valuable to your story as a way of encouraging active participation in the interview. Sometimes an interviewee may not completely understand exactly what you want and may be hesitant to speak for fear of saying the wrong thing.

Use silence to encourage dialogue. When the source finishes answering a question, wait a few moments before asking the next one. Some people are uncomfortable with silence and will rush to fill the silent void when they realize you are not immediately forthcoming with another question.

But do be aware that sometimes, no matter how hard you try, you may find that you simply can't get people to talk if they don't want to. In that case, it's time to think about a backup plan — alternate sources that may be able to provide the information you need for your story.

WRAPPING IT UP

As you come to the end of the interview, take a moment to glance at your list of questions and make sure you've asked everything you wanted to know. Then, before closing your notebook or turning off your tape recorder, ask the source one final question: "Before we finish, is there anything you would like to add that I haven't asked you?" It's a simple question but, amazingly, a significant one. Many reporters have found that giving interviewees one last chance to speak their minds resulted in material that was not covered by the planned questions and that added rich information to their stories.

As you prepare to leave, ask your source if it's all right to call or e-mail if you have any follow-up questions. Also, be sure to leave your own contact information with the source in case the person wants to get in touch with you later.

DOCUMENTING THE INTERVIEW FOR PRINT/ONLINE MEDIA

When writing for print and online media, one of the things you'll need to think about is how to document the information you will obtain during interviews. Should you use a note pad and pen, jotting down notes and quotations quickly as the interview proceeds? Or should you rely on a tape recorder to capture this material for you? There's no right or wrong answer to this question — it is something you'll have to decide for yourself. There are, however, advantages and disadvantages to both methods of recording information, which you can take into consideration when deciding which way to go.

Note Taking

Using a notepad is a convenient way of documenting an interview. You can carry the note pad in your pocket and pull it out as soon as you're ready to begin. As your source answers questions, you simply jot down as much of what the person says as quickly as you can. Note taking is also an efficient way of gathering information, as you have control over the process and don't have to take time to set up the tape recorder or worry about equipment malfunction.

A notepad works well when you are covering breaking news or have a tight deadline and don't have time to transcribe the tape between when you conduct the interview and when your story is due. Note taking also helps set the pace of an interview. A source watching you take notes may talk more slowly, knowing that you are trying to keep up. This gives you a chance to be thinking of follow-up questions as you write.

The challenge of using the pen and paper approach is learning to write quickly, and, as a result, beginning journalists sometimes find note taking to be a daunting process. It can be difficult at first to try to record everything the source says, especially when interviewing someone who speaks quickly or rambles from one subject to the next. However, note taking is a process that does get easier with time and practice. As you conduct more and more interviews, you will most likely find yourself developing your own form of shorthand, which will help you write faster. You'll also notice as time goes on that it becomes easier to determine how much to write down during an interview, as you begin to recognize what information is essential to your story and what is less important.

If you do opt to use a notepad and pen during the interview, be sure to indicate quotation marks around any comments from your source you plan to use as direct quotes in your story. Also, try to review and transcribe your notes as soon as you can after the interview while the information is still fresh in your mind. If you wait too long after the interview to go over the notes, you may find it difficult to read your own handwriting.

Tape Recording

In some ways using a tape recorder can give you more flexibility during an interview than a notepad can. Since the machine is recording information, you are free to give the interviewee your full attention and don't have to keep looking down at what you're writing. Tape recorders are useful because they capture everything that is said; so if you need to double-check a direct quote from your source, you have the person's words exactly as they were spoken. You don't have the problem of missing anything, which you might encounter when taking notes and trying to keep up with the interviewee. A taped interview can also be useful if a source later tries to claim he or she was misquoted in a story — the tape recording can be used as proof of what the person said.

The downside of using a tape recorder is that not all interviewees are comfortable having their words captured on tape. This can sometimes affect how quickly the source relaxes and warms up to you at the beginning of the interview. You want to be careful not to jeopardize the information you're seeking because the source is hesitant to speak because tape is rolling. Always ask if it is all right for you to tape an interview before you turn on the recorder.

The other factor to consider when using a tape recorder is that it is a machine, and machines occasionally malfunction. To reduce the chances of this occurring, test the recorder immediately before the interview, and bring an extra tape and a second set of batteries with you just in case. It's also a good idea to have a note pad with you and to jot down at least some minimal notes to get the main points of the interview on paper in the event that you get home and discover your tape recorder has failed.

Transcribing an interview tape can be a tedious process — it generally takes two to three times as long as the interview itself. To facilitate the transcription, purchase a tape recorder with a counter. When your source makes a comment worth noting, glance at the counter and jot down the number that registers at the time the comment is made. Later you can fast forward through the less important information and easily access the material you want to use in your story.

As mentioned earlier, there is no right or wrong answer to whether to take notes and/or record an interview. For your own benefit, however, it is recommended that while you are learning the basics of media writing, you start out using a notepad and pen, so you get the hang of how to take notes. Once you've gotten that down, you can try using a tape recorder and see how you like it. Ultimately, consider using both methods simultaneously — use the machine to record the interview but take detailed notes at the same time.

DOCUMENTING THE INTERVIEW FOR BROADCAST MEDIA

Broadcast reporters rely much more heavily on recording devices to document information than print or online reporters because part of their jobs involves capturing sound and images. A comment made by a source during a broadcast interview is referred to as a sound bite and is sometimes called an actuality because it signifies that the sound heard is the actual voice of the person being interviewed.

The goal of the broadcast interview is to obtain meaningful sound bites that characterize the essence of the story. Because of the time factor, only a fraction of what is captured on tape during a broadcast interview is likely to be included as part of a news segment. Much of the information will be used as background in helping you craft your story. Nonetheless, you want to treat each source as though you consider all the information he or she provides to be valuable to your story in order to help the person feel at ease and to encourage the one or two sound bites that will ultimately be used in the segment.

Even a source who readily agrees to be interviewed for a broadcast news segment may be intimidated by the prospect of making statements that will be captured on tape. To help your source feel at ease, talk to the person before the interview and explain that the camera is just a means to an end. Tell the source to concentrate on you when responding to questions rather than glance at the camera. Maintain eye contact with the person as much as possible during the interview to reinforce this. It sometimes helps to ask the same questions in different ways to give the source additional time think about how to respond and possibly give you a better sound bite.

Though the bulk of the information gathered during a broadcast interview will be recorded, always bring a note pad with you to an interview. You can use it to jot down questions to ask during the interview or observations that may help you put the story together during the editing process.

ALTERNATIVES TO THE FACE-TO-FACE INTERVIEW

There may be times when you are unable to interview someone face-to-face and need to rely on telephone or e-mail interviews to collect information. While these are certainly viable alternatives, they are not quite as effective as face-to-face interviews because you don't have the opportunity to see a person's body language or the visual cues that might be communicated during an in-person interview. Here are some things to know about these alternatives to the face-to-face interview.

Telephone Interviews

Both print and broadcast reporters rely on telephone interviews to connect with sources who are physically unavailable face-to-face. A freelance writer based in New York working on a story for a national magazine might want to interview several people located throughout the United States to get different points of view for the story. Since flying to various cities to conduct in-person interviews could be cost-prohibitive, the writer could make arrangements to interview the sources by phone instead.

A reporter at a radio station in Phoenix working on a story about a new diet pill might want to include comments from an official with the Food and Drug Administration based in Washington, D.C. The reporter could conduct a telephone interview with the FDA official, which could be broadcast live as part of the news story or recorded and aired later after the official's comments were edited.

The telephone interview is a good second choice for a reporter who cannot get to a source to conduct a face-to-face interview. Because the reporter and the source would still be conversing one-on-one, many of the same guidelines discussed earlier in regard to the in-person interview can also be applied to the telephone interview. If you plan to record a telephone interview, be sure to inform the person you are interviewing that you want to record the conversation and get the person's consent on tape.

E-mail Interviews

The e-mail interview is convenient because you and your interviewee don't have to be in the same place at the same time. You can develop a set of questions to send to your source, and he or she can answer them when it is convenient and return them to you. You don't have to worry about transcribing your notes or not being able to read your own handwriting.

The major shortcoming of the e-mail interview is that there is no spontaneity to it because the source sees the questions and has time to think about them before responding. The person can take time to craft a carefully thought-out answer devoid of unplanned or spur-of-the moment comments. For some types of stories, this lack of spontaneity is not that important, but in some cases it takes away from the candidness of the interview.

In an e-mail interview, you also lose the opportunity to ask on-the-spot follow-up questions, which, as noted earlier, can often lead to a more interesting direction for your story than you had initially envisioned. As a result, it is best to use e-mail interviews only as a last resort when gathering information for your stories, particularly if you do have the option of conducting a face-to-face or telephone interview instead.

DEALING WITH ETHICAL ISSUES

There are certain times when you will be faced with decisions during an interview that may pose ethical dilemmas. It is worthwhile to think about how you might handle some of these issues ahead of time so you are not taken by surprise when they occur.

Accepting Off-the-Record Information

Let's say you are in the middle of an interview that seems to be going well. Suddenly, your source says to you, "What I'm going to tell you next is off the record." In journalism, the comment "off the record" refers to something that a source is willing to reveal to you but doesn't want you to reveal to your audience. This can pose a challenge because someone may give you information off the record that is essential to your story. However, if you agree to let the source speak off the record, there is an implicit agreement that you are consenting not to use the information the source has shared with you.

There are several ways to handle this scenario. You can simply refuse to hear any information given off the record. Tell the source that everything said during the interview is considered on the record, and if the source doesn't want something revealed, it is better that he or she not even say it. You can agree to let the source speak off the record but define clear parameters as to where the off-the-record comments begin and end and at what point the interview goes back on the record.

You might suggest that instead of speaking off the record, the source agree to offer you the information "not for attribution," meaning that you can use the information as long as you don't attribute it to the source; or as "background," where the source agrees to be identified in general terms such as in the statement, "a government official familiar with the project said... ."

If you do agree to hear an off-the-record remark, make sure both you and the source agree on the terms so that you both understand what may and may not be used in your story. Also be sure to indicate in your notes exactly which material is off the record.

Altering Quotations

Consider the following situation: You're writing a feature story for a university alumni magazine and you interview a graduate of the university for your piece. Since your deadline is several weeks away, you feel no sense of urgency to transcribe your notes immediately after the interview, so you wait a few days before you do. When you finally get around to reviewing your notes, you realize that you can't read everything you've written down, including several quotations you had been planning to use in your story.

Although you can decipher most of what the person said, there are a few words you just can't make out. And since several days have passed since the interview, you can't remember the exact phrasing of the quotes. What do you do?

Should you use the quotes and guess at what the interviewee said in those few words you can't decipher, since changing a word or two probably won't alter the overall meaning of the person's statement? Should you abandon the idea of using the statements as exact quotes and simply paraphrase what the source has said? Or should you use the parts of the quotations that are legible to you and paraphrase the rest?

This is a dilemma that every writer faces at one point or another. Altering quotations is a topic that has generated much discussion within the profession and has even been the subject of a U.S. Supreme Court case (Masson v. New Yorker Magazine). According to the "Associated Press Stylebook and Briefing on Media Law," journalists should never alter quotations. This is the general rule of thumb at a number of major media outlets as well. If you cannot verify the exact phrasing of a quotation, you should not use it as a direct quote. Either use the pieces you can verify and paraphrase the rest, or just paraphrase the whole thing. You can also call the source and ask to verify what he or she said.

Along these same lines, you may encounter a situation where your interviewee says something very interesting or insightful, but he or she doesn't articulate it well – punctuating the statement with ums, and ahs, or speaking in fragments by starting a sentence, digressing to something else and then returning to the original point.

While you may want to use the source's information as a quote, you don't want to make the person appear incompetent or incoherent. In this case, the best approach is to use ellipses (…) in place of the ums and ahs to show that the words did not flow continuously or to indicate that the comments were not made as one complete thought but as several shorter statements that you have strung together.

Allowing Sources to Review Stories

Occasionally, when writing a print or online story, you will interview someone who will ask to see your completed article before it's published. The individual may want to verify the content of the story or check the accuracy of the quotations.

Generally, it is not standard practice for reporters to run their work by sources before going to press. This is a means of avoiding interviewees who suddenly have second thoughts and try to back out of having their information used in a story. What you can do instead is offer to read back any direct quotations you plan to use if you want to verify their accuracy. When writing about technical or scientific topics that may include complex information, it's also acceptable to double-check facts with your source to ensure the technical correctness of your writing. In both cases, you want to make it clear to the source that you will not change information unless it is inaccurate, not because the person doesn't like the way it sounds.

The primary exception to this rule is when writing public relations materials. It is not unusual in PR writing to allow a source to read a story or press release before it goes out; in fact, in some cases it is standard practice. Since many types of public relations materials are intended to represent the point of view of an organization rather than of an individual, it may be necessary to obtain an administrative stamp of approval before these materials can be released to the public.

Interviewing Victims of Trauma

Reporters covering breaking news sometimes have to interview someone who has just experienced a traumatic event — the relative of an accident victim, for example, or the survivor of a house fire. Even when interviewing someone for a feature story or public relations piece, you may be faced with asking interviewees questions of a sensitive nature that could potentially have an impact on their emotional well-being.

In getting caught up in the excitement of the news event and wanting to get as much information as possible, it's easy to forget that these people are hurting and need to be treated with care. Sticking a microphone in someone's face and asking, "How do you feel about the fact that you've just lost your son?" is not likely to produce the gripping response you may be hoping for. Instead, it is more likely to make you appear insensitive and uncaring to the audience.

The best approach when dealing with victims of trauma is to remember that they may be emotionally fragile and not willing or able to answer your questions in the way you would like them to. If someone doesn't appear ready or willing to answer questions right away, don't push the matter. Offer your business card and suggest that the person call you when he or she is ready to talk.

Sometimes victims of trauma do want to speak to reporters because it is therapeutic for them to talk about their loss. In that case, be sensitive in the way you ask questions. Instead of asking the mother of a car accident victim how she feels about the loss of her son, ask, "What will you miss most about your son?" or "Can you tell me something about your son so that others can understand what made him special?" Treating victims of trauma with care and compassion in order to gain their trust is more likely to result in compelling interview material than being persistent and aggressive.

Exercise 1: Categorizing Questions

The following questions were asked during an interview with a 25-year-old writer whose first novel has become a best seller. Identify which questions are closed-ended and which are open-ended. Then rewrite the closed-ended questions to make them open-ended ones that will help you gather broader information for your story.

Where did you go to college and what was your major?

How did you get interested in writing?

How did you develop the idea for this book?

Who are the main characters in the book?

How do you come up with your ideas?

What do you enjoy about your work?

Are you working on another novel?

Who are your favorite writers?

What are your hobbies?

Exercise 2: Developing Questions

You have been assigned to write a story for the student newspaper about the recently hired coach of the women's softball team at your school. Develop a list of 10 questions to ask during an interview with the coach.

You will also be interviewing the coach for the campus radio station. Review and re-work your list of questions and come up with three questions you could use during a live broadcast interview.

Exercise 3: Interviewing

Conduct a 20-minute interview with your favorite teacher. Set up the interview, do some background research, develop a list of questions and conduct the interview, following the steps outlined in this chapter. Then write a 1-page analysis of what took place at the interview, and explain what you would do differently if you had a chance to re-do the interview.

Exercise 4: Writing Profiles

Go through the notes from your teacher interview and identify information that you could use in a profile about the person you interviewed — quotes or sound bites, facts, anecdotes etc. Determine what information you would use in a print or online version of the story and what you would use in a broadcast version. Then explain how you decided what information to use in each type of story.

Name:	Date:

Exercise 5: Interviews

Conduct three separate, two-minute interviews with friends or acquaintances as though you were talking to them for a live broadcast news segment. Start by asking each person to talk about the classes he or she is taking this semester and then proceed with appropriate follow-up questions.

Tape record each interview and listen to the recordings. Then write an assessment of each interview, noting any changes you observed in your own interviewing style or technique from one interview to the next, and explaining why these changes might have occurred.

SPECIALIZED STORIES

This chapter:

- ☑ Explains how to write obituaries
- ☑ Discusses how to write stories from news releases
- ☑ Explains how to write speech and meeting stories
- ☑ Shows how to write roundup stories

It's now time to put your talents at gathering information, interviewing and news writing into practice. Your first assignment as a professional journalist will likely include writing one or more of the following types of news articles: obituaries, stories from press releases, speeches and meetings, and roundup stories.

OBITUARIES

An obituary is a report about someone's death. It should not be confused with paid funeral notices that funeral directors place in newspapers for a fee. Obituaries are more than news reports about people who have recently died. They are mini-biographies focusing on the lives of the deceased. They are among the most read or listened to stories because of their importance to the people involved.

Three types of obituaries exist:

News Obits. These include reports of prominent individuals. How prominently the obituary is displayed in the newspaper, Web site or broadcast depends on the stature of the deceased. Such obituaries are usually reserved for the very famous, such as George Harrison and Selena, or the very infamous, such as Timothy McVeigh or some other well-know terrorist.

Feature Obits. These types of obituaries were once reserved for very prominent people. However, Jim Nicholson of the Philadelphia Daily News has introduced the "common man" feature obit that details the lives of ordinary men and women. Honored as the nation's best obituary writer, Pulitzer Prize winner Nicholson writes obits about laborers, plumbers, security guards, pastors, housewives, truck drivers and storekeepers. These obits include biographical information, such as anecdotes, descriptions, quotations and other types of information about the person.

Appreciation. Someone familiar with the deceased may write an essay that focuses upon the impacts and contributions of the deceased.

The Obituary Lead

The lead of an obituary often includes the following standard information, which is usually obtained from funeral directors or family members:

- ☑ Identification of deceased, including full name, age and address.

- ☑ Unique or major attribute identifying the deceased.

- ☑ Time and place of death.

- ☑ Cause or circumstances of death.

The place and cause of death also can be in the second paragraph. Here are some examples of bad leads that were revised:

> **original:** Daniel J. Boorstin died Saturday of pneumonia at Washington's Sibley Hospital. He was 89.
>
> **revised:** Pulitzer Prize-winning historian Daniel J. Boorstin, who wrote more than 20 history books over his long career, died Saturday. He was 89.
>
> **original:** Roger E. Strangeland died of heart failure Feb. 27 at Methodist Hospital in Arcadia. He was 74.
>
> **revised:** Roger E. Strangeland, 74, former chairman and chief executive officer of The Vons Co., died of heart failure Feb. 27 at Methodist Hospital in Arcadia.

The original leads contain dull and routine information. The revisions are more specific and capture interesting facts about the people's lives and accomplishments. People are often described by their accomplishments, including their occupations, hobbies, civic accomplishments, philosophy or personality. The lead should stress that.

The Body of the Obit

Following the lead, the obituary should capsulize the person's life. The body of the obituary usually includes the following:

- ☑ Major accomplishments.

- ☑ Chronology of early life.

- ☑ Occupation and employment history.

- ☑ Honors, awards and offices held.

- ☑ Memberships in church groups, clubs and other civic groups.

- ☑ Military service.

- ☑ Surviving relatives.

- ☑ Funeral services, including location and any officiating clergy and other burial arrangements.

Note the structure of the third paragraph of the Boorstin obituary, which refers back to the lead, making for a good transition and unified story.

> Pulitzer Prize-winning historian Daniel J. Boorstin, who wrote more than 20 history books over his long career, died Saturday. He was 89.
> Boorstin died after midnight of pneumonia at Washington's Sibley Hospital, his wife, Ruth, said.

Reprinted by permission of San Gabriel Valley Newspaper Group Publisher.

Renowned for his books, Boorstin was appointed librarian of Congress in 1974 by President Ford and spent 12 years as director of the world's largest library.

It was also in 1974 that he won the Pulitzer for history for "The Americans: The Democratic Experience." The book was the third in Boorstin's "The Americans" trilogy and followed "The Colonial Experience" and "The National Experience." All sought to analyze the distinctive character of American institutions and culture.

Boorstin tackled world history with "The Discoverers," which looked at the human search for knowledge. That was perhaps the book he was most fond of, his wife said.

Boorstin's successor at the Library of Congress, James H. Billington, remembered Boorstin as a great historian and scholar. "This is a remarkable American of our times. He was an extraordinary historian, first and foremost of American historians. He was a polymath," he said.

Boorstin was born in Atlanta, reared in Tulsa, Okla., and educated at Harvard, Yale and Oxford universities. Before his appointment to the Library of Congress, he was director of the National Museum of History and Technology, senior historian of the Smithsonian Institution and a history professor at the University of Chicago for 25 years.

Stangeland's ties to Vons, which link the first three paragraphs, unify his obituary.

Roger E. Stangeland, former chairman and chief executive officer of The Vons Co., died of heart failure Feb. 27 at Methodist Hospital in Arcadia. He was 74.

The San Marino resident served as Vons' chairman and chief executive officer from 1984 to 1994, during which time Vons grew by acquiring 160 additional stores and became Southern California's leading supermarket chain.

Stangeland created Vons with a $5 billion leveraged buyout of Household Merchandising in 1985. It was the largest such transaction in retailing history at that time. He sold off the other businesses and became head of the now independent Vons, which was listed on the New York Stock Exchange in 1987.

Stangeland also was responsible for developing Vons' Pavilions and Tianguis divisions. He was board chairman of the Food Marketing Institute, the supermarket industry's leading trade organization, and received the group's Sydney R. Rabb Award, its highest honor in 1998. He also served on the board of the American Institute of Food and Wine.

Born in Chicago, Stangeland graduated with honors from St. John's Northwestern Military Academy in Wisconsin and earned a bachelor of science degree from the University of Illinois.

An avid and accomplished outdoorsman, hunter and fisherman, he started his business career by operating his own sporting goods business in Wauconda, Ill. In 1960 he joined Coast to Coast Stores in Minneapolis as head of the sporting goods department and in 1982 was promoted to executive vice president.

Active in civic and community affairs, he and his wife, Lilah, established the Roger and Lilah Stangeland Foundation and supported the Pasadena Playhouse. The couple also were members of the Annandale Gold Club and the Alisal Club. Stangeland was a Pasadena Playhouse director and chaired its development committee.

He and Lilah were married 53 years. He also is survived by daughter, Cyndi Olsen; two sons, Brett and Brad; two grandsons, Josh and Jason; and two granddaughters, Brooke and Tara.

A memorial service was held Monday at The Valley Hunt Club. Memorial services will be held today in Wauconda, Ill., and also on Saturday at St. John's Academy in Delafield, Wis.

The Boorstin death would likely be broadcast nationally and reported by the anchor:

One of America's most renowned historians died today.

Dainel J. Boorstin wrote more than twenty history books during his long career. One of those books, "The Americans: The Democratic Experience," won him the Pulitzer Prize for history.

Boorstin died of pneumonia at Washington's Sibley Hospital. He was 89 years old.

Reprinted by permission of San Gabriel Valley Newspaper Group Publisher.

Strangeland's death most likely would be aired only in Southern California:

The man responsible for developing Vons markets and its Pavilions and Tianguis divisions died today.
Roger E. Stangeland of San Marino died of heart failure at Methodist Hospital in Arcadia. He was 74.
Stangeland created Vons with a five (b)billion dollar leveraged buyout of Household Merchandise in 1985.
At the time, it was the largest transaction in retailing history.

Reporting the Good, Bad and Ugly

Some journalists avoid saying or writing negative information in obituaries. Other journalists say that obituaries should report the good and the bad. Negative information should be weighed on its newsworthiness, taste and impact on the community.

Some other points the obituary writer should keep in mind include:

A woman is said to be survived by her husband, not her widower. A man is survived by his wife, not by his widow.

A Catholic funeral Mass is celebrated, said or sung. Mass is capitalized.

Autopsies are performed to determine the cause of death. When an autopsy is planned, simply report that, "An autopsy will be conducted."

Don't label children as adopted, natural, or half brothers or sisters unless the family makes such a request.

Exact addresses usually are not reported since there have been many cases in which burglars have broken into homes of survivors while they were attending the funeral of their loved ones.

NEWS RELEASES

A news release is information relayed by print, video or electronic means about a person's or organization's activities or opinions. Media organizations daily receive hundreds of news releases. They come from major corporations, educational institutions, museums, the entertainment industry, government agencies, politicians and local groups, such as a garden or service club.

News releases announcing a group's upcoming fundraiser or promotions or honors within a company usually don't need additional sources. These are straightforward, noncontroversial stories that probably will be only a few paragraphs in a newspaper and ignored by broadcast news media. More often, however, reporters use news releases as tip sheets. They want more of the *how* and *why* of the story than the company issuing the news release might want to divulge. That's why reporters confirm the facts in the news release and use other sources to go deeper into the story than what the news release provides.

Reporters also need to be aware of such problems as leads that may be buried in the story and sources who may not be identified correctly or completely. Journalists who routinely make slight changes to news releases and then take credit for writing the stories are little more than lazy, unethical stenographers for the people sending in the news releases.

Writing News Stories from News Releases

Very few news releases are printed or broadcast without being rewritten or edited. Poorly written news releases and those promoting commercial products are likely to be tossed, as are those with little news value.

Try to localize the news release; make it relevant to your community. Most news releases are too general. For example, if a university or research institute in a remote city releases a study about a health issue, such as the benefits of drinking apple juice to prevent early memory loss, contact physicians or scientists in your community for comments.

Here is an example of a news release:

Bestselling Author Augusten Burroughs to Visit Holy Cross

Bestselling author Augusten Burroughs will give a talk, titled "Dry: Living Life Without Booze," on Wednesday, March 24, at 7:30 p.m. in the Hogan Campus Center Ballroom at Holy Cross. Burroughs will be available to sign copies of his books after the lecture, which is free and open to the public.

Massachusetts native Augusten Burroughs is the bestselling author of the novel "Sellevision" and the memoirs "Running With Scissors" and "Dry: A Memoir." Released in 2003, Dry tells the personal story of Burroughs' difficult emergence into adulthood, out of the closet, and through drug and alcohol rehab programs. During his talk, Burroughs will share with the audience the reality of alcohol dependence — blackouts, broken friendships and an apartment filled with nothing but empty bottles.

People Magazine describes Dry as "more than a heartbreaking tale; it's a heroic one. As with its predecessor, we finish the book amazed not only that Burroughs can write so brilliantly, but that he's even alive."

Burroughs' first memoir, "Running With Scissors," recounts his unusual childhood after his eccentric mother left him in the care of her psychiatrist. It is currently in production to be released as a feature film starring Julianne Moore.

Janet Maslin of The New York Times describes the book as "a bawdy, outrageous, often hilarious account ... In keeping with this book's dauntless comic timing, this guy doesn't miss a beat."

This event is sponsored by The Office of the President; Dean of the College; Student Affairs; Athletics; First-Year Program; the Center for Religion, Ethics and Culture; English department; Psychology department; and Wellness Programming.

For additional information contact Kristine Caputo at 555-555-5555.

Here's how this press release might be rewritten for print:

Bestselling author Augusten Burroughs will speak on "Dry: Living Life Without Booze" on Wednesday at 7:30 p.m. in the Hogan Campus Center Ballroom at Holy Cross.

Burroughs' memoir, "Dry: A Memoir," recount his battle with alcohol addiction. Burroughs also will be available to sign copies of his books, including his bestselling novel "Sellevision."

"Running With Scissors" recounts Burroughs' unusual childhood after his eccentric mother left him in the care of her psychiatrist. It is currently in production to be released as a feature film starring Julianne Moore.

The broadcast version would be even shorter:

One of America's bestselling authors will discuss his battle with alcohol addiction at Holy Cross on Wednesday.

Augusten Burroughs will also sign copies of his book "Running With Scissors" and his novel "Sellevision." The event will take place at 7:30 in the Hogan Campus Center Ballroom.

MEETING AND SPEECH STORIES

It is almost impossible to pick up a newspaper or listen to a news broadcast without reading or hearing about a speech or meeting that will or has taken place. Most reporters frequently write two types of speech or meeting stories: advance stories and coverage stories.

Advance Stories

These stories tell readers what is going to happen and where it will take place in case they want to attend. Most advance stories of speeches and meetings contain the following information:

☑ Who will be involved.

☑ What will occur.

☑ When it will occur.

☑ Where it will occur.

Advance stories for speeches and meetings are very short. They may run only one or two paragraphs. Television and radio broadcasts would only carry such stories if they involved very important or prominent people or topics of extreme importance to a large number of people.

Advance stories for speeches fully identify the speakers, report the day and time they will speak and what they will be talking about. They also might include who is sponsoring the talk or event. Advance stories for meetings identify the groups that are meeting — a city council, county board of supervisors or civic club — the day, time and place of the meeting, and the topic.

Here is an example of an advance story for print:

> Former Vice President Al Gore will deliver an address on global warming and the environment at Stanford University on March 11.
>
> The speech, to be introduced by Stanford Graduate School of Business Dean Robert L. Joss, is being co-sponsored by the Business School's View From The Top leadership lecture series and the Environmental Management Club.
>
> Gore's views on the environment were outlined in his best-selling book, "Earth in the Balance: Ecology and the Human Spirit." He says the warming of the earth is causing an imbalance in the environment that could have devastating effects on mankind.

Radio and television might cover it this way:

> Former Vice President Al Gore will speak at Stanford University on Thursday about a subject close to his heart — global warming and the environment.
>
> Gore says the warming of the earth is causing an imbalance in the environment that could have devastating effects on mankind.

Here's a local story about an upcoming city council meeting:

> The Azusa City Council will consider Monday whether to have restaurants in town post Health Department letter grades.
>
> After years of not forcing business owners to post grades, city officials will look at possibly changing that practice, which is common among other cities in Los Angeles County.
>
> Letter grades let people know how eateries rate in county health inspections.
>
> The meeting begins at 7:30 p.m. in City Hall, 213 E. Foothill Blvd.

Broadcast might cover it this way:

> Azusa may soon grade its eateries.
>
> The City Council is expected to take up a measure to post Health Department grades of its restaurants. Most other cities in Los Angeles County already require that the grades be posted.
>
> That decision is expected to take place this evening.

COVERING SPEECHES AND MEETINGS

Preparation is the key to successfully writing stories about speeches and meetings. That means you need to find out as much as you can about the speaker(s) or the agenda items of the meeting. Representatives of the speaker can provide you with the speaker's background and, in most cases, a copy of the speech. You still need to attend the speech. Speakers often stray from the prepared text of their speeches. Agendas of public meetings, such as those

Reprinted by permission of San Gabriel Valley Newspaper Group Publisher.

held by city councils and school boards, are available. Reporters also might talk to the city manager, school superintendent, council members or school board trustees before the meetings.

Here are some guidelines for covering speeches and meetings:

Arrive early. Broadcast journalists sometimes plug their tape recorder into the public address system, if possible. If that's not possible, the recorder should be placed near the microphone where the speech will take place.

Know the players. Get acquainted with the speakers before the speech or meeting, especially if you are not familiar with them.

Monitor the audience. Descriptions of the number of people in the audience and the actions of the participants add drama and color to your stories.

Take plenty of notes. Notes can be taken in two ways. At the beginning of their talks, good speakers have an introduction and forecast — an unfolding of what the speaker will be talking about. Take a page of your notebook and divide it into the number of columns corresponding to the number of topics the speaker expects to present. During the speech, place the exact quotations under the column heading. Another method is to use an outline format in taking notes much as you do for class lectures. The object is to get accurate, interesting and colorful quotes. You need direct quotations to report what was said in a speech. Tape recorders are an excellent tool for getting accurate quotes.

Stay after the speech or meeting. You may have questions that could change the focus of your story. Many leads come from talking to the speaker in private after the talk rather than what he or she said in public.

Leads of Speech and Meeting Stories

Leads must begin with the most important thing said or action taken during the speech or meeting. Inexperienced reporters sometimes write leads that are too broad. Here are some examples of bad leads for speech and meeting stories:

> **Original:** San Francisco Mayor Gavin Newsom on Saturday discussed his differences with the Bush administration regarding same-sex marriages.

> **Revised:** San Francisco Mayor Gavin Newsom on Saturday accused President Bush of political showmanship and discrimination after the Social Security Administration announced it wouldn't accept any marriage licenses — gay or straight — from San Francisco until the same-sex issue was resolved.

> **Original:** The Sierra Club released a report Tuesday evening that warned about increasing noise levels on public health.

> **Revised:** Greater numbers of people will be deaf by the year 2010 if noise levels continue to increase, the Sierra Club warned Tuesday.

> **Original:** The El Monte City Council on Tuesday night discussed ways to generate revenue from those who work but don't live in the city.

> **Revised:** The El Monte City Council on Tuesday approved a 1-percent tax on those who work but don't live in the city.

The Body of Speech and Meeting Stories

The basic structure of a speech or meeting story is a lead that summarizes the most important topic or topics. The second paragraphs of speech stories usually include background information, including the purpose of the speech and, perhaps, the number of people in attendance. Sometimes these are included in the lead. The third paragraph is usually a quote or paraphrased quote supporting the lead. Direct quotations are preferred, but use paraphrased quotations if the speaker does not give succinct sound bites.

When the stories have more than one important topic, select the most important news item as the lead for the story, and then briefly describe the other topics in the second paragraph. Continue writing about the first topic in the third paragraph, and then report on the other news items. You will have to use the transitional techniques described in Chapter 5 to make the story flow. For example:

The Los Angeles City Council approved an ordinance Tuesday that paves the way for city recognition of identification cards issued by the consulates of any nation, provided the cards meet security and other standards established by the city clerk.

The City Council also voted to support a state Senate bill that would require ammunition vendors in California to keep records of people who purchase ammunition and make it a crime to sell ammunition to a minor.

The identification cards have the support of immigrant-rights groups in the region, which have lobbied for the cards for several years. ...

ROUNDUP STORIES

Roundup stories may be among the most complex, yet one of the most common types of stories beginning reporters write. A roundup is a way for the news media to save time and space by combining similar types of stories. Roundup stories may summarize several different but related events. For example, a reporter might want to combine a number of weekend traffic accidents, crimes, drownings or sporting events into a single story.

The lead for a roundup story should tie all the facts together while emphasizing their commonality. For example:

Eight people, including two teen-age motorcyclists, were killed in traffic accidents this weekend.

The story would then describe the traffic accidents, starting with the most newsworthy.

The lead for a roundup story about a regional event with several sources should include a synopsis of the major facts. For example:

A powerful storm swept through Southern California on Tuesday evening leaving 10 people dead, 80 injured and causing $8.9 million in damages.

The reporters, or sometimes several reporters, would interview victims and other witnesses of the storm. They would also talk to people in law enforcement about the deaths and road conditions, representatives from the utility company about power outages and repairs, county and state officials regarding emergency aid to the storm victims, and weather forecasters.

After the lead, roundup stories about several different but related events focus on the most newsworthy accident, crime, fire or drowning. That is followed by the second, third and fourth most important events.

Exercise 1: Writing Obituaries

Write an obituary for a newspaper using the following information.

Also write a 30-second story for broadcast. Remember that about 15 typewritten lines, of 65 characters each, make up one minute of air time.

Identification: John Randolph

Age: 88

Circumstances of death: Died of natural causes at his home on Feb. 24

Funeral services: Memorial service is being planned for mid-March in Los Angeles.

Survivors: One daughter, Martha Randolph of Honolulu; one son, Hal Randolph of Los Angeles; a granddaughter; and a brother, Jerry Lippman of Edgewater, N.J. His wife, actress Sarah Cunningham, died in 1986.

Accomplishments: Born Emanuel Cohen in the Bronx, he legally changed his name in the 1940s. His family were middle-class immigrants from Romania. His father was a milliner who died at age 29 during a flu epidemic when his son was only 4 years old. His brother thought he should become an actor and got him his first audition. He began his stage training in the Federal Theater Project in the 1930s, later studying with Stella Adler and becoming one of the original members of the Actors Studio. He made his Broadway debut in 1938. In 1954, he and his wife were called before Sen. Joseph McCarthy's House Un-American Activities Committee, which was investigating alleged communist influence in the entertainment industry. They refused to answer questions. They became part of the Hollywood blacklist that denied them work.

Exercise 2: Writing Obituaries

Select an athlete, author, journalist, entertainer or politician who is currently living and write an in-depth obituary. Report that the person died of unknown causes last night and no services or funeral have been scheduled. Do not make up any facts. Consult at least five sources. List those sources at the end of the obituary.

Also write a 30-second piece for broadcast. Remember that about 15 typewritten lines, of 65 characters each, make up one minute of air time.

Exercise 3: Writing News from News Releases

Write a three or four paragraph news story from the following news release.

List what other sources you would use and what questions you would ask them.

Also write a 30-second broadcast story. Remember that about 15 typewritten lines, of 65 characters each, make up one minute of air time.

Former Irish President/U.N. Human Rights Official To Speak at University of Maryland on St. Patrick's Day

Mary Robinson, former President of Ireland and former U.N. High Commissioner for Human Rights, will deliver the University of Maryland's annual Anwar Sadat Lecture for Peace. In her speech, Robinson will reflect on the links between human rights and peace, drawing on her experiences as Ireland's head of state and as a top U.N. official.

Robinson will be available to speak to reporters prior to her speech. She also will answer audience questions.

"Mary Robinson's record, both as a champion of human rights and as President of Ireland, is now matched by her profoundly important endeavor to address some of the challenges posed by globalization, especially for the poorer segments of the world's population," says Shibley Telhami, who holds the University of Maryland's Anwar Sadat Chair.

Robinson became Ireland's president in 1990. She was the first head of state to visit Rwanda following that nation's genocide and the first to visit famine-stricken Somalia in 1992. She assumed leadership of the U.N. human rights program in 1997. Robinson stepped down from her U.N. post in 2002 and now directs the Ethical Globalization Initiative, a new, non-profit organization. The project describes its main objectives in 2004 as fostering more equitable international trade and development, strengthening responses to HIV/AIDS in Africa and shaping more humane migration policies.

The annual lecture series, part of the university's Anwar Sadat Chair for Peace and Development program, has attracted world figures including Kofi Annan, Nelson Mandela, Henry Kissinger, Jimmy Carter and Ezer Weizman.

WHEN: Wednesday, March 17 from 7 p.m. to 8 p.m.; media availability prior to her presentation

WHERE: Clarice Smith Performing Arts Center, University of Maryland, College Park Directions online: Parking is available in Stadium Drive Garage across the street.

Exercise 4: Writing News from News Releases

Write a three or four paragraph news story from the following press release.

List what other sources you would use and what questions you would ask them.

Also write a 30-second broadcast story. Remember that about 15 typewritten lines, of 65 characters each, make up one minute of air time.

Research to Create Lung Cancer Blood Tests Receives $3.4 Million
in Pennsylvania Tobacco Settlement Funds

A team of researchers from The Wistar Institute, Fox Chase Cancer Center, and the University of Pennsylvania has been awarded $3.4 million to pursue development of blood tests for lung cancer. The need for such tests is great — lung cancer kills more Americans by far than any other form of cancer, according to statistics compiled by the American Cancer Society.

As with most cancers, treatment for lung cancer is much more effective when the cancer is detected at an early stage. The Wistar-led research team will use a systems-biology approach primarily applying the recently developed tools of proteomics and genomics to find proteins and genes in the blood that indicate the presence of early lung cancer. They will then develop blood tests based on this information that could aid thousands of Pennsylvanians by detecting their cancers at an earlier stage than is currently possible.

"This funding allows us to bring together an expert team of basic scientists and clinicians to tackle a critical medical problem," said David W. Speicher, Ph.D., professor and co-leader of the molecular and cellular oncogenesis program at The Wistar Institute and principal investigator on the lung-cancer project. "Our aim is to develop powerful new diagnostic tools that should help save lives through earlier cancer detection."

The announcement of the grant was made today by Pennsylvania Health Secretary Dr. Calvin Johnson on behalf of Governor Edward G. Rendell. The grant was one of five health research grants totaling $22.5 million funded from Pennsylvania's share of the national tobacco settlement.

These non-formula grants — competitive grants based on research priorities and not dictated by a formula — will develop Centers of Excellence to reduce disparities in lung disease and pregnancy outcomes. "Center of Excellence" is a special designation given to medical or educational institutions conducting concentrated, specialized research.

"Our urban and rural populations suffer disproportionately from both poor pregnancy outcomes and the frequency and severity of lung disease," Secretary Johnson said. "This research makes sense because it will test prevention and treatment approaches for eliminating disparities and improving outcomes in these populations, and continues Governor Rendell's commitment to using tobacco settlement dollars on research that will improve public health."

Secretary Johnson said that the Department of Health will distribute an additional $58.7 million in tobacco-settlement funds through formula grants later this fiscal year. The law specifies that 13.6 percent of the tobacco settlement funds be distributed by a pre-determined formula to institutions that already receive funds from the National Institutes of Health (NIH) and the National Cancer Institute.

The tobacco master settlement law, Act 77 of 2001, says that each year settlement dollars will go toward addressing research priorities that are established and reviewed annually by a statewide Health Research Advisory Committee, which is chaired by the Secretary of Health.

The Wistar Institute is an independent nonprofit biomedical research institution dedicated to discovering the causes and cures for major diseases, including cancer, cardiovascular disease, autoimmune disorders, and infectious diseases. Founded in 1892 as the first institution of its kind in the nation, The Wistar Institute today is a National Cancer Institute-designated Cancer Center — one of only eight focused on basic research. Discoveries at Wistar have led to the development of vaccines for such diseases as rabies and rubella, the identification of genes associated with breast, lung, and prostate cancer, and the development of monoclonal antibodies and other significant research technologies and tools.

Exercise 5: Speech Story

You are a reporter for the San Gabriel Valley Tribune. You covered a speech given to the Concerned Parents' League on Sunday night. These are your notes of the speech. Write a story for Monday morning's edition.

Also write a one-minute broadcast piece. Remember that about 15 typewritten lines, of 65 characters each, make up one minute of air time.

Speaker: Don Miller, assistant coroner for Los Angeles County

Audience: Concerned Parents' League of Los Angeles

Size: Approximately 500

Topic: Drug Deaths in Los Angeles County

Place: Fairfax High School

Speech Highlights:

A coroner's job is to investigate deaths not due from natural causes. For example, when Julius Caesar was killed, he was stabbed 23 times and only one wound was fatal — the one to the chest cavity. It takes a coroner to determine this.

There are three types of drug deaths:

1) Accidental — something else happens to you while you're under the influence of drugs. We consider alcohol a drug, and most accidental drug deaths are due to alcohol being mixed with driving.

2) Excess amount, or lethal dose, sometimes a person doesn't know what he's getting when he buys drugs. Most drugs bought on the black market are incredibly impure. People who make money from selling drugs don't care much about quality. Sometimes a person doesn't know how many pills he's popping. Reds or downers slow down the respiratory system — the person feels drowsy and loses track of time so that he thinks it was hours ago that he took the previous pills when in reality he may have popped four just minutes ago.

3) Suicide — more people commit suicide with barbiturates (reds or downers) than with guns. But many of these deaths must be listed as accidental. Unless a coroner can definitely support suicide, he must list the death accidental. For 516 suicides in the state last year, 166 are listed caused by barbiturates with 143 of these from the seconal (reds) type.

Following are the figures on drug deaths in Los Angeles during the past years:

2000: 90

2001: 100

2002: 145, the second highest county for drug deaths in the state that year.

In the 2002 cases, all but one were under the age of 30. Basically, those dead from drugs are usually male and young.

2003: 165

115 deaths: heroin (25 females, 90 males)

20 deaths: Seconal

20 deaths: alcohol

5 deaths: Speed

The remainder were caused by lesser known drugs or combinations of drugs.

In California, a coroner can call for an autopsy when a body is found. Some states require parental approval. In about 40 percent of the cases, autopsies are performed.

Some of the cases have been ones like these (slides shown of the bodies as they were found):

- ☑ 3-month-old baby dead, the mother stated the child had suffocated. The autopsy showed the child had been given a drug overdose and found that the mother had been sedating the baby in an effort to keep him quiet.

- ☑ 13-year-old teenager — went home for lunch — found with her face down in the food — had been sniffing glue, passed out, and suffocated — listed as an accidental death.

- ☑ 23-year-old father of two — found in his car in the morning by his 4-year-old son — many bodies are left in cars — sometimes they are even driven to hospital parking lots and then abandoned.

- ☑ A 12-year-old found in the bathroom of his home — youngest heroin death in Los Angeles County — his father was found to be a pusher.

"Death is not pretty."

Background Information on Don Miller:

Age 41, coroner's assistant for Los Angeles County, native of Los Angeles, graduate of Cal State Fullerton with a degree in criminal justice; has worked in the coroner's office for the past three years; married with two children, ages 3 and 1.

In the past year, he has given nearly 100 such presentations to groups and organizations throughout the county.

He comments: "I'll speak to any group or parent free of charge because I can't do the type of work I do without feeling there ought to be some way I can help these kids. I'm always too late. But maybe, just maybe, I can shock someone into waking up and getting there early."

Exercise 6: Covering Speeches

Here is a transcript of President Clinton's address to the National Geographic Society in Washington, D.C. Write an eight or nine paragraph news story for print.

Also write a 30-second broadcast piece. Remember that about 15 typewritten lines, of 65 characters each, make up one minute of air time.

U.S.-China Relations in the 21st Century
William Jefferson Clinton
A Presidential Address to the National Geographic Society
11 June 1998

THE PRESIDENT: Thank you very much, President Fahey. I don't know what to say about starting the day with this apparition. But it's probably good practice for our line of work. I try to read every issue of the National Geographic, and I will certainly look forward to that one.

Chairman Grosvenor, members of Congress, members of the administration, and members of previous administrations who are here and others who care about the national security and national interests of the United States. First let me, once again, thank the National Geographic Society for its hospitality, and for the very important work that it has done for so long now.

As all of you know, I will go to China in two weeks time. It will be the first state visit by an American President this decade. I'm going because I think it's the right thing to do for our country. Today I want to talk with you about our relationship with China and how it fits into our broader concerns for the world of the 21st century and our concerns, in particular, for developments in Asia. That relationship will in large measure help to determine whether the new century is one of security, peace, and prosperity for the American people.

Let me say that, all of you know the dimensions, but I think it is worth repeating a few of the facts about China. It is already the world's most populous nation; it will increase by the size of America's current population every 20 years. Its vast territory borders 15 countries. It has one of the fastest growing economies on Earth. It holds a permanent seat on the National Security Council of the United Nations. Over the past 25 years, it has entered a period of profound change, emerging from isolation, turning a closed economy into an engine for growth, increasing cooperation with the rest of the world, raising the standard of living for hundreds of millions of its citizens.

The role China chooses to play in preventing the spread of weapons of mass destruction or encouraging it; in combating or ignoring international crime and drug trafficking; in protecting or degrading the environment; in tearing down or building up trade barriers; in respecting or abusing human rights; in resolving difficult situations in Asia from the Indian subcontinent to the Korean Peninsula or aggravating them. The role China chooses to play will powerfully shape the next century.

A stable, open, prosperous China that assumes its responsibilities for building a more peaceful world is clearly and profoundly in our interests. On that point all Americans agree. But as we all know, there is serious disagreement over how best to encourage the emergence of that kind of China, and how to handle our differences, especially over human rights, in the meantime.

Some Americans believe we should try to isolate and contain China because of its undemocratic system and human rights violation, and in order to retard its capacity to become America's next great enemy. Some believe increased commercial dealings alone will inevitably lead to a more open, more democratic China.

We have chosen a different course that I believe to be both principled and pragmatic: expanding our areas of cooperation with China while dealing forthrightly with our differences. This policy is supported by our key democratic allies in Asia, Japan, South Korea, Australia, Thailand, the Philippines. It has recently been publicly endorsed by a number of distinguished religious leaders, including Reverend Billy Graham and the Dalai Lama. My trip has been recently supported by political opponents of the current Chinese government, including most recently, Wang Dan.

There is a reason for this. Seeking to isolate China is clearly unworkable. Even our friends and allies around the world do not support us — or would not support us in that. We would succeed instead in isolating ourselves and our own policy.

Most important, choosing isolation over engagement would not make the world safer. It would make it more dangerous. It would undermine rather than strengthen our efforts to foster stability in Asia. It would eliminate, not facilitate cooperation on issues relating to mass destruction. It would hinder, not help the cause of democracy and human rights in China. It would set back, not step up worldwide efforts to protect the environment. It would cut off, not open up one of the world's most important markets. It would encourage the Chinese to turn inward and to act in opposition to our interests and values.

Consider the areas that matter most to America's peace, prosperity and security, and ask yourselves, would our interests and ideals be better served by advancing our work with, or isolating ourselves from China.

First, think about our interests in a stable Asia, an interest that China shares. The nuclear threats — excuse me — the nuclear tests by India and Pakistan are a threat to the stability we seek. They risk a terrible outcome. A miscalculation between two adversaries with large armies would be bad. A miscalculation between two adversaries with nuclear weapons could be catastrophic. These tests were all the more unfortunate because they divert precious resources from countries with unlimited potential.

India is a very great nation, soon to be not only the world's most populous democracy, but its most populous country. It is home to the world's largest middle class already and a remarkable culture that taught the modern world the power of nonviolence. For 50 years Pakistan has been a vibrant Islamic state, and is today a robust democracy. It is important for the world to recognize the remarkable contributions both these countries have made and will continue to make to the community of nations if they can proceed along the path of peace.

It is important for the world to recognize that both India and Pakistan have security concerns that are legitimate. But it is equally important for India and Pakistan to recognize that developing weapons of mass destruction is the wrong way to define their greatness, to protect their security, or to advance their concerns.

I believe that we now have a self-defeating, dangerous, and costly course underway. I believe that this course, if continued, not moderated and ultimately changed, will make both the people of India and the people of Pakistan poorer, not richer, and less, not more, secure. Resolving this requires us to cooperate with China.

Last week, China chaired a meeting of the permanent members of the U.N. Security Council to forge a common strategy for moving India and Pakistan back from the nuclear arms race edge. It has condemned both countries for conducting nuclear tests. It has joined us in urging them to conduct no more tests, to sign the Comprehensive Test Ban Treaty, to avoid deploying or testing missiles, to tone down the rhetoric, to work to resolve their differences including over Kashmir through dialogue. Because of its history with both countries, China must be a part of any ultimate resolution of this matter.

On the Korean Peninsula, China has become a force for peace and stability, helping us to convince North Korea to freeze its dangerous nuclear program, playing a constructive role in the four-party peace talks. And China has been a helpful partner in international efforts to stabilize the Asian financial crisis. In resisting the temptation to devalue its currency, China has seen that its own interests lie in preventing another round of competitive devaluations that would have severely damaged prospects for regional recovery. It has also contributed to the rescue packages for affected economies.

Now, for each of these problems we should ask ourselves, are we better off working with China or without it? When I travel to China this month, I will work with President Jiang to advance our Asian security agenda, keeping the pressure on India and Pakistan to curb their nuclear arms race and to commence a dialogue; using the strength of our economies and our influence to bolster Asian economies battered by the economic crisis; and discussing steps we can take to advance peace and security on the Korean Peninsula. I will encourage President Jiang to pursue the cross-strait discussion the PRC recently resumed with Taiwan, and where we have already seen a reduction in tensions.

Second, stopping the spread of nuclear, chemical and biological weapons is clearly one of our most urgent security challenges. As a nuclear power with increasingly sophisticated industrial and technological capabilities, China can choose either to be a part of the problem or a part of the solution.

For years, China stood outside the international arms control regime. In the last decade it has joined the Nuclear Nonproliferation Treaty, the Chemical Weapons Convention, the Biological Weapons Convention, and the Comprehensive Test Ban Treaty, each with clear rules, reporting requirements and inspection systems. In the past, China has been a major exporter of sophisticated weapons-related technologies. That is why in virtually all our high-level contacts with China's leadership, and in my summit meeting with President Jiang last October, nonproliferation has been high on the agenda.

Had we been trying to isolate China rather than work with it, would China have agreed to stop assistance to Iran for its nuclear program? To terminate its assistance to unsafeguarded nuclear facilities such as those in Pakistan? To tighten its export control system, to sell no more anti-ship cruise missiles to Iran? These vital decisions were all in our interest, and they clearly were the fruit of our engagement.

I will continue to press China on proliferation. I will seek stronger controls on the sale of missiles, missile technology, dual-use products, and chemical and biological weapons. I will argue that it is in China's interest, because the spread of weapons and technologies would increasingly destabilize areas near China's own borders.

Third, the United States has a profound stake in combating international organized crime and drug trafficking. International criminal syndicates threaten to undermine confidence in new but fragile market democracies. They bilk people out of billions of dollars and bring violence and despair to our schools and neighborhoods. These are problems from which none of us are isolated and which, as I said at the United Nations a few days ago, no nation is so big it can fight alone.

With a land mass spanning from Russia in the north to Vietnam and Thailand in the south, from India and Pakistan in the west to Korea and Japan in the east, China has become a transshipment point for drugs and the proceeds of illegal activities. Last month a special liaison group that President Jiang and I established brought together leading Chinese and American law enforcement officials to step up our cooperation against organized crime, alien smuggling, and counterfeiting.

Next month the Drug Enforcement Agency of the United States will open an office in Beijing. Here, too, pursuing practical cooperation with China is making a difference for America's future.

Fourth, China and the United States share the same global environment, an interest in preserving it for this and future generations. China is experiencing an environmental crisis perhaps greater than any other nation in history at a comparable stage of its development. Every substantial body of water in China is polluted. In many places, water is in short supply. Respiratory illness is the number one health problem for China's people because of air pollution.

Early in the next century, China will surpass the United States as the world's largest emitter of greenhouse gases, which are dangerously warming our planet. This matters profoundly to the American people, because what comes out of a smokestack or goes into a river in China can do grievous harm beyond its borders. It is a fool's errand to believe that we can deal with our present and future global environmental challenges without strong cooperation with China.

A year ago, the Vice President launched a dialogue with the Chinese on the environment to help them pursue growth and protect the environment at the same time. I have to tell you that this is one of the central challenges we face — convincing all developing nations, but especially China, and other very large ones, that it is actually possible to grow their economies in the 21st century without following the pattern of energy use and environmental damages that characterize economic growth in this century. And we need all the help we can to make that case.

In Beijing, I will explore with President Jiang how American clean energy technology can help to improve air quality and bring electricity to more of China's rural residents. We will discuss innovative tools for financing clean energy development that were established under the Kyoto climate change agreement.

Fifth, America clearly benefits from an increasingly free, fair and open global trading system. Over the past six years, trade has generated more than one-third of the remarkable economic growth we have enjoyed. If we are to continue generating 20 percent of the world's wealth with just four percent of its population, we must continue to trade with the other 96 percent of the people with whom we share this small planet.

One in every four people is Chinese. And China boasts a growth rate that has averaged 10 percent for the past 20 years. Over the next 20 years, it is projected that the developing economies will grow at three times the rate of the already developed economies. It is manifestly, therefore, in our interest to bring the Chinese people more and more fully into the global trading system to get the benefits and share the responsibilities of emerging economic prosperity.

Already China is one of the fastest growing markets for our goods and services. As we look into the next century, it will clearly support hundreds of thousands of jobs all across our country. But access to China's markets also remains restricted for many of our companies and products. What is the best way to level the playing field? We could erect trade barriers. We could deny China the normal trading status we give to so many other countries with whom we have significant disagreements. But that would only penalize our consumers, invite retaliation from China on $13 billion in United States exports, and create a self-defeating cycle of protectionism that the world has seen before.

Or we can continue to press China to open its markets — its goods markets, its services markets, its agricultural markets — as it engages in sweeping economic reform. We can work toward China's admission to the WTO on commercially meaningful terms, where it will be subject to international rules of free and fair trade. And we can renew normal trade treatment for China, as every President has done since 1980, strengthening instead of undermining our economic relationship.

In each of these crucial areas, working with China is the best way to advance our interests. But we also know that how China evolves inside its borders will influence how it acts beyond them. We, therefore, have a profound interest in encouraging China to embrace the ideals upon which our nation was founded and which have now been universally embraced — the right to life, liberty and the pursuit of happiness; to debate, dissent, associate and worship without state interference. These ideas are now the birthright of people everywhere, a part of the Universal Declaration of Human Rights. They are part of the fabric of all truly free societies.

We have a fundamental difference with China's leadership over this. The question we Americans must answer is not whether we support human rights in China — surely, all of us do — but, rather, what is the best way to advance them. By integrating China into the community of nations and the global economy, helping its leadership understand that greater freedom profoundly serves China's interests, and standing up for our principles, we can most effectively serve the cause of democracy and human rights within China.

Over time, the more we bring China into the world the more the world will bring freedom to China. China's remarkable economic growth is making China more and more dependent on other nations for investment, for markets, for energy, for ideas. These ties increase the need for the stronger rule of law, openness, and accountability. And they carry with them powerful agents of change — fax machines and photocopiers, computers and the Internet. Over the past decade the number of mobile phones has jumped from 50,000 to more than 13 million in China, and China is heading from about 400,000 Internet accounts last year to more than 20 million early in the next century. Already, one in five residents in Beijing has access to satellite transmissions. Some of the American satellites China sends into space beam CNN and other independent sources of news and ideas into China.

The licensing of American commercial satellite launches on Chinese rockets was approved by President Reagan, begun by President Bush, continued under my administration, for the simple reason that the demand for American satellites far out-strips America's launch capacity, and because others, including Russian and European nations, can do this job at much less cost.

It is important for every American to understand that there are strict safeguards, including a Department of Defense plan for each launch, to prevent any assistance to China's missile programs. Licensing these launches allows us to meet the demand for American satellites and helps people on every continent share ideas, information, and images, through television, cell phones, and pagers. In the case of China, the policy also furthers our efforts to stop the spread of missile technology by providing China incentives to observe nonproliferation agreements. This policy clearly has served our national interests.

Over time, I believe China's leaders must accept freedom's progress because China can only reach its full potential if its people are free to reach theirs.

In the Information Age, the wealth of any nation, including China, lies in its people — in their capacity to create, to communicate, to innovate. The Chinese people must have the freedom to speak, to publish, to associate, to worship without fear of reprisal. Only then will China reach its full potential for growth and greatness.

I have told President Jiang that when it comes to human rights and religious freedom, China remains on the wrong side of history. Unlike some, I do not believe increased commercial dealings alone will inevitably lead to greater openness and freedom. We must work to speed history's course. Complacency or silence would run counter to everything we stand for as Americans. It would deny those fighting for human rights and religious freedom inside China the outside support that is a source of strength and comfort. Indeed, one of the most important benefits of our engagement with China is that it gives us an effective means to urge China's leaders publicly and privately to change course.

Our message remains strong and constant: Do not arrest people for their political beliefs. Release those who are in jail for that reason. Renounce coercive population control practices. Resume your dialogue with the Dalai Lama. Allow people to worship when, where, and how they choose. And recognize that our relationship simply cannot reach its full potential so long as Chinese people are denied fundamental human rights.

In support of that message, we are strengthening Radio Free Asia. We are working with China to expand the rule of law and civil society programs in China so that rights already on the books there can become rights in reality.

This principled, pragmatic approach has produced significant results, although still far from enough. Over the past year, China has released from jail two prominent dissidents — Wei Jingsheng and Wang Dan — and Catholic Bishop Zeng. It announced its intention to sign the International Covenant on Civil and Political Rights, which will subject China's human rights practices to regular scrutiny by independent international observers. President Jiang received a delegation of prominent American religious leaders and invited them to visit Tibet.

Seeking to isolate China will not free one more political dissident, will not open one more church to those who wish to worship, will do nothing to encourage China to live by the laws it has written. Instead, it will limit our ability to advance human rights and religious and political freedom.

When I travel to China I will take part in an official greeting ceremony in front of the Great Hall of the People, across from Tiananmen Square. I will do so because that is where the Chinese government receives visiting heads of state and government, including President Chirac of France and, most recently, Prime Minister Netanyahu of Israel. Some have suggested I should refuse to take part in this traditional ceremony, that somehow going there would absolve the Chinese government of its responsibility for the terrible killings at Tiananmen Square nine years ago, or indicate that America is no longer concerned about such conduct. They are wrong.

Protocol and honoring a nation's traditional practices should not be confused with principle. China's leaders, as I have repeatedly said, can only move beyond the events of June 1989, when they recognize the reality that what the government did was wrong. Sooner or later they must do that. And, perhaps even more important, they must change course on this fundamentally important issue.

In my meetings with President Jiang and other Chinese leaders, and in my discussions with the Chinese people I will press ahead on human rights and religious freedom, urging that China follow through on its intention to sign the Covenant on Civil and Political Rights, that it release more individuals in prison for expressing their opinions, that it take concrete steps to preserve Tibet's cultural, linguistic, and religious heritage.

We do not ignore the value of symbols. But, in the end, if the choice is between making a symbolic point and making a real difference, I choose to make the difference. And when it comes to advancing human rights and religious freedom, dealing directly and speaking honestly to the Chinese is clearly the best way to make a difference.

China has known more millennia than the United States has known centuries. But for more than 220 years, we have been conducting a great experiment in democracy. We must never lose confidence in the power of American experience or the strength of our example. The more we share our ideas with the world, the more the world will come to share the ideals that animate America. And they will become the aspirations of people everywhere.

I should also say we should never lose sight of the fact that we have never succeeded in perfectly realizing our ideals here at home. That calls for a little bit of humility and continued efforts on our part on the home front.

China will choose its own destiny, but we can influence that choice by making the right choice ourselves — working with China where we can, dealing directly with our differences where we must. Bringing China into the community of nations rather than trying to shut it out is plainly the best way to advance both our interests and our values. It is the best way to encourage China to follow the path of stability, openness, nonaggression; to embrace free markets, political pluralism, the rule of law; to join us in building a stable international order where free people can make the most of their lives and give vent to their children's dreams.

That kind of China, rather than one turned inward and confrontational, is profoundly in our interests. That kind of China can help to shape a 21st century that is the most peaceful and prosperous era the world has ever known.

Thank you very much.

Exercise 7: Writing Roundup Stories

Write a traffic roundup story for Monday's paper based on your notes from various sources.

Also write a 30-second broadcast piece. Remember that about 15 typewritten lines, of 65 characters each, make up one minute of air time.

Accident 1
Source: Columbia Police Officer Steve Edwards

La Joi Richardson was in a westbound lane on Columbia Parkway.

Richardson lost control of her car, crossed the center line and was broadsided on the passenger's side by an eastbound car.

Happened around 5 p.m. Sunday evening.

Richardson's daughter, Jagara Brown, was in the car.

Richardson is 24; Jagara is 2.

Both were pronounced dead at the scene of the accident.

Brown was found on the street.

"When we arrived, the child was in a car seat but the car seat was outside of the vehicle at that point. There was no indication that the child was thrown from the car in any manner."

"The child may have been removed by a passerby in an attempt to do some kind of first aid on the child at that point."

Accident 2
Source: Sheriff's Deputy John Hays

Nick Gabbard and his wife Margaret Gabbard were killed Sunday on I-10 Freeway.

Nick is 55; Margaret is 47.

They were hit by a car going the wrong way on the freeway.

Accident happened at 5:30 a.m.

The driver of second car was also killed.

He was Philip Karnes.

Philip is 18.

Philip is a freshman at Westmont College.

Nick Gabbard is president of Washington Mutual Bank.

Margaret Gabbard hosts a local television talk show.

The Gabbards are known for their philanthropic activities.

Karnes may have lost control of his car.

The road was icy.

"On this area here, the pavement is somewhat worn and when you get into a situation when the temperature starts hovering around freezing, it doesn't take much."

The accident closed the freeway for approximately three hours.

Accident 3
Source: Highway patrol public information officer Barbara Loh

Michael Mulhill, 23, was in a motorcycle accident.

He hit a rock on the road on Bloomdale Highway south of Johnson's Bridge.

He skidded 50 feet.

Happened Sunday afternoon.

Taken by paramedics to Mercy Hospital.

Source: Mercy Hospital spokeswoman Jean Kearns

He's in critical condition.

Has back and head injuries.

Reported talked to Kearns late Sunday night.

Mulhill is 23.

Exercise 8: Writing Roundup Stories

Write an eight or nine paragraph roundup story for Tuesday's paper based on your notes from various sources.

Also write a one-minute broadcast piece. Remember that about 15 typewritten lines, of 65 characters each, make up one minute of air time.

Severe thunderstorm struck the area.

Happened around 5 p.m. Monday.

Hail the size of quarters, wind gusts of 90 mph and flash floods.

Another severe storm is expected early Wednesday.

Byron Steffens, manager of Duke Power Co.:

Power lines fell in many areas.

Blames high winds and heavy rain.

9,650 power outages throughout the area.

Crews will be working around the clock to restore electricity.

City Police Chief Tim Robbins:

Police responded to dozens of calls.

Three people were killed in car accident.

Tree limb fell on the front windshield of their car.

Driver swerved off the road and into an embankment.

About 20 people were injured from storm-related incidents such as falling debris.

Most required emergency-room treatment.

Fire Department Chief Stephen Duffy:

"We've got several power lines down, trees down, a lot of damage. So far, no major fires."

City Engineer George Bradshaw:

Estimates that damage so far exceeds $10.8 million.

"Valley and Ramona boulevards are flooded and have downed electrical wires. This a deadly area. Stay away from these areas."

Superintendent of Schools Martha Speaks:

"One of the roofs at the elementary school collapsed from the force of the hail and rain. Tiles from another roof at the same school blew away skidding like rocks across the baseball fields. The high school has severe damage after mud flowed into four classrooms. It is a sight beyond belief."

Airport Manager Mark Sutfield:

Several privately owned planes damaged.

"Two of the hangars have been completely destroyed. The force of the wind pushed one plane into a ravine near the airport. I've never seen anything like this in my 20 years here."

FEATURE-ARTICLE WRITING

This chapter:

☑ Talks about the differences between news and feature stories

☑ Explains the structure of a feature

☑ Provides examples of feature leads

☑ Discusses different types of feature stories

While news stories focus mainly on the basic facts of a situation, feature stories go a step further by exploring the details. Feature writing can be a rewarding process for those who are particularly interested in the "why" and "how" aspects of reporting.

Feature articles come in many shapes and sizes. They may be intended to inform, educate or entertain. They can take the form of travel, health, consumer-interest, business, how-to or human-interest stories. While in the past features were generally relegated to the "lifestyle" section of a publication, today you will find feature articles in all sections of a newspaper — even on the front page. They are a regular part of TV news broadcasts, and they add color to online publications, often by getting the reader involved in the story.

In print writing, a feature story might be used as a short piece called a sidebar, which accompanies a news story and provides additional details about some aspect of the article. When singer Britney Spears impulsively married a former high school chum in Las Vegas in 2004 and then immediately filed for an annulment, for example, the news was the short-lived nature of the marriage. To provide some context to Britney's story, however, several newspapers accompanied their articles about the quickie wedding and annulment with sidebars about other short-term celebrity marriages.

This same approach can be used in broadcast writing to help put a story into perspective. When a mountain lion attacked a young woman in a wilderness park in Orange County, Calif., local TV station coverage emphasized the brutality of the assault and the heroic rescue of the woman from the grip of the lion's jaws. To illustrate the seriousness of the attack, in a supplement to the main story one Los Angeles TV station described how two young children had been attacked by mountain lions under similar circumstances in an Orange County park in the mid-1980s. The story explained that those attacks had led to a ban on children in the county's regional wilderness areas.

Features can also take the form of longer stories that focus on a particular aspect of the news. In response to the mountain lion story, Los Angeles-based KCAL-TV created a segment called, "What to do if you're attacked by a mountain lion." The piece included background information on the nature of mountain lions and featured an interview with a Southern California park ranger. He explained why mountain lions might attack humans and offered tips on how individuals should respond if attacked.

Features can also work as stand-alone pieces that bring to light topics of interest, providing readers with information that may affect their lives. A story about the benefits of working out could be helpful to individuals interested in starting a regular fitness program. A print version of the story might discuss ways to use different types of exercise equipment and talk about the benefits of each. A broadcast version of the story is likely to show people using the equipment and might show someone demonstrating how each piece works.

Online features sometimes provide readers with supplements to their print or broadcast story counterparts by adding a level of interactivity. The print version of the working out story could appear online accompanied by an interactive quiz called, "How fit are you?" When readers completed the quiz, the instructions would refer them back to segments of the article that highlighted specific fitness options that might work for them based on their quiz answers.

CRAFTING THE FEATURE ARTICLE

There are many similarities between news stories and feature articles. Both require good research and reporting skills. Both incorporate quotes or sound bites that illustrate the points of the story and add depth to the information provided by the writer. A well-crafted feature story has a central theme just as a properly constructed news story has a main point to communicate to the audience.

But there are differences between news and feature articles as well. One primary difference is in the structure of a feature story. While news stories generally follow the inverted pyramid format, emphasizing the five Ws in their leads, feature stories use a variety of styles to capture the attention of the audience. There is more freedom in the construction of a feature story, which may appeal to individuals who want to break out of the parameters of the inverted pyramid and try their hand at more creative approaches to journalistic writing.

In many respects, feature writing incorporates elements of fiction writing — plot, characterization, description, dialogue. While the facts in a feature story must always be truthful, the presentation of these facts can be delivered in a more colorful package than the traditional news format allows. Good feature article writing employs the art of storytelling by setting a scene and engaging the audience in its details. The use of interesting language and the incorporation of elements such as suspense, conflict and emotion can be used to attract and sustain the interest of readers and viewers.

STRUCTURE OF A PRINT FEATURE

The visual depiction of a news story is the inverted pyramid, an upside-down triangle that presents the most important information at the top with less crucial facts and details trailing toward the bottom of the triangle. The shape of a feature is more rectangular, with the information presented in segments to the audience. The simplest version of this is what some writers such as Vicky Hay, author of "The Essential Feature," refer to as the "paper doll" model because a graphic depiction of it resembles a paper doll. This feature story model includes four basic components: lead, transition, body and ending.

Leads

As with a news story, the lead is the most crucial part of a feature. The lead is the hook, the piece of the story that captures the attention of readers and viewers and pulls them into the story. When writing features, you want to invest some time into coming up with well thought out leads that will command this attention. You can accomplish this by using your creativity and thinking about how to approach your stories from a variety of angles. Some writers will draft several versions of a feature story lead before choosing the one that is most appropriate for the story.

Unlike a news lead that emphasizes the five Ws, a feature lead can introduce a topic in many different ways. The lead can build suspense by creating a scenario that sets up the rest of the article. It can lay out a road map for the story or introduce characters who will figure prominently. It can pose a question that will be answered by the information contained in the feature. And in some cases, the lead may give no indication of the central theme of the piece. This theme may only become apparent to readers as the story slowly unfolds.

The main goal of the feature lead is to generate interest in what is to come, to pique the curiosity of those reading the story and make them want to find out more. Just as a good novel will draw the reader in with an enticing opening, a well-written lead has the potential to do the same for a journalistic feature.

When writing for print, there are many different types of leads you can use to hook your audience. Here are some options and examples:

Narrative

The narrative lead is used to set up a situation or set a scene for a story. It guides readers through a series of steps or chain of events that pull them into the story by making them feel like they're there. The narrative lead works well to create a sense of drama or suspense and engages readers by enabling them to connect with the scene being created. Consider this lead for a feature about why people enjoy hanging out in coffeehouses. The article appeared in the Village Advocate in Chapel Hill, N.C. The lead presents a scenario that many of the paper's readers will understand.

> The feeling is familiar — that uncomfortable sensation of dread that creeps up on you every Sunday afternoon as the weekend winds down and the threat of MONDAY MORNING looms like an ominous cloud.
> You've slept late and managed to fritter away most of the day, and now it's time to get down to business, to catch up on all the work you've put off all weekend. The only thought more depressing than the start of another week is the idea of spending the evening alone in the apartment with a pile of books.
> But all is not lost. With laptop in hand, you head off to Franklin Street to spend the evening doing your work in one of Chapel Hill's coffeehouses. Armed with a fresh cup of java and surrounded by a host of others with their own collection of reading material, you take comfort in knowing that the evening doesn't look nearly so bleak as it did just a few hours earlier.

Contrast

The contrast lead shows two opposing views of a topic or issue. It may present a set of facts and then follow with a statement that contradicts them. The contrast lead can be used to suggest tension or to create conflict in a story. It may take readers by surprise, leaving them wanting to read on to find out more, as in the following example:

> Mike Parker's mother loved to talk about her son. She would tell anyone who would listen about his accomplishments. How he'd learned to speak three languages by the time he was four years old. How he'd been a child prodigy who enrolled in high school when he was only 10. How he'd published his first article in The New Yorker shortly before his 12th birthday.
> But when Mike was arrested for murder last fall at the age of 14, suddenly his mother had nothing to say.

Summary

The summary feature lead is similar to the summary news lead because it presents the basic facts in the first few sentences of the story. You can use this lead to set up a problem or situation that will be addressed by the information contained in the remainder of the feature. The summary feature lead is appropriate for newspaper feature articles, as it quickly leads the audience to the heart of the story. This is important since newspaper features tend to be shorter than magazine features because of space limitations.

The following summary feature lead appeared in a story written about job-hunting resources available to soon-to-be college graduates.

> You've read dozens of job-hunting books, prepared a winning résumé, and mailed several hundred copies to as many companies as you could think of. But now it is nearing graduation day, and you still don't have a job awaiting you.

Perhaps it's time to take a different approach.

The lead is short and to the point, and it guides readers to the core of the story, which is an explanation of resources they can use to help them with their job search.

Descriptive

The descriptive lead uses words to paint a picture for the audience. A well-written descriptive lead provides enough details to help readers form a mental image of what is being described. The key to a good descriptive lead is the use of expressive language and the incorporation of literary techniques such as alliteration, metaphors and analogies. Consider the following lead from the Orange County Register:

> There is a little red jacket in Irvine that has never done what it was supposed to do.
> It has never sheltered a child from the cold or kept a kid dry. And no toddler has ever played in it or, God forbid, spit up on it.
> Instead of doing what it was made to do, this bold little garment took a detour — and became something far bigger than a little red jacket.
> It became the one thing that has bound three generations of boys.
> The jacket is like your Aunt Martha's heirloom doilies. Except instead of Martha passing the doilies down to Cousin Lou (and starting a family war), everyone gets a piece of the little red jacket. It is perpetually passed around. Sort of like the Stanley Cup.
> When a boy is born into the family, the red jacket arrives at the doorstep of that boy's mother.
> And that mother is obligated — not to mention honored — to slip her baby's arms into that jacket and have his picture taken somewhere around his first birthday, preferably before his first haircut.

Scene-Setting

The scene-setting lead is similar to a descriptive lead in that it relies on description to convey a sense of place. The scene-setting lead is often used to set a stage where a story can unfold. It can also be used in travel pieces as in the following example:

> Picture miles of glittering neon, chorus lines of costumed dancers, and the possibility of fortune and fame. Picture a city where lights glow 24/7 and people stream through the streets at all hours. Picture a place where nothing stands between you and your wildest dreams but the roll of a dice, the spin of a wheel, the pull of a handle and the blessings of Lady Luck. Picture Las Vegas.

Anecdote

The anecdote is often referred to as a story within a story. It is an appealing way to begin a feature because it can combine a number of lead writing techniques — narrative, description and contrast, for example. An anecdotal lead has a beginning, middle and end. The end of an anecdote will generally lead into the transitional paragraph that explains what the rest of the story will be about.

The anecdote can function as an introduction to the characters of the story, as in the following example written for the Smithsonian News Service to mark the 10th anniversary of the arrival of two giant pandas at the National Zoo in Washington, D.C.

> It seems like only yesterday. Two green crates marked, "Giant Pandas" stood in the middle of the animal enclosures at the Smithsonian's National Zoological Park in Washington, D.C., as anxious Zoo officials waited expectantly.
> Suddenly, a fluffy ball of black and white lumbered out of one crate. Waddling around her pen, she reportedly sniffed the new surroundings, picked up her water dish, promptly turned it upside-down and plopped it on her head. Ling-Ling, a 136-pound, 2-year-old female giant panda who had just arrived from China, was making herself at home.

Meanwhile, in the adjacent enclosure, there was silence from another large wooden box. After some time, a 1-1/2-year-old male, Hsing-Hsing, cautiously emerged. He peered around his new home carefully, then beat a rapid retreat into his den.

So it was that almost immediately after their arrival, outgoing Ling-Ling and shy Hsing-Hsing had already demonstrated their distinctive personalities.

That was 10 years ago, when the two giant pandas took up residence in the National Zoo. Though they've changed through the decade, the personable Ling-Ling and Hsing-Hsing continue to attract and entertain millions of visitors.

Sometimes an anecdotal lead will serve as an introduction to a broader topic. An anecdote used in the opening of an article in Flux magazine, the student publication of the University of Oregon, told the story of a young woman who had been adopted and who went on a quest to find her birth parents. The story began with a tale about how the woman traveled to Georgia to try and obtain her birth records but met with resistance from authorities. Initially, the lead gave the impression that the feature would concentrate on this woman's experience. However, after the transitional paragraph, the feature went on to focus on an organization that helps adoptees locate their birth parents, rather than continuing with this particular woman's story. It soon became evident that in this case the anecdote simply served as one example used to illustrate a bigger issue.

Second-Person

The second-person lead works well to establish a connection with readers through use of the word "you." This type of lead may sometimes have a more casual, conversational tone to it, as it is intended to paint a picture of a situation readers can relate to personally. While the lead may be written in second person to establish that reader connection, however, once the article moves into the transition paragraph, the writer should switch to third person.

The following example is the opening of a story on occupational stress, which appeared in a San Francisco Bay Area business magazine. The article was aimed at working professionals.

It's 4:30. You're just about ready to wrap up the day, and you begin to daydream about what to have for dinner. Suddenly your boss comes into your office with a stack of papers in her hand and says, "I know it's late, but I need you to write a report from this material for the meeting tomorrow morning. It should only take an hour or two."

Slowly your muscles tighten, and you can almost feel your blood pressure rising. The last thing you were planning on was working overtime, and you realize this means you will miss your photography class for the third week in a row because of someone else's poor planning. Muttering to yourself, you begin to shuffle through the papers and wonder why you allow yourself to put up with all the extra pressure.

Transition

To move from the lead to the body of your feature, you need a transitional paragraph or section that explains to the audience the point of your story. This is sometimes called the "nut graph," and it is used to form a bridge between the story's attention-grabbing opener and its central core.

The transition may be a simple, one or two sentence thesis statement that spells out where the story will go from here. A well-written transition section will show the audience how the lead relates to the rest of the story.

Here's the transition paragraph that followed the narrative lead for the article about hanging out in coffeehouses:

Hanging out in coffeehouses has become a Chapel Hill pastime, as the number of local coffee establishments continues to grow. For some, the shops offer a place to grab a quick cup on the way to the office; for others, they provide a place to hang out with friends and socialize. And, of course, for still others, they offer a safe place to help pass the time on a lonely Sunday night.

This transition paragraph lets the audience know what is forthcoming: a story about why people enjoy coffee-houses. At the same time, it shows a connection to the lead in its last sentence, with its reference to how people rely on coffeehouses to pass the time on a Sunday night.

Here's another example — the transition for the story on job-hunting resources for college students. This paragraph follows the brief summary lead by offering a solution to the problem posed by the lead.

> While the "resume blitz" is probably the most common job-search method used by college students, there are many other resources you can use that are more likely to get you the results you want.
> Job-hunting help can be secured from a number of sources, many of which are easily accessible to the college student. Here are a few suggestions to assist you in making the most of your job search.

The article then goes on to list 10 resources students can use to help them find employment after graduation.

Body of the Story

Once you've established a transition after the lead, it's time to move on to the body of your story. The body makes up the central core of a feature article, for it is here that you have the opportunity to provide your audience with information that builds on your lead and enables them to come away with a better understanding of your topic.

The body is where you include factual information you've gathered, quotations from sources that add color to these facts, statistics, background — whatever you can provide to help educate and inform your audience. It is here where you make your points, develop your theme and reveal to the audience the value of the information you have gathered.

If you were writing an article about how to buy a dirt bike, for instance, the body of your story is where you would provide readers with information about the various types of bikes, how they operate and what differentiates one from another. You might include statistics to show how many people ride dirt bikes and perhaps include quotations from an expert rider, salesperson or manufacturer of these bikes who could provide first-hand advice on how to choose the bike that is most suitable for your needs. The body of the feature is where you include as much information as you can to convince members of your audience that they have learned something from your story and that the time they've spent with it has been worthwhile.

The key to accomplishing all of this is good research. If you put sufficient effort into the information gathering part of your story, you will find that putting the pieces together can be a relatively painless process. Once you've determined the focus of your story, start thinking about what or who will be the most valuable sources of information. Do background research to see what others have written about your topic. Gather statistical information from databases, government sources etc. Talk to expert sources who can offer insights into your subject. Once you've spoken with them, go through your interview notes and choose quotations that best illustrate and support some of the other information you have gathered. This will add cohesiveness to your story.

You can organize the information in the body of your feature in a number of ways. You can write chronologically, telling the story in the sequence in which events occurred. If you were writing a celebrity profile, this approach would be appropriate because you could explain how the individual got from a starting point in life to the present state of celebrity.

Another format is to start with the simple and move on to the more complex. This works well when writing technical or scientific features such as when trying to explain how an engine works or why the rain forest is endangered. You might decide to compare or contrast elements of the story, as when writing a piece on how to choose a college or buy a used car. Or, you can use a problem and solution approach, presenting a problem at the beginning of your story and using the body to explain how to solve the problem. For instance, pose a question early on such as, "Why does healthcare cost so much?" Then use the results of your research to show the audience why it does and what can be done about it.

The body of your story is also where storytelling comes into play. This is where some of the fiction writing techniques mentioned earlier in the chapter can be implemented. Choose quotes that make the individuals or characters in your story appear three-dimensional, and show the essence of who they are and what they think. Use colorful, descriptive words and phrases that give the audience a clear picture of the images and emotions you are trying to convey. Present the material you've gathered through your reporting in a way that builds suspense or generates empathy.

When putting the body of your feature together, you also want to make sure the information flows logically and is easily understood by your audience. Be sure to include the necessary transitional phrases like *however, therefore, so, nevertheless* and *although* when changing topics within this section. This allows for a smooth transition from one area of the story to another.

Think of this segment of your feature as the heart and soul of your story. By putting some thought into what to include in the body of your feature story and how you present it, you can craft a feature that will be informative, entertaining and educational and that will leave a lasting impression on your audience.

Ending the Story

When writing a news article, it is not crucial to have a definitive ending to your story. The inverted pyramid format is designed to allow the news story to be cut as needed to fit the space allotted to it. Because of this, it is not unusual for a news story to simply end without any prior warning.

With a feature article, however, readers expect closure, something that ties together the elements of the story and brings them to some kind of resolution. So when writing a feature, you want to think about the ending from the start of your work on the story.

There are several ways to conclude a feature article to provide a sense of closure for your audience. The easiest way to round out your story is with a summary of the information you have provided in the article. You might include a brief re-cap of the main points or a closing statement that summarizes the central theme of your piece. The feature mentioned earlier about job-hunting tips for college students, for example, offered readers ideas about resources they could use to find a job after commencement and encouraged them to think creatively when exploring their options. The story presented 10 job-hunting suggestions and then finished in the following manner:

> Searching for a job can be a tedious, time-consuming process.
> Nevertheless, with a certain amount of diligence and perseverance — and a bit of creative thinking — you can land the job you have been working toward throughout those years in school.

The ending is simple and straightforward, and it summarizes the notion that if students persevere, they will be successful in their job search.

Another common way of ending a feature story is to use a quotation that will have a lasting impact on your audience. When you are sifting through the information you gathered from your interviews with sources to decide which quotes to use in the feature, keep an eye out for a strong quote that sounds like it might be appropriate to wrap up your story.

You may choose something that reflects the central theme of your article or best expresses the ideas of one of your sources. You could select a quote that sends a message to the audience or even just choose one that will leave them feeling good at the end of your story.

The article on hanging out in coffeehouses that was discussed earlier featured interviews with nine people, including a graduate student whose voice was heard throughout the story. Using a quote from her seemed an appropriate way to end the piece.

> "One of my favorite places to meet people is to say, 'let's go for coffee.' It's less expensive than going for dinner, you can go at any time of the day, and you can sit there for hours and hours. There's something romantic about being a student in a coffee shop."

One of the best ways to end your feature article is to close with something that ties the story back to the lead. This helps remind readers how the story began and shows that it has come full circle. Even the example given above achieves this in a subtle way. The ending is a quote from a student talking about how much she enjoys hanging out in coffeehouses. And as you may recall, the story opened with a narrative about the coffeehouse being a good place for students to go to hang out on Sunday evenings.

The following example is the ending of the story discussed earlier about occupational stress. That article began with an account of someone who appeared to be continuously stressed by the demands of a job. The story featured interviews with a variety of individuals who talked about ways to manage stress, including a counselor from a mental health center who offered her professional expertise on the subject. The ending of this story featured a quote from the counselor:

> "A person who is really stimulated in a job can work longer than a 9-5 day," she says. However, if an individual finds that none of the traditional stress reduction techniques are helping, "he has to re-evaluate what his job is doing for him or to him. Sometimes it takes a long time for someone to admit he really has to look for a job change."

Her statement appears to be appropriate advice for the stressed-out, dissatisfied employee introduced in the lead, thereby tying the end of the story back to its start.

STRUCTURE OF A BROADCAST FEATURE

Leads

When writing for broadcast, there are more limited options for feature leads because of the tight time element involved. Broadcast writers don't have the luxury of gradually introducing the audience to a story through the use of a lengthy narrative or anecdote. Even within these limitations, however, there are several lead options available to broadcast writers when introducing feature stories.

Delayed Lead. This lead can be used to build suspense or anticipation in a broadcast feature. It introduces a story gradually by starting with an introductory teaser statement and then moving into the main body of the story, as in the following example:

> Ice cream fans may soon have a chance to create their own creamy concoctions. A new contest invites ice cream lovers of all ages to come up with some innovative flavors.
> Ben & Jerry's Homemade is sponsoring the contest to mark the company's 25th anniversary. The company invites ice cream lovers to submit original recipes for their flavor creations. The three top entries will be produced by Ben & Jerry's and sold to consumers next year. The Vermont-based company is known for its unusual promotions.

The story could then go on to include interviews with company personnel talking about the organization's past promotions and how this contest fits with the company's marketing activities. The segment could also feature more details about how to participate in the contest and include comments from people planning to enter.

Quote Leads. An outrageous or attention-grabbing quote can sometimes be used to open a broadcast feature. While in a news story attribution frequently comes before the quote, in a feature this is not always necessary. In this case the focus should be on the impact of the quote and how it sets up the story that follows.

A quote lead may appear to be an easy way to start off a broadcast feature, but it can be tricky to write. If you are going to use this type of lead to begin a broadcast feature segment, you need to make sure the quote is sufficiently attention grabbing to generate viewer interest. Here's an example:

> "I'm not just going to Disneyland … I'm going to buy Disneyland!"
> That's what Fresno resident Karen McKinley said after winning 81 (m)million dollars in this week's Super Lotto drawing.

Body of the Story

Unlike print feature writing, there is no need for a transition in a broadcast feature. Once you've hooked the audience with your lead, you want to move right on to the core of your story. The body of a broadcast feature will include a mixture of lively copy, supporting images and interesting sound bites. A winning combination of these elements should engage viewers in your subject and leave them with something to think about when the segment is over.

The body of the broadcast feature is where the writer can build on the information presented in the lead. As in a print story, the body can include some of the same elements discussed earlier such as plot and characterization. The story about the lottery winner, for instance, could include a brief overview of the life of the woman who won the money contrasted with sound bites about what she expects her life to be like now that she's $81 million richer.

Broadcast features can also use a "story within a story" format similar to that of the anecdotal approach used in print features. A segment on a single mother of two small children trying to find affordable childcare might be used to illustrate a bigger story about challenges faced by single mothers.

Because of the time element involved, the body of a broadcast feature should be relatively concise, focusing on two or three main points. Too much information crammed into a short time segment will only confuse the audience. The body of a feature on salsa dancing, for example, could highlight the reasons for the dance's popularity, briefly show how it's done and talk about resources available to those interested in learning more about the subject.

Ending the Story

The ending of a broadcast feature is used to wrap up the story smoothly so the audience can tell when one story has ended and another is about to begin. It may be devised to leave viewers thinking about the consequences of the story. Sometimes a sound bite is used to close a broadcast story, just as a quote might be used to conclude a print or online feature. As in print, the quote needs to be compelling and relevant to the rest of the story in order to leave the audience with a sense of closure. The accompanying visual is also very important to a broadcast story because often the audience is likely to remember the image over what was said.

TYPES OF FEATURE STORIES

When writing features you have many options because of the wide variety of stories that fall into this category. This flexibility is one of the factors that make feature writing so appealing to aspiring journalists. Here is a sampling of some of the features typically used by print, broadcast and online news outlets.

News Feature

A news feature is usually connected to a breaking news story, taking an aspect of the news and exploring it from another perspective. As mentioned earlier in the chapter, when the news feature accompanies a breaking news story, it is called a sidebar and is frequently written to present an added dimension to the main story. The news feature can also function as a stand-alone story that runs a day or two after the initial news event. These follow-up or "second-day" features tend to be longer than the typical sidebar.

News features may include some of the basic facts from the original story to give the audience context, but they often introduce a new twist on these facts or provide added information intended to further educate the audience about the impact of the news event. After Sept. 11, 2001, for example, many print, broadcast and online media outlets relied heavily on news features to help news consumers make sense of the terrorist attacks on the World Trade Center towers and the Pentagon, and to give them a sense of the havoc wreaked on the nation as a result of these attacks.

CBS News, for example, ran several news features about Cantor Fitzgerald, one of the firms hardest hit by the attacks because of its location on the upper floors of the north tower of the World Trade Center. These stories showed TV viewers the devastating effect the attacks had on the surviving family members of the employees who'd worked for the firm and who had been killed by the terrorists.

Personality Profiles

The personality profile provides an in-depth look into the life of an individual, giving the audience the opportunity to better understand how the person lives and what he or she thinks and feels about the world. A well-crafted profile leaves people feeling as if they now know a little more about the subject's life than they did before reading or viewing the story.

The best profiles contain a combination of thorough background research and one or more in-depth interviews. Ideally, these interviews should result in insightful quotes that can be incorporated into the feature in a way that allows the people you interview to tell their stories in their own words.

Celebrity profiles are particularly popular with news consumers, as evidenced by the proliferation of magazines such as People and Us as well as such TV programs as "Entertainment Tonight" and "Access Hollywood". But a good profile doesn't necessarily have to highlight someone famous. Even the most unassuming person can make for an interesting profile with some ingenuity and creativity on the part of the feature writer. The trick to writing an attention-grabbing profile is to ask questions that encourage people to talk freely about themselves and to present this information in a way that shows the audience what makes these individuals worth writing about.

Sportswriter Bill Plaschke, for example, introduced his readers to a young woman named Sarah Morris in a touching portrait he wrote about her for the Los Angeles Times. In a wheelchair as a result of cerebral palsy, Morris was an avid L.A. Dodgers fan who wrote a regular column about the baseball team for her Web site, "Dodger Place." She did this despite the fact that the disease affected her arm movement, so she was only able to type her stories with a head pointer — an endeavor that could take all day.

Plaschke visited Morris in Texas where she lived with her mother and spent hours interviewing her, trying to get a sense of what her life was like. He then wrote a story about her for the L. A. Times, highlighting her devotion to "her Dodgers," and chronicling her interest in becoming a serious journalist. He discussed his visit to her in Texas, describing the rundown house where she lived, explaining the physical challenges she faced and talking about her commitment to her work. His emotionally charged depiction of her life touched many readers who wrote to the paper to comment on his story. It also ultimately resulted in Morris being hired to write a regular column about the Dodgers for the Web site "MajorLeagueBaseball.com."

Anniversary and Holiday Features

The anniversary or holiday feature is used to mark the occurrence of a day when something significant happened or to recognize a holiday or event that is widely celebrated. Broadcast news programs often use these types of features because they tend to be more lighthearted than other news segments and can add color to the newscast. A feature on what to do for your sweetheart on Valentine's Day, for example, might show members of a local barbershop chorus delivering singing valentines on Feb. 14. A piece to commemorate Veteran's Day could feature an interview with the community's oldest veteran as he recalls his war experiences.

The biggest challenge for the writer of the anniversary or holiday feature is to come up with a different angle each year for what is essentially the same story. Former Orange County News channel reporter Beth Bingham decided to add a new dimension to a Mother's Day feature when she produced a piece on children whose mothers had recently died and who were facing the holiday for the first time without them. Her segment showed the children planting trees in memory of their mothers and provided a poignant twist on the traditional Mother's Day holiday story.

Human Interest

The human-interest story encompasses a broad category of features that include many topics. Human-interest features can focus on just about anything that has an effect on how people live and how they deal with the challenges of everyday life. For this reason, human-interest stories can be entertaining to read and rewarding to write.

Some human-interest features are upbeat and uplifting, while others are intended to shed light on a serious or heart-wrenching situation that may leave the audience in tears. Human-interest stories generally require interviews with a number of sources who can speak knowledgeably about the topic. They typically are filled with quotes or sound bites, allowing readers and viewers to get the stories right from the mouths of these sources.

As a writer working on a human-interest story, sometimes your challenge is to find the interesting in the mundane. Orange County Register reporter Joel Zlotnik did just that when he wrote a feature about a 9-year-old girl getting a haircut for the first time in many years. What made this a compelling human-interest story was the fact that the girl got the haircut for a specific reason. She wanted to donate her long tresses to Locks of Love, an organization that turned donated hair into wigs for children who had lost their hair to cancer.

Travel

Travel features can transport their audiences to faraway places. They can introduce locals to some of the hidden treasures found in their own neighborhoods. Travel features allow audiences to explore unfamiliar cultures and experience new adventures — even if only vicariously.

Description is a key part of a well-crafted travel story. Your job as a writer is to provide enough details about a place to enable readers to picture it in their minds and picture themselves there. A broadcast feature will be able to include live shots to supplement the writing, but the words carry great weight with print and online travel stories — even if photographs accompany them.

A travel story should be well researched and should include pertinent details that can make it easy for people to begin planning their getaways to the destinations you have introduced to them. These details may include information about when to go, where to stay, what to see, how to get there, how much to pay and what to avoid.

How-To

The how-to feature does exactly what its name suggests. It gives readers and viewers instructions on how to accomplish something — find a job, buy a car, build a house, plan a vacation — the list can go on and on. While you may choose to write a how-to story about something you know how to do yourself, you don't need to be an expert on a subject to put together an effective how-to feature.

If you are interested in writing about a topic that is not your area of expertise, be sure to include interviews with individuals who are knowledgeable on the subject. For a story on how to apply for a student loan, for example, include an interview with the financial aid director of a university. When writing about how to secure an internship, talk to someone at a company that uses interns on a regular basis and find out what qualities he or she looks for when interviewing prospective interns.

How-to stories are popular because they leave readers and viewers feeling as though they've learned something — even if what they've learned is simply that they now want to find out even more about a topic.

Exercise 1: Story Ideas

Take a walk around your college campus. Jot down some possible feature story ideas based on what you see going on around you. Using these notes, outline five ideas for possible article topics you could use when writing for a campus publication.

Write one paragraph for each idea explaining:

- ☑ What the story would be about
- ☑ Why it might appeal to readers of a campus publication

Exercise 2: Types of Print Leads

The Collegiate Student Association at your university is sponsoring a Halloween costume contest Oct. 31 at the Student Union. You have been asked to write a feature article for the campus paper about the contest. Write four different versions of the lead for this article, choosing from the following formats.

- ☑ Narrative
- ☑ Scene-setting
- ☑ Contrast
- ☑ Anecdote
- ☑ Summary
- ☑ Second-person
- ☑ Description

Exercise 3: Broadcast Leads

Write a delayed lead for a broadcast version of the Halloween feature that could be used on the campus TV station.

Exercise 4: Profiles

Write a feature story about your favorite teacher, using the information you gathered from your interview in Chapter 10. Include material based on your interview, as well as information based on any background research you have done. Also include quotes from at least two other people who are familiar with the teacher.

Exercise 5: Story Assignment

Choose one of the following topics and write a feature story about it. For this assignment, you should do appropriate background research and conduct interviews with individuals who can provide some insight into your topic. Your story should include interviews with three sources.

Topics

> Fear of flying
>
> Hazards of roller coasters
>
> Pros and cons of plastic surgery
>
> Corporate sponsorship of college sports teams
>
> Trends in online journalism
>
> Everything you ever wanted to know about hot dogs
>
> Steps involved in starting a small business
>
> Impact of chain bookstores on independent booksellers

JOURNALISM ETHICS

This chapter:

☑ Explains what ethics is and why it's important to journalists

☑ Examines some of the ethical issues that journalists face

☑ Offers guidelines to avoid unethical behavior

Mel Opotowsky, former ombudsman for the Riverside Press-Enterprise in Southern California, received a phone call from a distraught father one morning. The man's wife was on trial on charges relating to the death of their two small children, who died in a freak automobile accident. Their 10-year-old son, who had witnessed the accident, had testified at the trial the day before, and his testimony was included in that morning's coverage of the trial.

Why, the man asked, did you have to identify my son? Didn't you notice that he had a different last name? Why didn't you ask us? We changed his name and moved him to a school across town so his classmates wouldn't stare at him. When I dropped him off at school this morning, one of his friends came up to him and asked if his mother was the woman on trial for killing her kids. Now he has to live through all this again. Why did you do this?

Opotowsky couldn't answer the man's questions but promised to look into it. When he questioned the story's writer, the reporter told him that he noticed the boy had a different last name but that he was on deadline and didn't think much about it. The reporter's editor and the copy editors said it was a hectic night and they were too busy and distracted to take the time to discuss identifying the boy by name.

"The paper hurt the boy," Opotowsky said, "because no one stopped long enough to think about what they were doing."

The newspaper and its staff did not break any laws. The Constitution's First Amendment gives the news media the right to report what courtroom witnesses say and to identify witnesses, no matter how young they are. But many working in the news media would agree that identifying the boy caused him unnecessary harm and that the reporter and editors who failed to question what they were doing acted unethically.

Ethics can be defined as moral judgments and standards of conduct for people or professions. It is a rational process in which we draw on our philosophies and moral codes to make decisions we feel are fair and honest.

Journalists and people working in public relations and other mass media can also turn to the codes of ethics established by professional organizations. The Society of Professional Journalists' code of ethics, for example, encourages reporters to minimize harm to the people they cover. It says journalists should "treat sources, subjects and colleagues as human beings deserving of respect" and that they should "show compassion for those who may be affected adversely by news coverage. Use special sensitivity when dealing with children and inexperienced sources or subjects."

The reporter and editors in Riverside that day clearly were not thinking about SPJ's code of ethics when they were working on the trial story.

Journalists have other ethical concerns besides minimizing harm. They must also make sure their work is honest, accurate and fair and does not plagiarize from other sources. Reporters must seek diverse sources for their stories and guard against conflicts of interest and unnecessary invasions of privacy. They should also be wary of using deception to get a story and establish guidelines on its use.

ACCURACY AND FAIRNESS

Journalists are in the truth-telling business. Readers and viewers expect reporters to "get the story right" and present it without bias. They want and need information that is balanced with all points of view presented so they can make decisions as important as whom to vote for or as trivial as what toothpaste to buy. Reporters must remain open minded and show no favoritism or prejudice in their stories.

The U.S. news media coverage of the invasion of Iraq in 2003 was criticized by some journalists and others who said the news reports did not question strongly enough statements by the White House or the military. Even when American lives and interests are at stake, people expect the news media to strive for accuracy and balance.

Reporters must also avoid stereotyping people or reporting rumors or unsubstantiated allegations. They should always confirm from independent sources the information they receive if there is any doubt about its veracity.

Editors and producers must make sure that the images they use accurately reflect what is in the story and that the headlines, photo captions and teasers are also accurate. Reporters must make sure their quotes are accurate and are not taken out of context. They should double check their facts and make sure they are all attributed to reliable sources. Reporters working for 24-hour TV news networks and news-oriented Web sites are constantly on deadline and often don't have as much time to double check information as their counterparts at newspapers, which have only one deadline a day. Broadcasters and Web producers must be careful that in the rush to be first with a story they don't report rumors or other inaccurate information.

Reporters and their news organizations must also be willing to publicly admit when a story does contain errors, even minor ones that would not result in a lawsuit, and issue corrections as soon as possible.

Reporters should be cautious about using anonymous sources. Identifying sources adds to a story's credibility because readers and viewers know the information is from someone who is in a position to speak with authority. Question the person's motives for providing the information and insisting on anonymity. A whistle blower worried about keeping his job may deserve protection, while a political operative trying to damage the reputation of an opponent while appearing to be above the fray may not. If you do promise not to reveal a source's identity, keep your promise, because ethical journalists are trustworthy.

PLAGIARISM AND FABRICATION

Plagiarism is using someone else's written work — even one sentence or phrase — without giving the author proper credit. Using other people's ideas is acceptable, but using their words verbatim is not. Fabrication is making up quotes and information; it is lying to your audience. Both plagiarism and fabrication damage the reporter's and news organization's credibility even more than inaccurate reporting does. At many organizations, it is grounds for immediate dismissal.

One of the most notorious recent plagiarism and fabrication cases involved former New York Times reporter Jayson Blair, who plagiarized stories from other newspapers rather than conduct his own interviews. Blair also fabricated quotes and other details for his stories. Blair resigned from the Times when he was confronted with the evidence against him. The paper's two top editors also resigned within weeks.

The Times published a 7,200-word Page-One story about Blair that listed stories the editors believed contained fabrications and plagiarism. The Times published the story in an attempt to regain the trust of readers who questioned the paper's credibility after they learned of Blair's action from other news media. The Times Page-One article helped the paper avoid being accused of trying to cover up the scandal.

Perhaps what is the most troubling aspect about the Blair incident is that very few of the people whom Blair quoted but never spoke to were shocked by what had happened. The Los Angeles Times in a follow-up article reported that many people whom Blair lied about interviewing had not complained to the paper because they assumed that reporters routinely steal from other newspapers and make up quotes in their stories.

Blair was not the first or the last reporter publicly fired for plagiarism and fabrication. The Los Angeles Times in 2003 fired a photographer for altering a photo he filed from Iraq. The Chicago Tribune in 2004 fired an 18-year veteran reporter for fabricating a quote. The news media make these breaches of trust public so their audiences will understand that they take truth telling seriously. These dismissals are often reported in journalism magazines and on Internet listservs, and the reporters' careers are destroyed.

Plagiarism is sometimes accidental. Reporters and others doing research for stories must make sure their notes indicate when information is taken word-for-word from a document, and they must put the work of others in quotation marks with proper attribution. They should also be knowledgeable enough about what they are writing about that they can say it in their own words.

DIVERSITY

The editors at The New York Times did not at first think the murder of Tejano singing star Selena Quintanilla-Perez in March 1995 was front page news. Former Times managing editor Gerald Boyd told a gathering in 2002 at the American Society of Newspaper Editors headquarters in Virginia that no one at the daily Page-One budget meeting reacted when the national editor mentioned her death. The story was added to the Page-One lineup only after Latinos in the newsroom noticed it wasn't part of the lineup and complained. Boyd said he was glad they complained because they saved the paper from overlooking one of the big stories of the day. The people deciding what went on Page One were mostly white (Boyd is black), and they were not aware how well known Selena was among New York's Spanish-speaking residents.

Had Latinos been among the gatekeepers deciding what is news at The New York Times, the paper probably would not have almost missed such a major story. The news media need diversity in their ranks to help avoid excluding major segments of their audiences. The news media have both an ethical duty and an economic imperative to be relevant to everyone in their diverse communities.

Diversity is also important in minimizing harm to people. The mainstream, white-owned news media in the 18th, 19th and most of the 20th centuries either ignored minorities or only reported negative stories about them. Reporters were often and sometimes still are insensitive to the people they write about when the topics are race, religion, ethnicity, sexuality, physical abilities etc. A diverse newsroom guards against causing harm to others.

Diversity among reporters also is part of accuracy and fairness, both to avoid stereotypes and to better report on a multicultural community. Reporters should also expand their list of sources so that it better reflects the communities they write about.

CONFLICTS OF INTEREST

Everyone has conflicting loyalties. We have loyalty to ourselves and want to excel and prosper professionally. We have loyalty to our extended families and want to nurture and protect them. We have loyalty to our communities and nation and want what is best for them. We also have loyalty to our employer and want the company to succeed both so we can continue to earn money and because we want to be proud of where we work. Journalists also have a loyalty to seeking and reporting the truth, and sometimes this loyalty is in conflict with the other loyalties.

Conflicts of interest arise when reporters, their bosses or their corporate owners have a stake in the outcome of a story. On a personal level, this can be socializing with, working for or accepting gifts from sources. Conflicts can also arise from affiliation with causes or organizations or investing in a business that you're writing about. Readers or viewers don't trust someone to fully report on a corporate scandal if they know the reporter is married to the company's public relations director. They would also question the veracity of a City Hall reporter who is dating a member of the City Council or other city official.

Reporters must also guard against activities that might hurt their credibility. They should not become involved in political or social causes if they are going to be reporting on them because the public will assume they are biased. They may someday also have to choose between reporting an unpleasant truth about a group they belong to and being a loyal member of the group.

Journalists who accept speaking fees from businesses or organizations risk being labeled as an employee of that group who can't be trusted to always be truthful. Reporters' credibility is also questioned when they accept free travel, lodging, food, tickets to amusement parks or sporting events, or other gifts from the people and groups they report about. Many news outlets have strict policies against accepting any fees or gifts, even if the contributor is not part of a reporter's beat.

Reporters also must not write about any business that they have an investment in or use their insider knowledge to invest in companies.

Keep in mind that credibility is what others think of you and your work. You might be able to maintain your loyalty to telling the complete truth, but your viewers and readers might not think so.

Sometimes a conflict cannot be avoided. Reporters do have to write about their own newspapers or stations occasionally, and they frequently report on the handful of conglomerates that own most of the broadcast media. Ethical journalists always include in their reports any potential conflicts. For example, an ABC reporter talking about a fatal accident at Disney World should include in the story that Disney owns ABC. When public radio and TV news programs report on a charity or business that supports their programs, they always mention that fact.

INVASION OF PRIVACY

The ethical concern involving the Riverside boy at the beginning of this chapter revolved around the issue of privacy. Reporters pursuing a newsworthy story unnecessarily invaded the boy's privacy and caused him harm.

The news media must be careful to avoid hurting or embarrassing innocent people when intruding on their privacy is not essential to the story. This is not as easy as it sounds. The public has a right to know what is said by people who set tax rates, determine how tax revenues are spent and set government policies. People also need to know to some degree about the private lives of people running for public office or who hold other powerful positions because character is one factor in whether we want them in positions of authority. The public also has an insatiable desire to probe into the private lives of celebrities and others who have thrust themselves or have been thrust into the public spotlight.

Ethical reporters do not reveal everything they know about newsmakers. They apply John Stuart Mills' Principle of Utility and weigh the good the information might do, such as putting a human face on AIDS, against any harm it might cause.

The story of Oliver Sipple is a good example of why reporters should question what they're doing and weigh any good their stories might do against any harm they might cause.

Sipple was living in San Francisco when President Ford visited the city in September 1974. He was in the crowd watching the president pass by when Sara Jane Moore, a follower of imprisoned mass-murderer Charles Manson, pulled out a gun and aimed it at the president. Sipple tackled Moore as she fired, missing Ford by only a few feet. Sipple was an instant hero. By saving the president's life, he had thrust himself into the public spotlight, which was something he did not want. Reporters clamoring to find more about him discovered that he was gay, a fact that Sipple's family in Detroit did not know. Although Sipple begged reporters to let him keep this part of his life private, the news media reported it anyway. The Los Angeles Times story carried the headline, "Hero in Ford Shooting Active Among S.F. Gays." The revelation ruined Sipple's life. His family stopped speaking to him, and he was not allowed to attend his mother's funeral. He became an alcoholic and was found dead in his small apartment in 1979. Sipple was 37 years old.

Homosexuality was not as accepted in 1974 as it is today, and a national hero who happened to be gay helped tear down stereotypes and build acceptance of gays. When Sipple begged reporters to let him keep his privacy, however, the reporters should have listened and asked themselves if the potential harm to Sipple from invading his privacy was greater than the potential good of reporting that he was gay.

Crime stories by their very nature involve invading people's privacy. Victims, especially rape victims, often don't want to be identified because they fear being stigmatized. Most news media outlets have a policy against identifying rape victims unless the victim wants to come forward and share her story. Identifying crime suspects also invades privacy. The fact that police have identified a suspect is newsworthy. However, most people assume someone suspected of a crime is guilty, and the person remains stigmatized even after investigators shift their focus elsewhere. If a person is identified in a story as a crime suspect, the reporter should follow up on the story to report whether the suspect was charged with a crime, and if he was not charged, explain why. The story won't undo all the harm to the person, but it shows the news media are trying to act responsibly.

Reporters and their news organizations should also discuss whether to give all the facts when writing about a suicide. They should consider among other things the newsworthiness of the victim and where the suicide occurred — in a public or private location.

Jay Black, Bob Steele and Ralph Barney, in their book "Doing Ethics in Journalism," offer a checklist to help journalists determine if invasion of privacy is warranted. They recommend, in part, that reporters:

- ☑ Question the importance of the information they are seeking. Is it something the public has a right or need to know, or it is something that the public simply desires to know?

- ☑ Ask themselves if the person is involved in the news event by choice or chance and how much harm will the invasion of privacy cause. They should also ask what level of protection the person deserves. Someone, like Sipple who became the focus of the news media through happenstance, may deserve a greater degree of protection than someone who intentionally steps into the public spotlight.

- ☑ Make sure they understand the story well enough to make a sound judgment on the impact of what they're doing.

- ☑ Consider telling the story in a way that minimizes invasion of privacy, perhaps by discussing the broader issue or including more "victims" rather than focusing the story on one person's experience.

- ☑ Discuss the story's potential harm with others in the newsroom and with outside experts, such as counselors or psychologists.

- ☑ Finally, and perhaps most importantly, ask themselves how they would feel if they or a loved one were the subject of this kind of scrutiny.

DECEPTION

Reporters should be wary of using deception to get a story. They are in the business of truth telling, and lying to sources may hurt their credibility with their audiences. Readers need to trust their news media because a democratic society depends on honest reporting in order to make educated decisions. The news must be as truthful as you can present it.

Since we put such a high value on truth, when, if ever, should a reporter lie or mislead in order to get a story? Some ethicists and journalists say "never." A lie is a lie no matter whom you tell it to. They say there is always an ethical way to get the story in an honest, forthright manner.

Others argue that "never" is too strong a word. They apply Mills' Principle of Utility. They say deception should be avoided, but if the story is big enough and there is no other way to get the story, then it's OK to lie to get the story.

"Doing Ethics in Journalism" also offers a checklist to help journalists determine if deception is warranted. The authors say *all* of the following criteria must be met to justify lying or using other deception to get a story:

- ☑ The information must affect a great number of people, perhaps protecting them from harm, and be of profound importance, such as revealing government or corporate corruption, cover-ups or major failings.

☑ Attempts to gather the information without using deception have been unsuccessful.

☑ Reporters and their news organizations must be willing to tell their audiences that deception was used to obtain the information and explain why it was necessary.

☑ The news outlets must commit the resources, both time and funding, to fully pursue the story and present it in a way that demonstrates journalism excellence.

☑ Any harm caused by the deception is far outweighed by the harm prevented by providing the public with the information.

☑ Reporters and their news organizations have carefully discussed using deception and considered how the deception will affect those being deceived as well as media credibility, their reasons for wanting the story, their organizations' policies on using deception, any legal consequences from the deception, and whether their reasoning and action are consistent with previous decisions.

A reporter who used deception to gather information showing a persistent pattern of bribes to city building inspectors could use this checklist to justify the deception, while a reporter who claimed to be the relative of an accident victim to persuade a hospital floor nurse to provide a medical update could not justify his actions.

Television reporters are often tempted to use deception to get stories. TV needs images to tell the story, and news producers sometimes use hidden cameras to obtain images for consumer-related stories. Hidden cameras are often the only way to get video of wrongdoing, but producers should ask themselves before deciding to use deception if the information is of profound importance. A story showing abuse in one nursing home may not meet the criterion of profound importance, while investing the time and resources to show that abuse is pervasive among a chain of nursing homes would be of profound importance.

Exercise 1: Truth and Objectivity

Most American journalists agree that balanced, objective reporting is one of the tenets of good journalism. They believe that if they report the story about a conflict in a neutral way and as fully as possible, their audiences will be able to decide for themselves who the aggressors and victims are.

However, some war correspondents argue that by objectively covering the conflicts in Rwanda and Bosnia in the 1990s, they failed to report what was really happening.

On one side of the conflict were rumors and second-hand, unsubstantiated reports from refugees about mass killings and other atrocities. On the other side were official government sources denying these reports and explaining that the stories were actually rebel propaganda. The reporters were not allowed into the areas to see for themselves what was going on.

Some journalists argue that remaining neutral and only reporting what can be substantiated helped governments cover up their atrocities.

CNN's Christiane Amanpour has said neutrality is not acceptable in a place like Bosnia where there was a clear aggressor.

"When you are neutral, you can become an accomplice, and in these kinds of situations, you are an accomplice to the most unspeakable crimes against humanity," the Los Angeles Times quoted her as saying.

BBC correspondent Allan Little said in the same Times article that in 1995 he knew, but could not prove, that ethnic Serb forces preparing to enter the Muslim town of Srebrenica would massacre civilians. The Serb military denied the rumor, and Bosnian-Muslim sources could only speculate. Little did not share his fears with his BBC audience because he could not confirm what he believed the Serbs planned to do.

Human-rights officials now say that up 7,000 men and boys were rounded up and slaughtered in Srebrenica.

Other journalists defend the reporter's traditional neutrality. They argue that reporters who give up their neutrality also give up their credibility because their audiences will believe that they are biased.

John Buckley of The Christian Science Monitor radio agreed that reporters should not back away from reporting genocide, "but far more worrisome is the possibility that if you allow yourself to demonize one side in a dispute, then you lose credibility," he said in the Times article. "And you risk losing your audience because people say, 'Right, we've heard one side of that today. Now maybe we should hear from a journalist speaking from the other side.'"

Are there circumstances when the news media should not remain neutral in reporting conflicts, or should they always remain a disinterested party in what they report? Explain.

Why should journalists be concerned that reporting what they suspect or believe but cannot substantiate will damage their credibility? Can they take on two roles at once: one of a neutral observer and one of an analyst offering opinions about the situation?

Sen. Hiram Johnson said in 1917 that the "the first casualty when war comes is truth." Governments on both sides of a conflict use propaganda to win both international and domestic support for the war effort. How should journalists handle their government's propaganda and the other side's propaganda?

Name:	Date:

Exercise 2: Conflicts of Interest

A reporter for The Post-Star, an upstate New York newspaper, found himself in trouble in 1999 when he decided to run for the local City Council. When his editors heard that he was a candidate, they instructed him to withdraw his name from the primary ballot.

The ballots had already been printed, however, and the paper ran a story stating that the reporter was no longer a candidate. The article stated that the paper "has a written policy forbidding newsroom employees from seeking or holding elected or appointed public office."

The paper also disciplined the reporter for violating newspaper policy.

Explain the reasoning behind The Post-Star's policy against employees seeking public office. Is this a good policy? Explain.

A reporter works at his job for about 40-50 hours a week, but he is a member of his community seven days a week, 24 hours a day. Does a news outlet have the right to tell its reporters that they cannot serve their community? Why should reporters be expected to show a higher loyalty to their work than to their community?

Is there is compromise position, a Golden Mean, between The Post-Star's absolutist policy against employees seeking public office and the reporter's desire to serve his community? Explain.

Exercise 3: Privacy

Nine people from Orange County, Calif., were among the 81 passengers who died when a Singapore Airlines jetliner hit a crane on a runway in Taiwan in November 2000. The first of the victims flown back to Orange County for burial was Fuad Memon, and his funeral was covered by the local news media. The story and photos dominated the Los Angeles Times' Orange County metro cover. Two photos accompanied the story, a small photo of the flower-draped coffin and a much larger one of Memon's wife and mother-in-law weeping over his coffin.

The story begins:

> As dozens of male relatives carried his wooden casket, draped in a red, black and gold scarf, past the entrance to the Islamic cemetery in Anaheim, Fuad Memon's 33-year-old widow wailed hoarsely in her grief.
>
> "You left me, you left me," Freba Memon said over and over in her native Persian, referring to the father of her two daughters, the medical student who would soon have followed his father's and brothers' footsteps into medical practice, but for last Tuesday's fatal crash of Singapore Airlines Flight 006 in Taiwan. ...
>
> Memon wasn't scheduled to fly back from Pakistan until the following day, but he had changed his plans and ended up on the fatal flight after one of his young daughters pleaded with him to return home.

Fuad Memon's death was certainly a newsworthy event. Was his funeral also newsworthy?

Is publishing the photo of the grieving family appropriate?

Should the paper have published the reason that he was on that particular flight?

What would be appropriate coverage of a funeral?

Is Memon's ethnicity a factor in how the Times covered this story?

Exercise 4: Deception

During the Gulf War in 1991, the Pentagon established a new policy, still in effect today, that banned the news media from covering the arrival of war dead at Dover Air Force Base in Delaware. Still photographers and TV crews in previous conflicts had covered the flag-covered coffins being removed from planes as a military color guard stood attention.

Freelance journalist Jonathan Franklin wondered if the policy was changed because the military was misleading the public about the number of casualties. He tried contacting the civilian mortuary in charge of handling the bodies, the airline shipping the bodies home and the officers in charge of contacting the families; but no one would talk to him.

Franklin then decided to go on the base posing as one of the morticians. He found that casualties were four times greater than what the Pentagon reported at the time and that many of the soldiers that the Pentagon said were killed in training accidents were actually killed by "friendly" fire. His story, which included the tactics he used to get the information, was published in the Bay Guardian in San Francisco and won second place in the Project Censored annual awards sponsored by Sonoma State University in California.

Was the information Franklin sought important enough to warrant using deception? Explain.

Use the deception checklist to analyze Franklin's story and explain whether the use of deception can be justified.

Chapter 14

MEDIA LAW

This chapter:

- ☑ Describes the elements of libel
- ☑ Explains libel defenses
- ☑ Describes laws pertaining to invasion of privacy
- ☑ Explains copyright and trademark laws
- ☑ Provides descriptions of some commonly used legal terms

Chapter 13 discussed journalists' ethical standards of behavior as determined by the individuals and their professional peers. Journalists who violate those standards risk losing their jobs and the respect of others, but they most likely won't find themselves the subject of a lawsuit.

However, reporters and public relations practitioners who make false accusations and violate laws protecting privacy, copyrights and trademarks may find themselves and their employers embroiled in costly lawsuits.

Here is an overview of the aspects of media law most important to journalists.

LIBEL — defamation, explain defamation — untrue harm, cause to reputation

In the United States, the First Amendment gives reporters tremendous freedoms. However, those freedoms compete with the protection of newsmakers' reputations. U.S. Supreme Court Justice Potter Stewart said it best, "The right of a man to the protection of his own reputation from unjustified invasion and wrongful hurt reflects no more than our basic concept of the essential dignity and worth of every human being — a concept at the root of any decent system of ordered liberty."

Libel is defined as a published or broadcast defamatory statement — it caused the individual some sort of harm — that is not true.

Technically, libel is based on written defamation, whereas slander is based on spoken defamation. But the courts over the years have included broadcasters when reviewing libel cases because TV and radio also reach a mass audience.

The threat of being sued for libel is perhaps the most serious legal problem facing journalists. Legal costs to defend million-dollar lawsuits can be disastrous to a news organization. In recent years, the Libel Defense Resource Center, a New York-based organization that monitors libel cases nationally, has reported a growing number of libel suits against the mass media, each exceeding $10 million. Although appellate courts overturn nearly 85 percent of such large libel judgments, the cost of fighting these suits can run into the millions of dollars.

Although many well-publicized lawsuits are filed against media giants — including ABC, CBS, the Wall Street Journal, the Washington Post, Time magazine and The New York Times — small-market news outlets are also targets. For example, the Alton (Ill.) Telegraph filed for bankruptcy court protection after losing a $9.2 million judgment. The paper did manage to stay in business when the plaintiffs agreed to accept $1.4 million. In another case, a medium-sized newspaper in Idaho was ordered to pay $1.9 million because the paper would not tell officials who told a reporter where to locate public records about wrongdoing by an insurance company. Although the judgment was set aside by a higher court, the newspaper had spent thousands of dollars on legal expenses by that time.

When a controversial story that may damage a person or a group arises, the reporter, the reporter's editor or producer, upper-management and frequently the organization's lawyers carefully check the story to ensure that it is accurate and that it is defensible in a lawsuit. But "smaller" stories, such as routine crime coverage or a company's boardroom battles, tend to be written and line-edited with less care. That's when careless writing can result in a lawsuit.

Reporters need not be lawyers, but they do need to understand the legal principles of journalism. They must be familiar with media law so they know when danger lurks in a story and when they should consult their organization's attorney. Journalists certainly are at risk daily because they deal with disclosures about people. Many stories contain information that is negative or harmful to someone or some organization.

Elements of Libel

A libel occurs whenever the elements of libel are present. Four elements, and sometimes a fifth, are necessary for a libel to occur.

1. The statement must be defamatory — it must hurt someone's reputation.

2. The statement must identify the alleged victim by name or by some other designation that is understood by people other than the victim.

3. The statement must be communicated — published or broadcast — so that at least one person other than the alleged victim and the reporter sees or hears it.

4. In most instances an element of fault must be present — and the reporter or publisher was guilty of actual malice (that is, the news organization knew the information was false) or at least was negligent in publishing it.

5. When the victim cannot prove that the published defamation was the result of actual malice, there must be proof of damages, losses that may be compensated in money. Before the Supreme Court added this requirement, state courts presumed that damages existed without proof of any actual injury.

Defamation. Reporters always should be alert for this first element necessary for a successful libel suit. Defamation means that a false communication ridiculed or disgraced a person to the extent that the person suffered financial loss or was shunned by friends and associates. The courts have recognized a variety of statements as defamatory, dividing them into two categories:

1. Using words that clearly would hurt a person's reputation. Classic examples are words such as "prostitute," "rapist" and "murderer."

2. The words themselves are not hurtful, but the context in which they are used is. For example, the National Enquirer reported that television director Arthur Fellows was "steady dating" a famous actress. Such a statement would not be libelous except for the fact that Fellows had been happily married to someone else for years. Fellows sued but lost the case because he could not prove that he had suffered any significant financial losses.

A story may be harmful to an individual's reputation and not be defamatory. Crime stories hurt the reputation of people under arrest. The subject of the story would prefer that the story not be published, but a reporter has an obligation to report the news. Because this report is accurate and part of a public record, defamation is not present. The defamation element can be defined as injuring another's reputation without good reason or justification. If a

2 levels for defamation

Negligence - non prominent

Malice - prominent person has to prove

story erroneously reports that a local resident ran from an illegal brothel that was burning, when in fact he was in Europe on vacation, the report would be defamatory. This, combined with the other elements, likely would result in a successful libel suit against the newspaper that published the report.

Reporters must be sure of their facts, especially when a story contains information that is harmful to another's reputation. Accuracy has no substitute.

Identification. In a libel suit, a plaintiff also must prove identification. A person may be identified without using his or her name. Identification means that at least one other person who read the story was able to identify the individual by the description or circumstances provided. The classic example is the situation that led to the famous Supreme Court decision in New York Times v. Sullivan. The plaintiff was a Montgomery, Ala., city commissioner. What prompted the lawsuit was a New York Times ad alleging police misconduct against civil rights activists in the South (including Montgomery), but the ad never mentioned Sullivan either by name or as a city commissioner. He was able to convince a jury that the criticism of the conduct of the local police injured his reputation because many people knew that one of his responsibilities as a city commissioner was to oversee the police.

At times reporters want to report on an ongoing investigation but will not use any names unless arrests have been made. In such instances, vague references to possible suspects might be safe, but a reporter must be sure that even the sharpest reader is unable to identify the suspect, or, worse yet, misidentify the person and defame someone not being investigated. Once an arrest has been made and the name becomes part of the public record, it is safe to identify the suspect.

If a story is defamatory and is about an organization but does not identify the group's members, it still can be dangerous. The courts have ruled that individuals within the group may sue for libel if the group is small enough that the libel affects the reputations of individual members or if the statement does not name but refers to and defames a specific individual within the group. In short, don't expect your publication to escape a libel suit by permitting a vague identification to slip through.

Publication. The courts assume that if an item is published or broadcast, a third party will learn of it. For example, a newspaper is responsible for its content, even letters to the editor. If a story or photo caption contains a statement from an outside source, it is safe only if it is true. News organizations also may be sued for disseminating a defamatory item that first appeared in another publication or broadcast, in a wire service dispatch, or in a public speech. All the parties who disseminate the message to the public are responsible for accuracy of the content.

Fault. New York Times v. Sullivan is a landmark Supreme Court case because for the first time the court, in its 1964 ruling, differentiated between public officials and private individuals in libel lawsuits. The court ruled that public officials who sue for libel must prove actual malice, which the court defined as publishing a falsehood with knowledge of its falsity, or with reckless disregard for the truth. This is equivalent to knowingly publishing or broadcasting a lie or not caring that it is a lie.

Over the years, the court extended the actual malice rule to public figures such as sports and Hollywood celebrities and to people who are community activists or try to sway public policy. The leaders of the National Rifle Association and National Organization for Women would fall into this category. Oliver Sipple, the man described in Chapter 13 who saved President Ford's life, would also be a public figure.

So today there are two levels of fault in libel cases:

1. Public figures and public officials, who have thrust themselves or been thrust into the public spotlight, have to prove actual malice.

2. Private individuals, who are not known to the general public, have to prove negligence.

The negligence test requires reporters to carefully check the facts when working on stories that can harm someone's reputation. Use multiple sources, and make sure the information is accurate.

Libel Defenses

On test

State and federal courts have recognized three major defenses for libel: truth, privilege, and fair comment and criticism. Retraction is also a defense in many states.

Truth. The most obvious of the libel defenses is truth, which is an absolute defense in every state. Perhaps better terminology for this defense might be accuracy. Reporters rely heavily on sources who supposedly are telling the truth. If several sources say the same thing, one must assume that such agreement constitutes accurate information, or truth. One-source stories that level charges at someone may present problems in court if the source claims, and is able to document, that the accusations against the plaintiff are false.

Reporters also must be sure that if they are sued for libel, they can produce sources, either people or documents, at the trial. For example, if a reporter bases a story on a discussion with an anonymous source, the reporter must be sure that the source will testify if a libel suit is filed. If the source refuses to agree to testify, the reporter should consider holding the story until other sources are found.

Journalists who rush to print or broadcast bits and pieces of "sensational" information are flirting with danger. They must be aware that photos and video can be misleading and sources sometimes lie or exaggerate. Editors must be sure that each story and image has a solid foundation in the truth.

Crime reporting is difficult work. Good reporters sprinkle generously in their stories the words "alleged" and "suspected." Words such as these, however, might not offer much protection in a lawsuit. Journalists must remember that a person is innocent until found guilty by a court. Most crime stories are reported before and during a trial, before the judge or jury determines guilt or innocence. Remember, until a verdict is determined, someone accused of murder or crimes is a suspect, not a criminal; do not call the person a murderer or thief.

Privilege. News organizations are protected if they accurately report what is said at public governmental meetings, even if what is said at the meeting is false and defamatory. The concept of privilege comes from the U.S. Constitution, which provides an absolute privilege for congressional members involved in debates on the floor of Congress. This privilege has been extended to government officials at local, state and national levels. This allows officials to speak freely without fear of being sued for slander or libel.

The courts have extended this privilege to the news media because reporters need to be free to report what public officials are saying. Journalists have a qualified privilege to report on government proceedings and documents without fear of a libel suit provided that they produce a fair and accurate report. The qualified privilege defense may not protect a slanted report, quotes taken out of context or quotes given outside the meeting place, say in the hallway.

Qualified privilege might not apply to sealed records or non-public proceedings. If a source leaks to a reporter a sealed record or information from a closed proceeding and the information is published but turns out to be false, the court may rule that the report was not privileged. Also, some states have refused to grant privilege to court documents that have been filed and open to the public but have not yet been reviewed by a judge.

The police beat can be treacherous for a reporter. Police files may not be public records. Police frequently jot down notes that become part of a file but may never be placed in a public record. Reporters who have good relationships with law enforcement officers are permitted to review police files that may make false charges against a suspect. A story based on such a report may not be protected by the qualified privilege defense. Information about a person's arrest and booking, however, usually are privileged.

Although the qualified privilege defense provides reporters with broad protection, ethical considerations demand that reporters make every effort to determine the truth of charges made about someone in a public meeting. Government officials can be wrong and might damage a person's reputation by making false but legally protected statements. Reporters add to the problem when they quote those officials without confirming their accusations. Because of the privilege defense, the person has no recourse, but ethical journalism demands that reporters check the veracity of their sources.

Fair Comment and Criticism. The fair comment defense allows the mass media to offer opinions about public (not private) performances of people who offer their work for public approval and who voluntarily place themselves before the public. The actions of politicians, musicians, athletes, actors and others are legitimate targets for fair comment. Reviews of movies, restaurants, plays and music as well as sports commentary frequently criticize a production or team. The courts consistently have protected such expression, considering it a legitimate exercise of a free press. Fair comment is protected from libel lawsuits as long as the opinion is based on facts and is a critique of a person's public rather than private performance.

Retractions. In the rush to make deadline, reporters can easily make errors in reporting stories, and editors and producers can accidentally change the meaning of sentences or write misleading headlines. When this occurs, the paper runs a correction as soon as the error is brought to someone's attention.

In nearly two-thirds of the states, publishing a correction or retraction reduces the chances of a successful lawsuit or at least lessens the damages awarded.

PRIVACY

Most people believe that the press has no business prying into certain areas of their lives. Some things are simply no one else's business. Surveys taken during the past few years indicate growing unhappiness with the news media, and one reason is that the average person believes the media have no sense of decency when it comes to revealing personal information. People believe they have a right to be left alone.

The fact is that privacy and freedom of the press clash. On the one hand, people are eager to protect their privacy. On the other hand, journalists claim a First Amendment right to publish whatever they believe the public should know.

In 1960, legal scholar William Prosser wrote that the concept of invasion of privacy breaks down into four legal rights:

1. Intrusion on a person's seclusion or solitude, or into private affairs.

2. Public disclosure of embarrassing private facts about someone.

3. Publicity that places the person in a false light in the public eye.

4. Appropriation, for the user's advantage, of the person's name or likeness.

Courts in most states have recognized these four kinds of invasion of privacy. Reporters, producers and editors should be most concerned with the first three legal rights.

Intrusion

Reporters and photographers who go to extremes to gather news or to videotape a subject may fall victim to an intrusion lawsuit. These suits could result when a journalist intrudes into a newsmaker's physical solitude or private affairs. Snooping, eavesdropping or capitalizing on modern technology such as miniature electronic listening devices, miniature video cameras and telephoto lenses may place news gatherers on dangerous ground.

Journalists have wide latitude in gathering news, but when they overstep the bounds of good sense and decency, a court may find in favor of someone who files an invasion of privacy suit. For example, when gathering news, journalists should be aware of the legal risks in entering private property, especially private homes, even if they are accompanying police or rescue workers. Photographers in public places generally may shoot any subject within view for news purposes but not for commercial or advertising purposes. Occasional exceptions exist, but the general rule is that anything within camera range of a public place may be photographed for journalistic purposes. If the picture has even a little newsworthiness, and if no false impression is created with a misleading voice over or caption, it usually is safe.

In the past few years, however, news organizations have been sued because of journalists' newsgathering behavior — as opposed to being sued because of the content of what appears in the media. Many of these lawsuits allege not only invasion of privacy but also intentional infliction of emotional distress.

In one of the first of these newsgathering lawsuits, the court curbed media "ride-alongs" with law enforcement officials that were a popular genre of "reality" TV shows. The courts have ruled that allowing camera crews to accompany law enforcement officers into private homes, even when they have search warrants or arrest warrants, violates the Fourth Amendment protection from unreasonable searches. Media attorneys now are cautioning news organizations of the legal hazards of photographing or videotaping police activities when they accompany officers onto private property, even if the photos are never published and the video is never aired.

In recent years, the courts have shown impatience with the use of hidden cameras and secret taping. In a 1999 decision, the California Supreme Court ruled that ABC could be sued for having reporter Stacy Lescht pose as a psychic and use a hidden camera to videotape the conversations of workers who were paid to give psychic advice over the telephone. Lescht used a camera hidden in a flower on her hat and a microphone attached to her brassiere to get her story. The court found that her actions were unduly intrusive even though the story revealed the newsworthy fact that the people working for "psychic hotlines" did not always take very seriously the advice they were giving to the 900-line callers.

ABC also was slapped with a $5.5 million jury verdict for having two "Prime Time Live" staffers take jobs at the Food Lion grocery store chain in North and South Carolina. The staffers used hidden cameras to record alleged health hazards in food processing. The verdict was eventually reduced to a token $2 by a federal appellate court. However, ABC had spent at least $1 million for its legal defense.

Journalists who quote from private conversations "overheard" on Internet discussion groups without seeking permission might also be accused of intrusion. Internet chat rooms and discussion groups have become a forum for heated debate about social and political issues. The courts have not yet decided if these discussions should be treated as private, as they are in telephone conversations, or as a public forum.

Disclosure of Private Facts

Lawsuits that charge public disclosure of private facts are the most common legal action involving privacy issues. These facts usually are true, but they are painfully embarrassing and personal and generally not known by others. Most important, they are facts that are not newsworthy. In determining whether a fact is newsworthy, courts have established four criteria:

1. What is the nature of the story?

2. What is the subject of the story?

3. How intimate are the revelations?

4. What is the degree of embarrassment?

Truth plays no role as a defense in this form of invasion of privacy.

In addition to the newsworthy defense, public record plays a significant role for the mass media. Stories written from the public record usually are protected. However, although two Supreme Court decisions upheld the media's right to publish public records, several courts have allowed lawsuits for the publication of information that was in a public record. For example, an appellate court upheld a lawsuit against a newspaper that published the name of a murder witness, even though that information was in a public record in the coroner's office.

Rape Victims. While most news organizations choose not to publish the names of rape victims, the U.S. Supreme Court has said that the mass media could report the name of a rape victim if a reporter lawfully obtained the information. However, information gathered from other sources may not have the same protection.

Juvenile Offenders. Though many states prohibit publishing the names of juveniles involved in crimes, the U.S. Supreme Court has said that the First Amendment protects the publication or broadcast of juvenile names as long as the names are gathered legally. The news media have broad protection in disseminating information about private and public people. Publishing or broadcasting private information may be legal, but reporters, producers and editors must also examine the ethics of what they are doing. Many believe that children who commit crimes should be rehabilitated rather than punished and that publicizing their names stigmatizes them for life. Publication of youthful suspects' names is often determined by the child's age and the seriousness of the crime.

False Light

Sometimes a story, videotape or photograph is altered or presented in such a way that it communicates a false message to the reader. Journalists must be sure that video's voice over and photographs' captions are accurate and do not provide false information that might embarrass the people shown. News organizations are particularly sensitive to false light today because digital images are easily manipulated. They must be sure they know the circumstances in which the video or photo was taken, and they must be sure they trust the people providing the images.

False light is similar to libel in that it allows someone to sue when portrayed falsely. In an invasion-of-privacy suit, the reputation of the person portrayed falsely is not harmed but the person suffers embarrassment and humiliation. In a libel suit, the reputation of the person portrayed falsely is harmed. The key to preventing a suit in this category of privacy is accuracy.

COPYRIGHT/TRADEMARK INFRINGEMENT

Another legal issue in the mass media involves copyright, which is the ownership and control of one's creative work, including stories and photos in newspapers and on the Internet, broadcast-news programs and video footage, books, and work created for the entertainment industry. Trademarks, which are product names and logos, are also protected and must be used correctly to avoid lawsuits.

Copyright

Owners of copyrighted material have the exclusive right to reproduce the work, to create derivative works based on it, and to distribute or display the work. Anyone else who is involved in these things without permission is guilty of copyright infringement. Violating this exclusive right by reproducing someone's work without his or her consent is plagiarism, which is unethical, and, beyond that, is likely to lead to a copyright infringement lawsuit.

Copyright laws protect the style of presentation — the actual words, not the underlying factual information or ideas. News and other information cannot be copyrighted. In addition, historical or scientific information cannot be copyrighted. And ideas, processes and inventions may not be copyrighted — but may be protected by patent law.

However, journalists could not go about their jobs very well if they could not use excerpts from copyrighted works. Congress has established the Fair Use Doctrine and guidelines for determining which uses of copyrighted works are fair use. Critics reviewing books, movies and musical recordings can quote and broadcast excerpts from the works. Reporters can also quote from other news organizations or other sources, providing the quotes are not too long and are properly cited.

Trademarks

Like copyrights, trademarks are protected and must be used correctly to avoid lawsuits. Some guidelines for successful use of trademarks include:

- ☑ Make sure a trademark is capitalized or set off in distinctive type.
- ☑ Use the trademark as an adjective, followed by the generic product name (Frisbee flying disc, Kleenex tissues); or as a noun (Would you like a Coke?).
- ☑ Never use the trademark in a plural form (three Polaroid cameras, not three Polaroids).
- ☑ Never use the trademark as a verb ("Photocopy the term paper," not "Xerox the term paper").

Crimes and Legal Terms

Reporters must have knowledge of legal terms and the legal process. Just a few of the most important legal terms are explained here.

Larceny is the legal term for the wrongful taking of property. Its non-legal equivalents are stealing and theft.

A **thief** does not use threats or violence in committing a larceny, whereas a **robber** uses violence or threats in committing larceny.

A **holdup** is a robbery, even if nothing was taken from the victim. The term attempted robbery should never be used.

A **burglar** is one who makes an unauthorized entry into a building. If a burglar is caught in the act and uses a weapon, that person is a **robber**.

A **felony** is a serious crime, an offense punishable by prison or death.

A **misdemeanor** is a minor offense that carries a potential penalty of no more than a year in jail.

A **grand jury** indicts — accuses or charges.

Defendants enter formal pleas at an **arraignment**, in which the person is brought to court to answer to a criminal charge. This is different from a **preliminary hearing**, which shows probable cause that a crime has been committed and a likely suspect exists.

The person charged in court can be freed on **bail**, the security given for release of a prisoner.

Parole is a conditional release of a prisoner with an indeterminate or unexpired sentence.

Probation allows a person convicted of some offense to go free, under suspension of a sentence during good behavior and often under the supervision of an officer of the court.

A **verdict** is a finding of a jury or of a judge if a jury trial is waived.

Judges declare, but do not order, **mistrials**.

Attorneys general or similar officials give opinions, not rulings.

A defendant may be judged **not guilty by reason of insanity** but not "innocent by reason of insanity."

Statements are either written or oral (not verbal).

The correct terminology is **sheriff's deputy**, not deputy sheriff.

Narcotics are drugs, but not all drugs are narcotics.

A jury that fails to reach a verdict is a **hung jury** or is **deadlocked**.

Exercise 1: Dangerous or Safe?

Determine whether these sentences raise legal concerns or are safe to publish.

1. A Thousand Oaks mother who kidnapped her 5-year-old daughter after a court awarded custody of the child to an unrelated Van Nuys man is being held on $120,000 bail. *dangerous*

2. Nathan Collier, a 21-year-old Canoga Park man, committed suicide today. An empty gun and a note, which stated "Life is Unbearable," was found beside him. The coroner is investigating his death.

3. The district attorney charged her with blackmail, and a well-informed source told reporters she was guilty of larceny as well. *dangerous*

4. Las Vegas has become America's sin city. More prostitutes, drug lords and panhandlers walk the streets of this gambling mecca than anywhere else in the world.

5. Great news for fans of Peter O'Toole: He finally sobered up enough to begin work on another film.

6. It was revealed Thursday that the presiding judge was charged 25 years ago with drunken driving. *dangerous*

7. The Democratic nominee charged that his opponent was arrested as a peeping Tom while a teenager. *dangerous*

8. "The new film underscores my point, Jim Carrey can't act his way out of a paper bag," Tribune critic Jim Smith wrote. *safe* *safe*

9. Who could best play the role of a drunk better than actor Mark Sutter, who has more DUIs than anyone else in Hollywood?

10. The Tribune's restaurant reviewer complained, "When we finally got our food, it was unfit to give to my dog."

11. Political science professor Fred Federic today called the Democratic candidates for president "a bunch of arrogant and incompetent boobs."

12. Police said the victim, Margaret Henderson of 5151 State Road, was too intoxicated to be able to describe the assailant.

13. "We state again in this editorial that Mayor Bloomberg is a liar."

14. Police said he is wanted in California on bank robbery charges and is considered by police to be a shyster lawyer.

15. Kerr McGee is pumping some 500 acre-feet of perchlorate into the Colorado River, and no one seems to care, the California Conservation League charged today.

16. During debate on the Senate floor, U.S. Sen. Jim Marcus said his opponent was "a scam artist who is unworthy to be in this chamber."

17. Police shot and wounded Mark Smith, a 29-year-old mail worker, after he rushed toward them with a knife.

18. Eighty-year-old Laura Sortmoth was charged today with attempting to pass counterfeit $20 bills.

19. Most waitresses who work in Marie Callender's restaurants are prostitutes, he alleged.

20. "O.J. Simpson was guilty for those murders," Judge Ito told the reporter while leaving the courthouse.

Exercise 2: Manslaughter

Using the following facts, write a story for a newspaper, a television broadcast and an Internet news site.

Terry Williams, 55, of Compton, a former detective with the Los Angeles Police Department until his retirement last March after 22 years, was arrested Thursday.

He is believed to be guilty of manslaughter after his pickup truck careened into the back of a car on Sunset Boulevard near Gower Street in Hollywood.

The other car was driven by a Martha Davis, a 43-year-old Los Angeles woman.

She was killed when her automobile was pushed against a utility poll.

Williams said he was drunk when the accident occurred. He said he was sorry.

Williams retired from the force after being shot in the hip by a gang member during a shootout.

Chapter 15

WRITING FOR PUBLIC RELATIONS

This chapter:

- ☑ Describes the practice of public relations
- ☑ Reviews the basics of public relations writing
- ☑ Discusses the relationship between media and public relations
- ☑ Provides an overview of written public relations materials
- ☑ Explains how to write a news release

Not everyone who studies news writing will choose to work as a print or broadcast journalist. Some will take the skills they learn in school and apply them to other areas of the communication profession, such as public relations.

Public relations is a growing field within college and university mass communication programs. Whereas in the past, individuals entering the public relations profession did so by starting out in journalism, that has changed in the last 25 years. It is now possible to major in public relations and take specialized courses that specifically relate to professional practices in the field.

But what exactly is public relations? Some people erroneously think of it as "working with people." But there is much more to the profession than just that. Others believe that public relations practitioners are nothing more than glorified press agents who try to promote their causes no matter what the cost.

While promotion is a part of the public relations profession, today the field is much more sophisticated than it once was when publicity and promotion made up the bulk of the business. Today's public relations practitioners wear many hats. They work to build relationships with the various public groups served by their organizations. They counsel management and help strategize about the organization's future. They communicate information, both internally and externally.

Public relations practitioners may be responsible for putting on special events, responding to media inquiries, conducting research or writing news releases. They may organize fundraising activities, write feature stories or organize news conferences. The list goes on and on.

In fact, many public relations practitioners will tell you that the best part of their job is the variety — every day brings a new set of activities and challenges that allows them to hone their communication skills. And these same practitioners are likely to say that the skill most valued in the profession is the ability to write clearly and effectively.

Writing is a key component of the public relations profession. It is not possible for organizations to convey information to the various public groups they serve without knowing how to communicate this information in a clear-cut manner. On a day-to-day basis, public relations practitioners are involved in preparing a wide assortment of written materials. These include news releases, brochures, newsletters, annual reports and public service announcements, among others.

This chapter will discuss the relationship between writing for the mass media and writing for public relations and will explain how writing is used in the practice of public relations.

BASICS OF PUBLIC RELATIONS WRITING

Public relations practitioners are employed by organizations to communicate information to the various public groups that may have a vested interest in the activities of the organization. These include both external groups, such as members of the general public who use the products and services provided by the organization, as well as internal groups, such as employees who are responsible for the day-to-day operations of the company. The publics of an organization may include employees, stockholders, news media, community members, government regulators and consumers.

While the messages communicated to these different groups can vary, there is a need for these messages to be clear and easy to comprehend. This is similar to the approach used in news writing. As discussed in previous chapters, media organizations strive to inform their readers and viewers about issues by presenting the facts in a straightforward manner. Public relations practitioners may also use this fact-based approach — to inform members of the public about events and activities they are sponsoring, for example, or to keep the public up to date in the event of a crisis.

But one of the differences between writing news and writing public relations materials is that some of these materials will be written to persuade as well as to inform. Organizations may use public relations materials to promote products or generate support for causes. The writing for these types of materials may need to include more persuasive language than that used in a news story, which strives for objectivity.

Even when writing to persuade, however, it is important to be careful not to go overboard in using exaggeration and inflated statements to get a point across. This approach can have a negative effect on the public's reaction to the information an organization is trying to convey. It is also important not to engage in unethical practices when writing for public relations by making statements that are not truthful. The Public Relations Society of America, a national organization for public relations practitioners, publishes a code of ethics, that states, "We adhere to the highest standards of accuracy and truth in advancing the interests of those we represent and in communicating with the public."

RELATIONSHIP BETWEEN MEDIA AND PUBLIC RELATIONS

The media act as a liaison between organizations and the various public groups these organizations serve. By communicating information through the media, the public relations practitioners can reach a mass audience. Because the media have the ability to touch millions of people, it is to an organization's advantage to cultivate good working relationships with members of the media in order to gain access to the general public.

The relationship between journalists and public relations practitioners can sometimes be a tenuous one because of the different nature of their jobs. As mentioned above, journalists strive to be objective in their reporting, while public relations practitioners may need to be persuasive. As a result, some journalists may regard anything supplied by a public relations practitioner as biased just because of where it came from.

Despite this reservation about the potentially biased nature of the information, members of the media do regularly rely on information supplied through public relations to help them craft the stories for their newspapers and newscasts. There are issues that journalists would not be aware of if not for the public relations practitioners who bring them to the attention of the news media. It is to the advantage of both groups to try to work together in a way that will ultimately benefit the members of the public they are trying to reach.

From a public relations perspective, practitioners can accomplish this by finding out which journalists are likely to be interested in the their organizations' activities and by making an effort to develop good working relationships with journalists. This can be achieved by finding out what kind of information the journalists are interested in receiving and learning how they want to be given this information.

For example, the public relations director of a university should make the effort to find out who the education reporters are at the local news organizations, since these are the people who are liable to be interested in the activities of the university. Once this is known, the director can contact these people and find out what kinds of news items they might be interested in writing about. That way when something happens at the university, the public relations director can determine whether reporters will consider it newsworthy. The director can also find out how the reporters would like to be informed about these news items — from news releases or via phone calls or e-mails pitching the story.

Taking the time to understand the needs of reporters can enhance the working relationship between journalists and public relations practitioners and can help reduce the tension that has traditionally existed between the two groups.

WRITING PUBLIC RELATIONS MATERIALS

Public relations practitioners use a wide range of written materials to reach their various audiences. Some of these materials are written to inform, some to persuade and some to educate. A public relations practitioner needs to determine the nature of the audience that will receive the information in order to assess the best approach to use when crafting these written materials.

For example, suppose the American Cancer Society were sponsoring a walk-a-thon to raise money to find a cure for lung cancer. A public relations writer for the organization would send out a news release to the media informing them about the walk-a-thon, in the event they wanted to cover it for their news outlets. This news release would be written to inform.

The writer might also publish a brochure promoting the event to the general public and encouraging people to participate. This brochure would be written to persuade. At the same time, the public relations practitioner could write an article for the organization's newsletter, explaining the rationale for the walk-a-thon based on the number of fatalities caused by the disease. This article would be written to educate.

Here is a sampling of the different types of public relations materials organizations can generate to inform, persuade and educate various public groups about their activities:

News Releases

Organizations use news releases to announce information that may be of interest to the general public. News releases may be written to publicize new products, promote special events or encourage support for charitable causes. They can be used by organizations to announce the appointment of personnel, such as when a company hires a new CEO. Organizations may also use news releases in the aftermath of a crisis. After the World Trade Center attacks on Sept. 11, 2001, for example, both United and American airlines issued news releases to keep the public informed about how the companies were responding to the crisis since their planes and passengers were indirect targets of the attacks.

The primary end-users of news releases are the news media because, as mentioned earlier, they have access to the general public. Consequently, when organizations have news to announce, their public relations personnel prepare news releases to be distributed to the appropriate media outlets.

Because they are primarily intended for the media, news releases should be written in the same format used for news stories — in inverted pyramid style with a summary lead. This makes it easy for reporters to determine what the news is. Reporters receive dozens of news releases every day and don't have time to go through all of them in detail. It is to an organization's advantage to ensure that a news release contains newsworthy information that is easily identifiable and well written. If a journalist has to wade through the first few paragraphs of a news release to find the news, the release is liable to end up in the trash. The section at the end of this chapter will explain how to write a news release.

Video News Releases

The electronic variation on the news release is the video news release. It is a pre-produced news and image package prepared by an organization and sent to television stations to be used as part of their newscasts. Organizations may create VNRs to increase their opportunities for broadcast coverage of their products and services.

VNRs are more complex to generate than traditional news releases because they involve production as well as writing. They can also be risky to produce because acceptance of the video news release may vary from station to station. While some broadcast media outlets may incorporate portions of a VNR into a newscast or even run a package as is, some stations have policies that prohibit their use.

The average video news release is about 90 seconds long. It may be accompanied by B roll, or background footage, that can be used by stations that want to develop their own news segments based on information contained in the VNR.

Brochures

Organizations use brochures for many purposes — to inform, persuade or educate, and, in some cases, to accomplish a combination of the three. A brochure could include a concise overview of a product or service. It might be used to promote a cause or to motivate people to take action on an issue.

A cultural organization such as the Art Institute of Chicago, for example, would be likely to produce a brochure that gives an overview of the highlights of its collection and includes information about membership, hours of operation and cost of admission. A company like the Nike Corp. might use a brochure to introduce a new running shoe and to promote the features of the product. An activist organization such as Greenpeace could use a brochure to educate the public about the plight of the whales.

A typical brochure consists of a sheet of paper divided into sections or panels and folded several times for ease of handling. Most brochures usually include a combination of copy, photographs and attention-grabbing headlines and subheads. The art of producing a successful brochure is to include the right blend of copy and graphics in order to encourage readers to pay attention to the message conveyed within the publication.

Newsletters/Magazines

Many companies publish newsletters or magazines aimed at their various target publics. These publications use a combination of news and feature stories to keep readers informed about what's going on within an organization.

Some of these publications are intended as a means of internal communication to keep employees apprised of organizational changes, update them on personnel-related issues or help foster a sense of community among company workers. Others focus on external publics such as shareholders, association members or residents of the local community.

The Southern California division of the American Automobile Association, for example, publishes a bimonthly magazine for its members called Westways. The magazine not only keeps members updated on the organization's products, services and legislative activities, it also includes travel articles and features about restaurants and places of interest in the Southern California area. The National Communication Association publishes a newsletter for members called Spectra that features information about upcoming conferences and job openings. Many universities publish alumni newsletters and magazines to keep their graduates updated about school activities and to encourage them to donate to their alma maters.

Today, many organizations publish electronic versions of their newsletters or magazines instead of — or sometimes in addition to — the print versions. Users can access these publications through organizational Web sites. In the case of employee publications, these electronic newsletters may be accessed through a corporate intranet, which is an internal version of the Web available only to the company's employees.

Annual Reports

Annual reports offer a capsulized overview of a company's activities for the year. On the corporate level, they are of interest to stockholders who have invested money in the organization. On the nonprofit level, they are valuable to donors who support the organization and want to know how their dollars have been spent.

An annual report usually includes a message from the CEO or director of the organization. It may include descriptions of programs and activities the company has engaged in over the year, as well as projections for the upcoming year. The bulk of the report consists of detailed financial information about the organization's profits and losses, or, in the case of a nonprofit organization, an accounting of how grants and donations have been applied to organizational programs.

Annual reports are important documents for organizations, and their construction entails extensive research and attention to detail. They require a public relations writer to process complex financial information and translate it into easy-to-understand copy that will help readers grasp the fiscal activities of the organization.

Public Service Announcements

For-profit companies frequently use paid radio and television advertisements to promote their products and services. Nonprofit organizations don't have the same resources as their for-profit counterparts and instead rely on unpaid public service announcements to communicate information about their causes over the airwaves.

Public service announcements, or PSAs, are short broadcast pieces put together in a manner similar to that of commercials. They are usually written as 15- or 30-second spots and sent to TV and radio stations to be aired on a space-available basis.

Many PSAs are designed to communicate messages about health and safety concerns. They may offer advice to parents on how to talk to their children about drug use or point out the importance of wearing a seatbelt when driving. Public service announcements can be used to educate listeners and viewers about social issues such as homelessness or teen pregnancy.

Radio PSAs are usually written in script format. A television PSA may be produced in video format with appropriate sound and images and submitted to a station as a package, similar to a video news release. Because PSAs are meant to be heard or watched, they should be written in a conversational manner and should adhere to the guidelines of effective broadcast writing.

While a commercial is assured on-air exposure because it has been paid for, there is no guarantee that a public service announcement will air at all. It is up to the discretion of the station manager to determine whether there is room for it. This may depend on the number of public service announcements received, the quality of the PSAs and the amount of airtime available. Public services announcements are often aired late at night when they are not competing with paid commercial time.

Web Sites

In recent years, Web sites have become invaluable tools for organizations, as they offer a means to display information that can be easily accessed by the public. An organizational Web site is ideal for publishing information about a company's history, products and services, employment opportunities, etc. Some Web sites even include a "newsroom" section specifically designed for easy access by the media. Here an organization can post news releases, copies of the annual report, and other items that could be of use to reporters.

Some corporate Web sites are quite elaborate and designed to be interactive in order to draw in visitors and keep them actively engaged on the site. The Ben & Jerry's Web site, for example, contains ice cream recipes, online games and electronic greeting cards, while the Disneyland Web site shows users an illustrated map of the theme park and allows people to purchase their tickets online.

While the design and maintenance of an organizational Web site may be handled by a computer technician, responsibility for the copy is likely to fall to the organization's public relations specialist. In addition to coming up with a concept for the site, this person will be in charge of ensuring that information is kept up to date and that it is consistent with other organizational materials such as brochures and newsletter articles.

Writing an Effective News Release

As explained in the previous section, the news release is the primary public relations tool that organizations use to communicate information to the media. Because of this, a public relations practitioner needs to know how to craft a news release in a way that increases its chances of being read by reporters. The key is to write the news release in a format that reporters instantly recognize — inverted pyramid style with a summary lead.

In addition to the summary lead, there are several other elements that typically make up the basic framework of a news release. The body of the release following the lead will generally include some follow-up factual information, as well as quotes from personnel at the organization who may be relevant to the news item. This is similar to the makeup of a news story, which would also contain facts and quotes. A news release should also include some brief background information about the organization, the name of a contact person and the date the information can be released to the public.

Here's an example of a typical news release that adheres to the criteria outlined above.

Carlsbad College
16 Academy Road, Chilton, Ill. 60634
(413) 337-4900
www.carlsbad.edu

Contact: Jonathan Sparks
(413) 337-4978
jsparks@carlsbad.edu

February 15, 2004

FOR IMMEDIATE RELEASE

Carlsbad College to Sponsor Women and Media Panel

The top of the news release should identify the organization issuing it. This identifying slug should include the organization's name, address, phone number, and e-mail or Web site address.

The name of a contact person from the organization should also be included near the top of the release. This contact is usually the person who wrote the news release and who can answer any questions reporters might have about the information contained within it.

The first dateline shows the date when the information is being distributed to the media. This helps reporters keep track of when they receive news releases from various organizations.

A second dateline indicates the date the media can release information to the public. This may not be the same as the date the news release is distributed to the media.

For example, a company may send a news release to a newspaper in mid-April to announce a new product that will make its debut on May 1. The company may not want the news announced to the public until the day the product is officially unveiled. In that case, the release tagline would say: For release on May 1, 2004.

If the organization wants the media to make the information available to the public as soon as they receive the news release, the second dateline should say "For Immediate Release," as illustrated in the example provided.

A brief headline should give an overview of the news contained in the release. This headline should be similar to the kind that might be used to introduce a news story.

Three veteran journalists will discuss the role of women and media at a panel discussion called, "Women in Communications: How Far Have We Come?" The session will be held in Lionel Auditorium at Carlsbad College on Saturday, March 6, at 1 p.m. The presentation is the kick-off event for the school's celebration of National Women's History Month.

Susan Clarkson, Dana Perry and Janice Hunt will discuss their experiences working in the media. Clarkson is a 30-year veteran of the Chicago Tribune and was one of the first female sports reporters for the paper. Perry has worked in television for 20 years and was a correspondent for CNN during the Gulf War. Hunt is a producer with CBS News in New York, where she has worked since 1974.

"We're very honored to have such a prestigious corps of women on campus to share their experiences with students," said Carlsbad President Candace Blake. "Many of these women have opened doors for today's women in media."

The panel discussion launches a month-long roster of activities celebrating National Women's History Month. Additional events will feature presentations by author Amy Tan and astronaut Sally Ride, as well as the campus premiere of "The Heidi Chronicles" by playwright Wendy Wasserstein.

Carlsbad College is a small liberal arts college founded in 1906. The school has approximately 1,000 undergraduate and 200 graduate students. Carlsbad launched the country's first women's history program in 1974.

The opening paragraph of the news release should be written in inverted pyramid style with a summary news lead. This makes it easy for reporters to identify what the news is. In the example provided, the 5Ws and H are all compactly addressed in the lead paragraph of the news release from Carlsbad College just as they would be in a news story.

Following the opening, the body of the news release will contain additional facts that build upon the summary news lead. In the example provided, the lead explains that three journalists will talk about women and media during a panel discussion at Carlsbad College. A follow-up paragraph identifies the women and explains their qualifications for speaking on this panel.

The body of the news release may also include quotes from individuals affiliated with the organization announcing the news. In this case, the news release contains a quote from the college president. A reporter then has the option of using the quote provided or of contacting the quoted individual directly to obtain additional information and quotations for a story.

The body of this news release includes information about upcoming activities scheduled at Carlsbad College during National Women's History Month. An enterprising reporter interested in covering future school activities can contact the person listed at the top of the release to find out details about these activities for a future story.

The end of a news release will usually include a brief description of the organization issuing the release. This description should only be a few sentences long and should give some background information about the organization. This is particularly important to organizations that may not be widely known to members of the media. In the example provided, information about Carlsbad College includes a sentence about the school having the first women's history program in the country. This tidbit of information might be of interest to reporters since it could be connected to the school's practice of celebrating National Women's History Month.

Admission to the women and media session is free. For additional information, call (413) 337-4976, or check the Web site at www.carlsbad.edu/womenandmedia.

The final paragraph of the news release should include a phone number, e-mail address or Web site address that can be provided to the general public in the event that they want more information about the news item. This phone number or e-mail address will probably be different from that of the contact person listed at the top of the release unless the person who wrote the release is also responsible for the activity being announced.

Exercise 1: Promoting Your School

Visit the Web site of your college or university. Choose five items found on the site that you consider to be newsworthy. Then write a short explanation of why you think these are worth writing about and how you would promote them to the media and/or the general public.

Exercise 2: Writing News Releases

Write a news release using the following information:

The Carson Recreation Center will offer a water safety instruction class for college students.

The class will meet for 10 weeks, starting Sept. 18.

A certified water safety instructor will teach the course.

College students who are at least 18-years-old will be eligible to participate in the class. Previous swimming experience is required.

Participants will receive a certificate of completion at the end of the course.

The Carson Recreation Center has been offering physical fitness and recreational activities to members of the local community for the last 20 years. The Center is located in downtown Carson.

The address is 5405 Tremont St., Carson, NJ, 80745. The phone number is (619) 445-0897.

The cost of the course is $60.

The director of the Center is Carl Butler. He said, "We have always offered swimming classes, but this is the first time we've offered a water safety instruction class. Students who complete this course will be eligible to work as lifeguards, which will expand their options for summer jobs."

The class will meet at the Center on Saturdays, from 9 a.m.- noon.

Exercise 3: Writing News Releases

Write a news release using the following information:

The Screen Actors Guild Museum will sponsor an exhibit called, "The Art of the Movie Poster." The exhibit will feature vintage movie posters from well-known Hollywood productions.

The exhibit will include 200 posters from such classic films as "Casablanca," "An Affair to Remember" and "It Happened One Night."

The museum is located at 1654 Vine St. in Los Angeles. The phone number is (213) 442 8195, and the Web site is www.sagmuseum.com.

The exhibit will run from Nov. 1 until March 31.

An opening wine and cheese reception will kick off the exhibit on Nov. 1. The time of the reception is 6 p.m.

The museum is open Monday-Saturday, 10-6 p.m. It is closed on Sundays.

The Screen Actors Guild Museum was founded in 1982 by actor Jimmy Stewart. It features changing exhibitions related to the movies and to those who are affiliated with the film industry.

Most of the posters are on loan from private collectors throughout the world.

Some of the posters were donated by stars who appeared in the movies they represent. For example, Julie Andrews donated a poster from "The Sound of Music."

Admission to the exhibit is $4 for adults, $2 for seniors and children under 12.

Carol Samson is the exhibit curator. She said, "It has taken nearly two years to organize the exhibit because there are so many pieces involved. We are grateful to the many collectors who have graciously agreed to let us use their posters in the show."

Exercise 4: Preparing a Brochure

Prepare a brochure about the vintage poster exhibit from the previous exercise. The goal of the brochure is to inform members of the public about the exhibit and to encourage them to attend. Make an outline of what you would include in the brochure, and explain how you would craft the brochure in a way that would make it persuasive as well as informative.

Exercise 5: Writing Feature Stories

You have also been asked to write a short feature story about the exhibit for the Screen Actors Guild newsletter. The readers of this newsletter are patrons of the museum and donors who contribute to the organization.

Based on what you know about the exhibit, make an outline of what you would like to include in this newsletter article that is likely to be of interest to the publication's audience. List information that you already have, as well as any information you don't have that might be needed to complete the article. Then make a list of the resources you will need to consult to gather this additional information.

Exercise 6: Critiquing Web Sites

Visit the Web site of your favorite music or clothing company. Critique the site from a public relations perspective to determine how well it promotes the organization it represents. Use the following criteria as a guide:

- ☑ What kind of information is contained on the Web site?

- ☑ Is it easy to find information about products or services? Why or why not?

- ☑ Does the site contain news and information aimed specifically at the media? If so, explain what this includes.

- ☑ Does the Web site contain any interactive components? If so, what are they?

- ☑ What do they add to the effectiveness of the site?

- ☑ When was the site last updated?

- ☑ What information might you add to make the site more valuable to Web users?

·················· Chapter 16 ··

WRITING FOR ADVERTISING

This chapter:

☑ Explains the purpose of advertising in the mass media

☑ Discusses jobs in the advertising industry

☑ Describes advertising strategies

☑ Explains the basics of writing advertising for various media

After sharpening their writing skills in college courses, some students find they would like to pursue an area in the communication field that allows them to use their imagination and creativity. The area that offers the biggest challenge, and the biggest reward, to creative writers is advertising.

Advertising has been a highly visible part of the American culture since it became a vital part of mass media in the 19th century. Today, as advertisers face tough new challenges from ad clutter and new media technologies such as satellite radio and premium television channels that eliminate advertising, there is a great deal of opportunity in the field for people with fresh ideas and creative ways to express them.

WHAT IS ADVERTISING?

One of the most important characteristics to remember about advertising is that it is a paid message. Unlike the information generated by news or public relations writers, advertising appears in the mass media because the advertiser has paid for its space in print and online media or its time in broadcast media.

The other important characteristic that makes advertising different from news and public relations is that it is almost always persuasive in nature. Advertisers spend millions of dollars yearly to plan, produce and disseminate persuasive messages about their products or services. While advertising does give the consumer information, it is designed to meet a communication objective — to make the consumer aware or increase awareness of a product or service, or to make the consumer aware of a product's benefits.

A variation of advertising are public service announcements, which are persuasive messages for a charity or non-profit organization. The news media run the ads for free as a public service as space and time allows.

WORKING IN ADVERTISING

Many people think of advertising as a glamorous job environment where people earn big salaries, have power lunches with celebrities and produce million-dollar Super Bowl commercials. While successful advertising copywriters are very well paid, do sometimes work with celebrities and may even eventually work on a Super Bowl commercials, more often they labor under tight deadlines and work hard to keep their advertising ideas and copy creative while achieving communication objectives.

Advertising copywriters can work at advertising agencies, as freelancers, or within the advertising department at a company. A good working knowledge of advertising copywriting is necessary for anyone working in advertising, as people are often called upon to evaluate advertising copy someone else has written.

Copywriters at an advertising agency are part of the creative department, usually working under a creative director. While agency structures can vary, in larger agencies an advertising copywriter works with an art director in what is called a "creative team."

Copywriters and art directors work together to develop ideas and concepts that creatively express the criteria set by the advertising strategy or creative platform. This is not to say that copywriters always do words and art directors only do visuals. Often, a copywriter comes up with an idea for just the right visual or an art director suggests the perfect headline. Both people learn to think of the words and visuals interchangeably. Those colorful animated figures or chatty sports celebrities or the carefully choreographed musical numbers don't just happen. They are carefully researched, carefully developed and painstakingly produced to persuade.

Once the creative team has come up with several ideas, or concepts, they like, they take them to the creative director for evaluation. Very few ideas make it all the way from conception to a fully produced television commercial or magazine ad.

While advertising copywriters spend much of their time writing ads, they also write other marketing communication materials, some of which are quite creative and some which are simply informational. Other types of writing include copy for brochures, for packaging, for point-of-purchase displays, for tags on products and even for small one-page "stuffers" included in grocery bags or with monthly bills.

WRITING "ON STRATEGY"

Before discussing advertising writing, it is important to briefly discuss creative strategy. While strategic thinking is important in all aspects of business, it is absolutely vital in planning and executing successful marketing, advertising and advertising copy.

A company's creative strategy comes out of its advertising strategy, which in turn comes out of its marketing strategy. The creative strategy is the document that tells creative people what to be creative about — whether to emphasize a product benefit or a consumer benefit, whether the product is new or is being introduced to a new target audience, whether the product or service has been changed or improved, and whether the advertiser wants consumers to switch brands or repeat purchase.

The creative strategy is the "thinking" part of advertising writing. You could say it gets to the "reason why" of the copy. Think of it as a roadmap to keep everyone on the creative team moving in the same direction toward the same destination. The creative strategy keys on the elements that have been determined to emphasize and reinforce the brand. All elements of the creative strategy are based on marketing research. Most importantly, the document has been reviewed and approved by management at all levels, so creatives are not working in the dark.

The format of a creative strategy differs from one ad agency or company to another. In fact, the creative strategy may even be called something different — perhaps a creative platform or a creative brief. While strategy formats are seldom the same, all usually have several components in common:

- ☑ One concise strategy statement about all the other components
- ☑ Communication objectives tied to the company's overall marketing and advertising objectives
- ☑ Target audience(s)
- ☑ Characteristics of the brand
- ☑ Benefit(s) to consumers
- ☑ Tone of advertising

Once the creative strategy is refined and approved, the creative team begins generating ideas, concepts and advertising copy.

BASICS OF ADVERTISING WRITING

While advertising writing is often very creative, it must also adhere to rules — some very rigid, others not so. First, advertising copy must be correct. If claims are made, they must be backed up because regulatory agencies make sure that advertisers' claims are legitimate. The Federal Trade Commission is empowered to regulate deceptive advertising. Under the 1971 advertising substantiation program, advertisers are required to make documented evidence available to consumers to support any claims they make about their products.

The other reason to avoid misleading or false claims in advertising writing is that the advertiser loses credibility. The steady stream of corporate scandals in the last few years makes credibility more important than ever. Once credibility is lost, it is almost impossible to regain. Also, today's consumers are extremely sophisticated, intelligent and have access to almost unlimited information. They are hard to fool, quick to question and slow to forgive deception.

Another rule that should never be broken is that good advertising copy must always attract attention. In today's media-rich environment, people are bombarded with thousands of advertising messages as they go about their busy daily routines. Thus most advertising messages are lost in a sea of ad clutter. Creative advertising copy, along with the right visual, breaks through the clutter and attracts attention. If it doesn't, it fails.

In regard to advertising writing, attracting attention to the ad is its most important component. It is in these first few seconds that the writer must attract consumers and pull them into the ad. In a print ad, the headline and/or the visual must grab attention. In a radio or television commercial, it is the first sound or word or visual that does it. In a brochure, it is the cover. In a direct mail piece, it is the phrase or words on the outside of the mailer. On a Web site, it is the color and composition of the site itself.

Ad creators have many ways to attract attention, and currently one of the most popular is the use of sex, particularly for ads tailored to target an audience like college students. Look through the current issue of Cosmopolitan or Maxim or tune to MTV or listen to radio shock jock Howard Stern to see how sex is used to attract attention and sell products such as perfume, clothing, grooming products and automobiles.

Another way to attract attention is the use of powerful visuals. These do not necessarily have to express a sexual theme to be successful, but they are extremely important to reach younger audiences who are accustomed to receiving information via visual images. These are people who spend much of their leisure time playing video games or sitting in front of television screens, computer screens or wide screens at the multiplex. They have short attention spans and are accustomed to large-scale action.

The challenge for advertising writers is to put the right words, no matter how many or how few, with the right visuals to capture attention and draw the consumer into the ad.

Other successful attention-getting devices include very specific offers of discounts, special promotions or special features as well as dramatic references to or demonstrations of the product's benefits. Writers must look to the creative strategy to determine what the target audience is like and whether the ad describing the product's benefits or service matches the target audience's needs.

The fact that the target audience may be in a very different demographic group than the advertising writer points to one important factor for beginning copywriters. The successful copywriter learns to think outside himself or herself, to experience what it's like to be in other people's shoes. Writing assignments, particularly for beginning copywriters, may be ad copy for dentures, baby powder, retirement plans or life insurance. The challenge is to be creative, stay "on strategy," attract the attention of the target audience and stress the benefits of the product or service.

All good advertising copy stresses benefits. One of the questions advertising writers constantly ask when they put themselves in the place of their target audience is, "What's in it for me?" The creative strategy tells writers which benefits to stress. Then the writer must stress that benefit or benefits in such a way that the target audience clearly sees how the product will help them.

In writing benefit-driven copy, advertising writers focus on the target audience, not the product or service they're writing about. Good ad copy is about benefits, not features. It speaks directly and clearly to the audience member and what he or she wants, dreams of, hopes for or fears. The product or service is then offered to solve the problem or meet the need.

Another flexible rule for advertising copy is that it always includes a call to action. This is where writers tell the target audience what they want it to do — dial a telephone number, go to a retail outlet, fill out and mail the coupon, redeem the coupon, or go to a Web site. Traditional ad copy experts maintain that readers, viewers or listeners do not perform the action you want them to unless you tell them to.

The reason this rule is flexible is because many of today's ads carry a minimum amount of advertising copy. Often a toll-free number and a Web site are simply included in the ad with no formal call to action.

Regardless of whether the call to action is included in the ad copy, ads should always include information — even if it's very small and at the bottom of the ad — on how consumers can obtain more information about the product or service, and find out how to buy it and where to buy it. The ad will not be successful if consumers can't act on the information given them.

Another unbreakable rule for advertising writing is that it should always be in the present tense and it should include active, not passive, verbs. Something that happened in the past or will happen in the future is not "real," or timely, and passive forms of verbs simply do not convey the excitement or interest advertising copy must generate.

Those rules lead to the last rule — write, rewrite and rewrite. Then get out the red pencil and edit, edit, edit. That is the secret of lean, tight, to-the-point copy. Good copywriters should have one of Mark Twain's best quotations hanging in their offices: "Eliminate every third word. It gives writing remarkable vigor."

BREAKING THE RULES

It has been said that you must know the rules before you can break them. This is particularly true for advertising writing. The rules an advertising copywriter must know and abide by are those for correct punctuation, spelling and grammar. These are never broken. Rules for sentence construction, however, are often violated in advertising copy.

Why are these rules broken? Because advertising copy is written in a conversational style, that is, written as if the writer is speaking to the receiver personally. That means sentence fragments are often used in advertising copy because that is the way people actually speak to each other. Single words are also used in advertising copy.

The focus in advertising copy, both for print and electronic media, is a smooth flow between concise and easy-to-understand ideas. The writer must use short, simple words, constructed into short simple sentences. Also, avoid slang or jargon unless the ad is directed to a very specific audience; people who are unfamiliar with the terminology will become confused and miss the point. Sexist terminology should always be avoided.

An advertising writer must remember that the person viewing or hearing the ad may be talking to someone, driving on a busy street or engaging in a host of other distractions. People seldom fully "attend" advertising messages. At best they glance at them and give full attention only if they are attracted by something in the ad.

A last rule for good advertising writing is to be specific and avoid superlatives. People are exposed to thousands of advertising messages daily and do not see or hear generalities or unsubstantiated superlatives. The product may be "new and improved" but a good advertising writer will find a better way of saying so. The product may be convenient or good-tasting, but chances are so is the competition. As for superlatives, the biggest, greatest, newest or best may be just that, but the consumer has heard it all before and it is generally meaningless.

The basics of advertising writing discussed above apply to all advertising. There are, however, some rules that apply to writing for specific media.

WRITING FOR PRINT

In coming up with an idea for a print ad, advertising writers generally think of the components of the print ad and how they may or may not be used. These components consist of:

☑ Headline — almost always used

☑ Visual — may or may not be used

☑ Subhead — may or may not be used

☑ Body copy — may or may not be used

Headlines

The importance of the headline in a print ad cannot be overstated. Perhaps advertising pioneer David Ogilvy said it best in "Confessions of an Advertising Man": "On average, five times as many people read the headline as read the body copy. When you have written your headline, you have spent 80 cents out of your dollar. If you haven't done some selling in your headline, you have wasted 80 percent of your client's money."

A hard-working creative director, whose name is now lost in history, said of the headline, "If you have five days to write an ad, spend four of them on the headline."

That should be enough to make a beginning advertising writer understand the value of the headline in a print ad. It acts as the attention-grabber, the vehicle for drawing the reader into the ad and, if possible, communicates the product's benefit.

Traditional copy experts say the headline should not be more than seven or eight words and should include the brand or product name, but these rules are often ignored today in favor of keeping headlines edgy, interesting and powerful.

There are numerous types of headlines but no specific rule as to which to use when. Some ads consist entirely of a headline, with no supporting body copy. That is possible but usually requires a very clever headline and often accompanied by a very powerful visual.

Another type of headline is the news headline, which gives the reader news about the brand. This headline may also stand alone — that is, without copy, if it accomplishes the objective.

In testimonial ads, the headline, enclosed in quotation marks, does the selling and draws the attention. By using the quote from a customer, celebrity or trusted expert, the headline emphasizes the power of first-hand experience.

A headline that emphasizes the benefit or claim the writer wishes to emphasize can also be very effective by putting the emphasis right where it belongs.

Headlines can also emphasize many other elements: the brand itself, the tone of the advertising (emotional, fun, serious) or the audience to whom it is directed.

Assuming the ad has a powerful visual, what is called the "head-viz match" is critical to the ad's success. By making sure the headline matches the visual, each element reinforces the other, and they work together to make a powerful sales pitch. This is the equivalent of saying the sum is greater than the parts. When the visual and the headline do not match, the consumer is confused and likely will simply flip the page or move on to other parts of the publication.

The headline should always be in the same typeface as the ad. This serves as a form of continuity between the elements as well as giving the ad a clean, flowing appearance.

Subheads

The subhead almost always appears just before or after the headline. It serves to reinforce or elaborate on the headline and should also draw the reader into reading the body copy. The subhead should be in the same typeface as the headline, but smaller in size.

Most copywriters and creative directors do not use subheads extensively. The general feeling is that a good headline and a good visual should do the job. A general rule of thumb is that an ad with long body copy should use a subhead or subheads to draw the reader into the body copy and guide the eye through long copy.

Body Copy

In today's fast-paced, visually dominated, short-attention-span world, many creatives put less and less emphasis on body copy. They say a writer cannot assume readers will take the time to read several paragraphs of copy to get the message being communicated.

While that may be true, there is still a place for body copy, and every advertising writer must be adept at crafting good body copy. A "copy-heavy" ad is usually an ad for a highly specialized or very expensive product, service or point of view. People about to invest thousands of dollars on a new car, new computer or retirement plan want to know more about the product being advertised. That is where good writing and smart strategy achieve objectives.

No matter how clever or interesting body copy is, it will not be successful unless it is "on strategy." It also must complete the thought expressed in the headline and reinforce the key element being emphasized, whether it's the benefit or the brand.

There are several rules for writing good body copy. As stated earlier, the writer must speak to the reader in a friendly, conversational tone, and that means present tense; active verbs; and short, simple, familiar words and phrases (the sentence fragments referred to previously). Long body copy should also be written in sentences and paragraphs of varying length, often broken up by short subheads. Avoid the clichés and superlatives that call copy's credibility into question. Most importantly, be sure any claims can be substantiated and documented.

Graphic or typographic techniques can help emphasize words or phrases or to separate thoughts. Use bullets, lists, underlining, boldface, italics, capital letters, arrows, boxes, borders or color to draw readers' attention to specific points. Art directors will want to use these sparingly, as they can make the ad too "busy" and distracting to the eye; however, they can be quite useful in conveying large amounts of information to readers.

Here's the copy and description of the visual elements for a print advertisement for a hypothetical product, Yummy peanut butter:

> VISUAL: Yummy peanut butter jar full of peanuts, with peanuts overflowing and scattered around the jar
>
> HEADLINE: Go ahead and count 'em.
>
> SUBHEAD: You'll find there's still 463 peanuts inside every jar of Yummy peanut butter.
>
> COPY: That's why Yummy peanut butter tastes so good. Every bite is bursting with the peanutty taste of fresh peanuts. Lots of fresh peanuts.
>
> And isn't that why you love peanut butter?
>
> The ad would have a logo for Yummy Peanut Butter accompanied by text stating, "Why you love peanut butter."

WRITING FOR ELECTRONIC MEDIA

Many copywriters contend that writing for radio and television is the most disciplined writing in advertising because the writer has 10 seconds, 20 seconds, 30 seconds or 60 seconds to do it all and say it all — to attract attention, communicate the benefit or expression of the brand and close with a call to action.

The other challenge of electronic media advertising is that it is fleeting, that is, it is gone at the end of its allotted time. There is no opportunity for the listener or viewer to go back and listen or look at it again, as there is in print advertising. Listeners and viewers have to "get it" in a memorable way or the ad is not successful.

The above considerations are primarily the reason early electronic ads contained so much repetition. While some copy experts feel repetition is still necessary, it is seldom employed today, and if it is it generally comes in a cleverly disguised form.

Whether writing for radio or television or both, a good copywriter keeps in mind the advantages and limitations of both and writes to the strengths of the medium.

Radio

Radio has been called the "theater of the mind," and while it often takes a backseat to television, it can be extremely creative and effective, especially for an advertising campaign with a limited budget. While a buffalo stampede or a jetliner taking off may be too big-budget for a television commercial, either is very easy to create for radio, where a writer creates visuals with sound.

Radio copywriters must always remember they are writing for the ear not the eye on radio. For that reason, copy must be short, simple and easy to understand. Do not use long, compound sentences with dependent phrases or clauses or multi-syllable words.

Just as in print copywriting, think of the elements available and how best to use them: words, sound effects, music and silence.

The last element, silence, is the equivalent of white space in a print ad. It can make all the other elements more interesting and emphatic. It can add drama, build suspense or help emphasize a key point. A good copywriter learns to use silence as effectively as words, sound effects and music.

Radio has several formats for ads, with the most common being the dialogue, the announcement and the musical. The dialogue is generally a scenario played out with characters making key points through conversation with each other. This format may or may not utilize an announcer at the end to emphasize a selling point.

The announcement format is just what it says it is — a straightforward announcement about the product or service. The announcer may be a professional announcer, a celebrity or even a customer giving a testimonial.

The musical format centers primarily on a jingle or song produced to attract attention and convey information about the product or service in a memorable way. Jingles are produced in different formats to accommodate different variations of radio commercials: a "full sing" is a 30-second singing version of the jingle; and the "donut" is with singing at the opening, a musical "bed" in the center for copy to go over, and a musical close. A "tag" has a musical bed in the center and a singing close of about five to 10 seconds. Jingles are produced to 10-second, 20-second, 30-second and 60-second versions to maximize their use.

A 10-second ad has 20 to 25 words; a 20-second has 40 to 45 words; a 30-second has 60 to 65 words; and a 60-second has 120 to 125 words.

Here's a 30-second radio ad for Yummy peanut butter:

> SOUND EFFECT: peanuts dropping into empty jar
> CHILD: (speaking slowly) One... two....
> Announcer: Big, plump fresh peanuts.
> CHILD: (speaking slowly) Fifty-four...
> ANNOUNCER: They come in a jar y'know. A Yummy peanut butter jar.
> Child: (speaking slowly) One hundred fifty...
> ANNOUNCER: There are 463 peanuts in every jar of Yummy peanut butter. That's why it tastes so good.
> CHILD: (speaking slowly) Three hundred...
> ANNOUNCER: And isn't that why you love peanut butter?
> CHILD: (with finality) Four hundred sixty three!
> ANNOUNCER: Yummy peanut butter. Four hundred sixty three fresh peanuts in every jar.

Television

To say television is pervasive in our society is to understate the obvious. It has been said that the average pre-schooler in America sees over 5,000 TV ads before learning to read. Volumes have been written about the social and cultural aspects of television advertising in Western society.

Writing ad copy for television has many rules that are constantly violated, some for good reasons, some not. A good rule for a television copywriter to remember is "less is more;" that is, using the medium's inherent capability of visuals and sound to its fullest may call for fewer words and more action.

One rule that should never be violated, however, is the rule of clarity in television advertising. In television, the writing must be clear; the message must be delivered visually and orally. A commercial must gain attention, persuade and be memorable, all while the viewer is talking to a friend, going to the bathroom, getting a snack or channel-surfing.

Despite viewer distractions, writers should remember that their job is to sell the product or service first and entertain the viewer second. If the viewer is entertained while being sold, that's great, but only products with a long, well-established brand identification can afford to entertain viewers instead of selling them.

Television advertising must fully utilize the visual aspects of the medium to re-emphasize the brand image or personality. Take full advantage of this opportunity for continuity of the brand itself.

Keep words to a minimum unless the format of the commercial demands lengthy dialogue or announcements. People watch visuals, movement, color, interesting people and interactions; they don't necessarily sit and listen to all the words. Be sure the message is presented visually, with words to accentuate or reinforce key elements of the message.

Formats for television commercials vary. Some of the most common are giving a demonstration, using a spokesperson or announcer, showing a problem and demonstrating how the product will solve that problem, and storytelling/slice of life.

Demonstration. This format is the most obvious for television, since the writer can show a product or service in use. Copy in this type of format is usually straightforward, but that doesn't mean it can't be dramatic or humorous. Showing a product being used can be a powerful, persuasive message.

Spokesperson/Announcer. The spokesperson/announcer format, as would be expected, is heavier on copy. The speaker may be a celebrity, a well-known personality heavily identified with a brand or an average person. The announcer is also used in this format, usually for products such as automobiles or pain relievers. While the personality of the speaker carries a lot of emphasis, words are crucial in this format, particularly for an announcer.

Problem/Solution. This format is a specialized kind of demonstration format, where television is used fully to emphasize benefits of a brand. This format can also utilize the storytelling/slice of life format, which is often used to sell household products such as detergents, floor cleaners and drain openers.

Storytelling/Slice of Life. Telling a story can entertain as it sells — nothing is more interesting to people than other people in engaging situations. After all, that is the stuff of entertainment programming in the mass media, be it novels, movies, television shows or magazines. This format is particularly useful in setting up characters and situations with which the brand's target audience can identify.

Here's a 30-second TV ad for Yummy peanut butter:

Visuals	Audio:
CLOSE-UP OF A SMALL HAND DROPPING PEANUTS INTO YUMMY PEANUT BUTTER JAR	BOY: (speaking slowly) One... two
	ANNOUNCER VOICE OVER: Big, plump, fresh peanuts.
SLOW PULL OUT TO SHOW SMALL BOY COUNTING AND DROPPING PEANUTS INTO JAR	BOY: Fifty-four...
	ANNOUNCER VOICE OVER: They come in every jar of Yummy peanut butter.
	BOY: One hundred fifty...
	ANNOUNCER VOICE OVER: There's four hundred sixty three fresh peanuts in every jar of Yummy peanut butter. That's why it tastes so good.
BOY PUTS A PEANUT IN HIS MOUTH AND CHEWS AS HE CONTINUES TO CONCENTRATE, COUNT AND DROP PEANUTS INTO JAR	

CLOSE UP OF YUMMY PEANUT BUTTER JAR OVERFLOWING WITH PEANUTS, SOME ARE SCATTERED AROUND JAR	BOY: Four hundred… ANNOUNCER VOICE OVER: And isn't that why you love peanut butter?
TEXT IS SUPERIMPOSED OVER THE IMAGE: "WHY YOU LOVE PEANUT BUTTER."	BOY: Four hundred sixty three ANNOUNCER VOICE OVER: Yummy peanut butter. Four hundred sixty three fresh peanuts in every jar

Writing for Direct Mail

Advertisers are particularly fond of direct mail, as it is highly targeted and its results can be measured more directly. While it can be effective, it also presents particular challenges to writers.

Attracting attention is crucial with direct mail. Most people are accustomed to receiving a stack of unsolicited mail daily, and the dull, uninteresting pieces that do not catch the recipient's eye or interest go unread into the wastebasket. The use of color, unusual shapes and sizes, and engaging words on the outside can motivate readers to open a piece before deciding to discard it.

Today's new technologies in computer mailing and the use of mailing lists also give writers powerful new tools for personalizing messages to direct-mail recipients. Often a personal message calling the addressee by name can be printed on the front of an envelope or mailer, gaining attention in a unique way unavailable in any of the mass media.

In writing for direct mail, it is particularly important for writers to feel empathy for their readers. This may be difficult for young writers preparing copy for a retirement home or baby shampoo; however, it is imperative that direct mail demonstrate knowledge and enthusiasm for the product.

Many of the same rules that apply to body copy apply to copy for direct mail; however, writers often have the luxury of more space and not having to conform to a publication's printing specifications. This can mean more flexibility in use of color, types of paper stock, even die cuts (where a piece is cut out to an unusual shape) or foldouts that produce excitement and add to opportunities for selling.

Two other rules for writing direct mail is always remember the power of the word "free" and always make it easy to respond to the ad. When people are told about a free offer, there is a good chance they will be enticed to open the piece and find out the details. Be sure the details are there in a straightforward, clear and easy-to-understand form. Then be sure to tell the readers what you want them to do.

Here's a mailer for Yummy peanut butter:

COVER: Look inside for a yummy offer on Yummy peanut butter.

INSIDE
HEADLINE: Now you have 464 reasons to love Yummy peanut butter

COPY: How could we make those 463 fresh, plump peanuts in every jar of Yummy peanut butter taste even better? By giving you 25 cents off your next jar.
Let's see. That works out to just over 0.0005 cents savings per peanut. And we thought we couldn't possibly make Yummy taste even better!
The ad would include the coupon and have a logo for Yummy Peanut Butter accompanied by text stating, "Why you love peanut butter."

Internet

While writing for traditional mass media presents plenty of challenges, writing for Web sites presents even bigger challenges. The medium is still so new that researchers don't know what kinds of ads are most successful at drawing attention and selling products and services. Also, probably more so than any other mass media, the World

Wide Web is an environment where advertising is particularly unwelcome. People use the Web to access information, and advertising, particularly pop-up advertising, has generated a lot of negative reaction.

Rules for writing cyber copy do not differ that much from writing other advertising copy. In fact, in many instances the self-selected audience may be more interested in the product or service advertised than is generally seen in other mass media. After all, the person did seek out the site where the advertising is seen.

Copywriters for the Internet have a number of factors to consider. First, take full advantage of the interactivity of the medium. Leading a potential customer through a series of click-and-proceed paths is far more powerful than passive media such as newspapers, radio or magazines.

Also keep in mind that when users visit a site, the visit can be very brief — perhaps seconds — therefore writing cyber copy can be much like writing for billboards. The opportunity to communicate is brief, and the message must "shout," not speak.

As with other mass media, ad clutter is fast becoming a major problem with Internet advertising. The environment is cluttered, often with competitors, and ads must be concise, attention-getting and attractive. Visitors must have a reason to click on one ad and ignore the others.

Here's a Web site ad for Yummy peanut butter.

VISUAL: Yummy peanut butter jar full of peanuts, overflowing and scattered around the jar.
HEADLINE: Why you love peanut butter.
SUBHEAD: Visit yummypb.com for 463 reasons to love Yummy peanut butter.
Clicking on the URL will take visitors to the Web site.

Exercise 1: Print Ads

Create the text and images for a newspaper advertisement for a musical group.

Create another ad for a home-delivery pizza company.

Exercise 2: Radio Ads

Create the text for a radio advertisement for a musical group.

Create another ad for a home-delivery pizza company.

Exercise 3: TV Ads

Create the text and images for a TV advertisement for a musical group.

Create another ad for a home-delivery pizza company.

Exercise 4: Direct-Mail Ads

Create the text and images for a direct-mail advertisement for a musical group.

Create another ad for a home-delivery pizza company.

Exercise 5: Internet Ads

Create the text and images for a Web-page advertisement for a musical group.

Create another ad for a home-delivery pizza company.

Reporters' Resources

REPORTING

Acronyms has nearly 3,000 definitions for acronyms, abbreviations and initials. www.acronymfinder.com

Attorneys at Law. Martindale-Hubbell provides a directory of lawyers. www.martindale.com

The Art of Interviewing. www.journalism.org/resources/tools/reporting/interviewing

Beginning Reporting — A Website for Reporters and their Teachers was compiled by Jim Hall, Fredericksburg, VA www.courses.vcu.edu/ENG-jeh/BeginningReporting/Introduction/home.htmResources

CIA World Factbook gives detailed international information. www.cia.gov/cia/publications/factbook/

"Creative Interviewing: The Writer's Guide to Gathering Information by Asking Questions" 3rd ed. by Ken Metzler. (Allyn & Bacon, 1997).

Drug Policy Information Clearing House www.whitehousedrugpolicy.gov

Encyclopeadia Britannica Online www.britannica.com

Factiva.com proves information on the business community. www.factiva.com

Federal Bureau of Investigation www.fbi.gov

Federal Communications Commission www.fcc.gov

Federal Trade Commission www.ftc.gov

FedStats offers links to government statistical information. www.fedstats.gov

Food and Drug Administration www.fda.gov

Infopeople Best Search Tools Chart www.infopeople.org/search/chart.html

The International Trademark Association includes a list of all registered trademarks. www.inta.org/

"Interviewing for Journalists" by Sally Adams and Wynford Hicks. (Routledge, 2001).

"Interviewing: Speaking, Listening and Learning for Professional Life" edited by Rob Anderson and George M. Killenberg. (McGraw-Hill, 1998).

"Interviews That Work: A Practical Guide for Journalists" 2nd ed. by Shirley Biagi. (Wadsworth, 1991)

The Journalist's Toolbox has links to Web resources for reporters. www.journaliststoolbox.com

Library of Congress www.loc.gov

"Math Tools for Journalists" by Kathleen Woodruff Wickham. (Marion Street Press, 2003).

MSN Encarta is an online encyclopedia. www.encarta.msn.com

National Center on Disability and Journalism. www.ncdj.org

National Lesbian and Gay Journalism Association Stylebook Supplement offers gay, lesbian, bisexual and transgender terminology www.nlgja.org/pubs/stylebook.html

National Institute for Computer-Assisted Reporting www.nicar.org/

Reporting Techniques and Tools. www.journaliststoolbox.com/newswriting/reportingtechniques.html

National Writers Union serves freelance writers. www.nwu.org

NewsPlace.org has links to news sources, reporting resources, journalism skills, breaking media-related news and more. www3.niu.edu/newsplace

Obituaries. How the Sharon, Pa., Herald handles obituaries. www.sharon-herald.com/localnews/obituaries/smsobits.html

100 Questions and Answers About Arab Americans: A Journalist's Guide, produced by the Detroit Free Press. www.freep.com/jobspage/arabs/index.htm

The Poynter Institute offers a comprehensive list of journalism resources. www.poynter.org/content/content_view.asp?id=896

Religion source is a database of expert sources created by the American Academy of Religion. religionsource.org

Search Engines

    All the Web — www.alltheWeb.com

    Alta Vista — www.altavista.com

    Ask Jeeves — www.ask.com

    Excite — www.excite.com

    Google — www.google.com

    Hotbot — www.hotbot.com

    Teoma — www.teoma.com

    Vivisimo — www.vivisimo.com

STAT-USA is a federal site with economic data. home.stat-usa.gov

Subject Directories

    About — www.about.com

    Academic Info — www.academicinfo.net

    Looksmart — www.looksmart.com

    Yahoo — www.yahoo.com

"Teaching undergrads WEB evaluation: A guide for library instruction" by Jim Kapoun. C&RL News (July/August 1998): 522-523.

"Toolkit for the Expert Web Searcher" by Pat Ensor, www.ala.org/ala/lita/litaresources/toolkitforexpert/toolkitexpert.htm

U.S. Census Bureau www.census.gov/statab/www/ccdb.html

Weapons terms are provided by gun dealer Hallowell and Co. www.hallowellco.com/abbrevia.htm

Web Search Strategies www.learnwebskills.com/search/main.html

The White House www.whitehouse.gov.

WRITING AND STYLE

American Copy Editors Society. copydesk.org/

"The Associated Press Broadcast News Handbook" by Brad Kalbfeld. (The Associated Press, 2004).

"The Associated Press Guide To Internet Research And Reporting" by Frank Bass. (Perseus Books, 2004).

"The Associated Press Stylebook and Briefing on Media Law" edited by Norm Goldstein. (The Associated Press, 2004).

Copy Editor. www.copyeditor.com

"Elements of Style" by William Strunk Jr. This is the original 1918 edition. http://www.bartleby.com/strunk

Grammar and Style Notes. andromeda.rutgers.edu/~jlynch/Writing

Guide to Grammar and Writing, hosted by Capital Community College, Hartford, Conn., includes a grammar hotline. www.ccc.commnet.edu/grammar/

The SLOT: A spot for Copy Editors. www.theslot.com/

HyperGrammar offers interactive grammar exercises. www.uottawa.ca/academic/arts/writcent/hypergrammar/grammar.html

"The New Fowler's Modern English Usage" 3rd. ed. edited by R.W. Burchfield. (Claredon Press, 1996).

"When Words Collide" 6th ed. by Lauren Kessler and Duncan McDonald. (Wadsworth Publishing Co., 2004).

ETHICS, NEWS JUDGMENT AND LAW

Bureau of Justice Statistics, U.S. Department of Justice offers crime statistics compiled by the federal government. www.ojp.usdoj.gov/bjs

Columbia Journalism Review offers a guide to covering courts. www.cjr.org/Resources/crime99/ or www.soros.org/crime

Communications Law Institute www.cde.psu.edu/C&I/Commlaw.html

Dart Center for Journalism and Trauma. www.dartcenter.org

Fairness and Accuracy in Reporting (FAIR) monitors media bias and censorship. www.fair.org/fair

First Amendment Center is affiliated with the Freedom Forum and Newseum. www.fac.org

First Amendment Online is maintained by the University of Minnesota Law School. 1stam.umn.edu/

The Freedom Forum defends the First Amendment. www.freedomforum.org

Freedom of Information Center is a unit of the Missouri School of Journalism. http://foi.missouri.edu

The International Journal of Communications Law and Policy. www.digital-law.net/IJCLP www.digital-law.net/IJCLP

Libel Defense Resource Center is a clearinghouse to monitor and promote First Amendment rights in libel, privacy and related fields of law. www.ldrc.com

National Public Radio Ethics and Style Guidebook www.npr.org/inside/styleguide/stylmain.htm

The Newseum, an interactive museum of news. www.newseum.org

Online Journalism Review includes information on public policy and journalism resources. www.fairness.com/resources/by-relation?relation_id=5854

The Pew Research Center for the People & the Press studies attitudes toward press, politics and public policy issues. people-press.org

Reporters Committee for Freedom of the Press htpp://www.rcfp.org

Student Press Law Center is a useful guide for students covering campus crime or dealing with libel or access issues. www.splc.org/

Victims and the Media is the Web site for the Victims and the Media Program at Michigan State University's School of Journalism. www.victims.jrn.msu.edu/

MULTIMEDIA

Institute for Interactive Journalism at the University of Maryland helps the news media use new technologies to engage their audiences in public policy issues. www.j-lab.org

National Organization of Broadcasters. www.nab.org

Newspaper Association of America. www.naa.org

The Online News Association is open to journalists around the world who produce news for the Internet or other digital platforms. www.journalists.org/

White Noise Productions offers an overview of video production and a glossary of terminology. www.whitenoiseproductions.com

PUBLIC RELATIONS

"Handbook for Public Relations Writing" 4th ed. by Thomas Bivins. (NTC Business Books, 1999).

International Public Relations Association. www.ipra.org

PR-Education.org. lamar.colostate.edu/~pr/

PR newswire is a leading source of news releases distributed on the Internet to the news media. www.prnewswire.com

Public Relations Division homepage for the Association for Education in Journalism and Mass Communications (AEJMC). lamar.colostate.edu/~aejmcpr/

Public Relations Society of America. www.prsa.org

"Public Relations: The Profession and the Practice" by Dan Lattimore, Otis Baskin, Suzette Heiman, Elizabeth Toth, and James Van Leuven. (McGraw-Hill, 2004).

"Public Relations Writing — Form and Style" 7th ed. by Doug Newsom and Jim Haynes. (Wadsworth, 2004).

"Public Relations Writing and Media Techniques" 5th ed., by Dennis L. Wilcox Allyn & Bacon, 2004.

MISCELLANEOUS

American Society of Media Photographers. www.asmp.org/

American Medical Writers Association www.amwa.org/

American Society of Feature and Sunday Editors is an international organization of editors dedicated to the quality of features in newspapers. www.aasfe.org/

American Society of Journalists and Authors says it's nation's leading organization of freelance writers. www.asja.org

American Society of Newspaper Editors Many newspaper associations are featured on this Web site. www.asne.org. Internship information: www.asne.org/kiosk/careers/interndate.htm

Asian American Journalists Association www.aaja.org/

Associated Press Managing Editors www.apme.com/index.shtml

Association of American Editorial Cartoonists www.detnews.com/AAEC/AAEC.html

The Association of Capitol Reporters and Editors is a national organization whose members cover state governments. www.capitolbeat.org

The Associated Press. www.ap.org

California Chicano News Media Association www.ccnma.org

Editor and Publisher magazine. www.editorandpublisher.com

Foundation for American Communications (FACSNET) provides journalists with online resources and background information about public issues. www.facsnet.org/

Hollywood Foreign Press Association is best known for its annual Golden Globe Awards. www.goldenglobes.org/

International Federation of Journalists defends the freedom of the press. www.ifj.org

International Museum of Cartoon Art cartoon.org/

Investigative Reporters and Editors (IRE) www.ire.org/

Journalism and Women's Symposium describes itself as an organization for women journalists that combats gender bias and fosters education. www.jaws.org

International Association of Business Communicators www.iabc.com/homepage.htm

National Lesbian and Gay Journalists Association www.nlgja.org

National Newspapers Publishers Association members are publishers of African-American owned newspapers. www.nnpa.org/

National Press Club. npc.press.org/

Native American Journalists Association www.naja.com

Newspaper Association of America www.naa.org

Radio-Television News Directors Foundation www.rtnda.org/rtnda/

Religion Newswriters Association www.religionwriters.com/

Reporters Sans Frontieres (Reporters Without Borders) defends press freedom around the report www.rsf.org/

Society for News Design www.snd.org/

Society of Environmental Journalists. www.sej.org/

Society of Professional Journalists. spj.org

Women in Journalism offers interviews with women journalists who have made significant contributions to society through careers in journalism since the 1920s. npc.press.org/wpforal/ohhome.htm

Index

features, 259
high impact stories, 7–8
as information, 3–4
information gathering, 181–186
radio and, 23–24
resources for, 339–343
writing from news releases, 226–227
"News About the News, The" (Downie, Kaiser), 2, 6
news databases, 183–184
news obits (obituaries), 223
news releases, 185, 226–227, 301
effectiveness of, 304–307
video news releases, 302
Newsday (New York City), 20
newsletters, 302
newspapers, 20–23, 123–124. see also writing
definitions for, 21
Internet sites of, 26
inverted pyramid in, 124–128
leads for, 101–102
USA Today, 8
newsworthiness, 4
Nicholson, Jim, 223
"Nightly Horrors" (Nimbi, Combs), 6
Nimbi, Dan, 6
nonessential clauses/phrases, 34
"not for attribution," 210
note taking, 208, 229
nouns, 31–32
capitalization of, 58
possessive, 32
prepositional phrases as, 77–78
novelty. see unusualness
numerals, 57, 58–60

O

obituaries (obits)
body of, 224–226
leads for, 224
negative information in, 226
types of, 223
objectivity, 85–86
"off the record," 83, 210
Ogilvy, David, 323
"on background," 83
"On Press" (Wicker), 4–5
"on the record," 83
on-the-spot interviews, 204
open-ended questions, 206
Opotowsky, Mel, 273
orphan quotes, 82. see also quotations

P

packages, 21, 23
parallelism, 79–80
parentheses, 41
partial quotes, 82. see also quotations
participles, 36
parts of speech, 31–32. see also grammar
passive voice, 35–36, 87
periods, 41
personal titles, 58
personality profiles, 260
Pew Internet and American Life Project, 26
Pew Research Center for the People & the Press, 2, 7, 8
Philadelphia Daily News, 223
phoners, 23
phrases, essential vs. nonessential, 34
place words/phrases, 76
plagiarism, 274–275
planned interviews, 204
Plaschke, Bill, 260
police beats, 290, 291–292
popular names, 58
possessive nouns, 32
possessive pronouns, 32, 76
PR Newswire, 184
prefixes, 60
prepositional phrases, 77–78
prepositions, 32
press releases. see news releases
primary sources, 83
"Prime Time Live," 292
Principle of Utility, 276, 277
print, 21–23. see also newspapers; writing
abbreviations in, 57
advertising, 322–323
feature articles for, 251–258, 259–261
numerals used in, 59–60
quotations in, 82
summary leads for, 101–102
privacy
disclosure of private facts, 292
invasion of, 8–9, 276–277
media law and, 291–293
privilege, 290
problem/solution format, 326
producers, 23
prominence, 5
promotion, 299. see also public relations
pronouns, 31–32, 76–77
agreement of, 33–34
cases, 33
demonstrative, 76–77
possessive, 32, 76

covering events with, 228–229
leads in stories about, 229
spokesperson format, 326
spot news, 6
standups, 23
STAT-USA, 184
state names, 58
Steele, Bob, 277
stereotyping, 85–86, 274, 276–277
Stewart, Potter, 287
storytelling format, 326
straight news, 6
style, 55–62. *see also* "Associated Press Stylebook and Briefing on Media Law" (Associated Press)
acronyms and abbreviations, 56–58
books for, 55–56
capitalization, 57, 58
consistency in, 56
resources for, 341
subheads, in advertising, 323
subject directories, on Internet, 185, 186
suffixes, 60–61
summary leads, 21, 101–102, 253–254
active voice for, 103
attribution in, 108
double-element, 108–109
five W's in, 104–108
localizing, 109–110
news elements in, 103–104
tone set by, 102–103
"sunshine laws," 182
Super Bowl (2004), 1, 8

T

"tag," 325
tape recording, of interviews, 208–209
target audiences, for advertising, 321, 328
technology, 9–10. *see also* Internet
telephone directories, 182
television, 20. *see also* broadcast media
advertising for, 325–327
public service announcements, 303
writing for, 24–26
throwaway leads, 164–165
Timberlake, Justin, 1
time words/phrases, 76
timeliness, 5, 20
tone, of stories, 102–103
trademark infringement, 293–294
transitions
in feature writing, 255–256
of logic, 75–76
of thought, 75–77

transitive verbs, 36–37
trauma victims, 211–212
travel features, 261
truth, libel and, 290

U

umbrella leads, 108–109, 165
uniqueness, 102
unusualness, 4–5
upload, 26
URL (Uniform Resource Locator), 26
U.S. Congress, 185, 293
U.S. Constitution
First Amendment, 8, 273, 287, 292
Fourth Amendment, 291–292
on privilege, 290
U.S. Supreme Court
on disclosure of private facts, 292
on libel, 287, 289
USA Today, 8

V

verbosity, 78
verbs, 31. *see also* active voice
agreement with subjects, 34–35
strength of, 88
transitive *vs.* intransitive, 36–37
voice, 35–36, 87
victims, 211–212, 277, 292
video news releases (VNRs), 302
visuals in advertising, 321
VOs (voice overs), 23

W

Wall Street Journal Online (Dow Jones), 184
Weaver, David, 8
Web sites. *see* Internet; *individual names of Web sites*
Webster's New World Dictionary, 60
Westways (American Automobile Association), 302
what element, in leads, 106
when element, in leads, 106–107
where element, in leads, 107–108
White House Web site, 184
who element, in leads, 104–106
Who's Who in America (Marquis), 183
why elements, in leads, 108
Wicker, Tom, 4–5
Wilhoit, Cleveland, 8
Winfrey, Oprah, 2
wire services, 21, 184
women, identification of, 86
word repetition, 77
word usage, 55, 83–84. *see also* grammar; style